JOURNAL FOR THE STUDY OF THE OLD TESTAMENT
SUPPLEMENT SERIES
328

Editors
David J.A. Clines
Philip R. Davies

Executive Editor
Andrew Mein

Editorial Board
Richard J. Coggins, Alan Cooper, J. Cheryl Exum, John Goldingay,
Robert P. Gordon, Norman K. Gottwald, John Jarick,
Andrew D.H. Mayes, Carol Meyers, Patrick D. Miller

Sheffield Academic Press
A Continuum imprint

Reading Hosea in Achaemenid Yehud

James M. Trotter

Journal for the Study of the Old Testament
Supplement Series 328

Copyright © 2001 Sheffield Academic Press
A Continuum imprint

Published by
Sheffield Academic Press Ltd
The Tower Building, 11 York Road, London SE1 7NX
71 Lexington Avenue, New York, NY 10017-653

www.SheffieldAcademicPress.com
www.continuumbooks.com

British Library Cataloguing-in-Publication Data

A catalogue record for this book is available from the British Library

Typeset by Sheffield Academic Press
Printed on acid-free paper in Great Britain by Antony Rowe Ltd, Chippenham, Wiltshire

ISBN 1-84127-197-7

CONTENTS

Acknowledgments

As with any major accomplishment in life, this work could not have been produced without the instruction, support and encouragement of many people. I wish to begin by acknowledging the love and nurture of my family. The interest and commitment that led to this investigation grew out of the intellectual and religious environment created by my grandparents and parents. I offer them my deep gratitude for providing me with such an excellent foundation.

I would like to express my thanks to Carol Newsom and Jon Berquist. They both provided many valuable insights from their readings of earlier drafts. The final is much better as a result of their input. I particularly wish to thank Gene M. Tucker, not only for his valuable contributions through reading and commenting on various stages of this work, but also for his friendship and encouragement over the last decade. He always seems to offer just the right word at just the right time. Thanks, Gene.

Finally, I want to thank Rachel, my companion and partner through life. She has given selflessly and lovingly through many difficult years. More than she or anyone else could know, this project owes much of its existence to her encouragement, friendship and love. It is to her, my wife and best friend, that I dedicate this work.

ABBREVIATIONS

AB	Anchor Bible
ANET	James B. Pritchard (ed.), *Ancient Near Eastern Texts Relating to the Old Testament* (Princeton: Princeton University Press, 1950)
BASOR	*Bulletin of the American Schools of Oriental Research*
BWANT	Beiträge zur Wissenschaft vom Alten und Neuen Testament
BZAW	Beihefte zur *ZAW*
CBQ	*Catholic Biblical Quarterly*
CRBS	*Currents in Research: Biblical Studies*
GKC	*Gesenius' Hebrew Grammar* (ed. E. Kautzsch, revised and trans. A.E. Cowley; Oxford: Clarendon Press, 1910)
HSM	Harvard Semitic Monographs
HTR	*Harvard Theological Review*
HUCA	*Hebrew Union College Annual*
IDBSup	*IDB*, Supplementary Volume
IEJ	*Israel Exploration Journal*
JAAR	*Journal of the American Academy of Religion*
JBL	*Journal of Biblical Literature*
JSOT	*Journal for the Study of the Old Testament*
JSOTSup	*Journal for the Study of the Old Testament*, Supplement Series
JTS	*Journal of Theological Studies*
LCL	Loeb Classical Library
NCB	New Century Bible
NRSV	New Revised Standard Version
OBT	Overtures in Biblical Theology
Or	*Orientalia*
OTL	Old Testament Library
SBLDS	SBL Dissertation Series
SBLMS	SBL Monograph Series
VT	*Vetus Testamentum*
WBC	Word Biblical Commentary
ZAW	*Zeitschrift für die alttestamentliche Wissenschaft*

Chapter 1

HISTORICAL READERS AND READING HISTORICALLY

The reading of the final form of the book of Hosea which follows draws heavily from both the traditional interpretive practices of historical-critical approaches to biblical studies and newer interpretive strategies drawn from contemporary literary criticism. In relation to contemporary literary-critical methodology, this proposed reading is most concerned with the process or experience of reading, placing it within the broad theoretical spectrum of reader-response criticism. However, the concern with the reception of the book of Hosea within a particular historical horizon (early Achaemenid Yehud, c. 539–516 BCE—that is, from the beginning of Persian rule over Yehud to the completion of the Jerusalem temple) aligns this reading more closely with historical-critical approaches to the text than has been true of some other recent biblical studies informed and shaped by recent trends in literary criticism. In fact, as will be indicated below, New Historicism represents a literary-theoretical perspective which combines the concerns of reader-oriented literary analysis regarding the reception of a text by the reader with an analysis of the socio-historical setting of any particular reading of a text. Thus this perspective provides an opportunity to bridge the gap that has developed between the common concerns of historical-critical biblical studies and recent biblical analyses which are primarily informed by modern literary theory.

Reading the Prophets and Historical-Critical Scholarship

For the last 200 years biblical scholars have recognized that many of the prophetic books were not written in their final form by the prophet by whose name they are now known to us but rather are the products of composite authorship over a period of years. This recognition has led to a variety of fruitful investigations by form and redaction critics seeking to isolate the original speeches of the prophets, discussing the form of these speeches and their original social settings, and separating the various redactional layers and attempting to place them in their historical periods of origin. Such investigations are extremely useful for analyzing the process by which the prophetic books came to have their present shapes, for sifting out the various strata of material that compose the prophetic books (which can then be used in reconstructing the different historical periods from which these strata arose), and in searching for the 'historical prophet'.

One significant contribution of critical prophetic studies has been the identification of several possible contexts of production and reading of the prophetic materials. One context of interpretation is the setting in which a prophetic speech was first spoken and heard (in the case of Hosea, during the third quarter of the eighth century in Israel). Reading prophetic material in this context requires the sifting of the 'original' or 'genuine' prophetic speeches from the redactional alterations and additions that have recontextualized these speeches during the course of their transmission history.

A second context of interpretation is related to the different redactional editions and stages through which the existing material has passed. This is not really a single context but a spectrum of contexts, each related to a different intermediate redactional stage through which the material passed before reaching the final form. Every new juxta-position of previously independent units, alteration in the wording of an existing text, and/or editorial additions to a text, creates a new text and provides a new interpretive context, both textual and socio-historical, in which to read both the pre-existing material and the additions and alterations; that is, the new text resulting from the sum of the redactional processes.

A third context of interpretation is the setting in which the final form—that is, the last redactional stage—was produced and received. As with all of the intervening redactional stages, the final form represents a recontextualization of the pre-existing material for a new socio-historical setting. The resulting text must be read as a new (or at least different) text in the social situation of its production and reception. This reception of the final form is then multiplied in an effectively infinite number of settings, commonly called the history of inter-pretation (or reception).

The intrinsic value in distinguishing the various redactional levels and their unique contexts of reception lies in the fact that each redactional shaping of the material in a new situation changes the way in which the new text is read. It is not only the redactional additions which can be interpreted in relation to their socio-historical setting of production but also each distinct redactional product composed of the pre-existing text, any alterations to or deletions from the pre-existing text, and all additions to that text. The editorial changes and redactional additions to a prophetic speech inevitably alter the way in which the speech is received. The effect of this alteration is further compounded by the changed temporal and social setting in which the new text is produced and read.

The focal point of this book is the last of these various contexts of reading. This is not an effort to delineate the compositional history of the text but an endeavor to suggest a possible reading of the final form of the book of Hosea within a particular socio-historical context. Choosing to focus on the final form of the book is not an attempt to deny the validity or value of these other approaches but simply represents the selection of one possible aspect of the interpretation of the text. Modern critical commentaries on the prophetic books have often focused on separating the various layers of material preserved in the final form and then interpreting each of these layers in relation to the historical setting in which they are believed to have been written. This study attempts to do something similar with the final form of the book: to propose how the finished product of the redactional process might have been read in a historical setting soon after the completion of the process. In other words, the primary concern is not an understanding of the diachronic development of the Hosean traditions but a synchronic reading of the final form within one specific socio-historical horizon.

A recent study of Isaiah by Edgar Conrad represents an approach to prophetic literature similar to that proposed here.[1] His concern in this work is to present a reading of the whole of Isaiah informed by recent developments in literary-critical theory. He recognizes the need to broaden the definition of reading from an excavative technique, through which one extracts meaning from texts, to a process—an experience through time—in which meaning is created and experienced. His assessment of Isaiah demonstrates a literary sensitivity not always found in traditional historical-critical analyses.

1.   Edgar W. Conrad, *Reading Isaiah* (OBT; Minneapolis: Fortress Press, 1991).

Although Conrad's effort has much to commend it, his work demonstrates a lamentable animosity toward historical-critical scholarship. He
seems to find little or no value in efforts to analyze parts of the whole
text or discover levels of redactional activity. Indeed, anything beyond
the text as it stands, including historical information from the time of
writing, is considered spurious information. The roots of this animosity
lie in the fact that Conrad accepts New Criticism's rejection of any role
for authorial intention or historical setting in the interpretation of texts.[2]

Conrad, quoting profusely from some of the earlier writings of Stanley Fish, argues that the problem with historical-critical scholarship is
its attempt to read texts in the light of authorial intention and historical
setting.[3] Conrad has correctly perceived that both authorial intention
and historical setting are not objectively 'there, in the text', but a more
nuanced critique is needed. The 'problem' of historical-critical scholarship is not, as he contends, its emphasis on reading texts in the light of
their historical background or the author's intentions. Rather, the problem of *some* historical critics has been the identification of their reading
of the text with the one meaning of the text and the belief that their
interpretations of a text were objectively there in the text, unaffected by
their interpretive conventions.[4]

The most startling incongruity in Conrad's work is that he appears to
share this 'problem'. He continually talks about 'the implied audience

2.   See particularly Conrad, *Reading Isaiah*, pp. 1-4.

3.   For example the following statement: 'When historical critics claim that
meaning emerges from authorial intention, they locate the origin of that meaning in
the text rather than in the reading process' (Conrad, *Reading Isaiah*, p. 4). In criti-
cizing M. Sweeney, Conrad makes the following claim: 'The redactors' intentions
are no more inherent in the text than those of the prophet. His own interpretive
strategies, imposed from outside the text, have shaped the text and have yielded
intentions' (*Reading Isaiah*, p. 20).

4.   According to S.D. Moore, 'This notion of the Bible is as fundamental to the
critical reader as to the evangelical reader. The *modus operandi* of the critical
scholar is an unceasing attempt to "get it right," to bring his or her interpretation
into alignment with the real meaning of the text—usually, with the intention of the
author—conceived as "in there," awaiting discovery, in principle independent of
the activity of the interpreter. Such assumptions need rethinking even in light of the
moderate positions of the early Fish or of Wolfgang Iser, who redefined interpretation as a two-way, dynamic process. Textual meaning is established as much
by the reader as by the author; prior to the interpretive act, there is nothing *definitive* in the text to be discovered' ('Negative Hermeneutics, Insubstantial Texts:
Stanley Fish and the Biblical Interpreter', *JAAR* 54 [1987], pp. 707-19 [715-16]).

encoded in the text'[5] and describes his own approach to the text as a combination of M.H. Abrams's pragmatic and objective classifications of theories of textual interpretation.[6] Conrad does not appear to recognize that his 'implied audience encoded in the text' is no less an interpretive construal than authorial intention or historical setting proposed by others. Nothing is objectively in the text prior to interpretation—that is, as humans we only have access to the text through our interpretive practices. All aspects of our reading of a text, authorial intention, historical setting, implied audience, and so on, are interpretations or construals shaped by our interpretive conventions (see below, 'Reading the Prophets and Literary Theory').[7]

In spite of his rejection of historical-criticism, Conrad does, however, see some similarities between his work and the recent redaction-critical studies of Isaiah by R.E. Clements, R. Rendtorff and M. Sweeney. He praises what he views as a shift in the understanding of redactors from mechanical collectors to creative editors to authors of the final forms.[8]

5.   Conrad, *Reading Isaiah*, p. 2. Also, 'I view the implied reader and the implied audience as theoretical constructs encoded in the text' (*Reading Isaiah*, p. 31).

6.   Conrad, *Reading Isaiah*, pp. 27-33. M.H. Abrams, *The Mirror and the Lamp: Romantic Theory and Critical Tradition* (New York: Oxford University Press, 1953).

7.   Two quotes from Stanley Fish are appropriate: 'Perception is never innocent of assumptions, and the assumptions within which it occurs will be responsible for the contours of what is perceived. The conclusion is the one I have reached before: there can be no category of the 'given' if by given one means what is there before interpretation begins' ('Why No One's Afraid of Wolfgang Iser', in *idem, Doing What Comes Naturally: Change, Rhetoric, and the Practice of Theory in Literary and Legal Studies* [Durham, NC: Duke University Press, 1989], pp. 68-86 [78]). Also, 'To put it another way, mediated access to the world is the only access we ever have; in face to face situations or in the act of reading a novel, the properties of objects, persons, and situations emerge as a consequence of acts of construction that follow (and because they follow they are not, in any simple sense, free) from a prestructured understanding of the shapes any meaningful item could possibly have. What this means is that we know "real people" no more directly than we know the characters in a novel; that "real life" objects are no less "ideated" than fictional objects; that ordinary language is no more in touch with an unmediated reality than the language of literature' ('Why No One's Afraid of Wolfgang Iser', p. 81).

8.   Conrad, *Reading Isaiah*, pp. 12-17. While this progressive movement in the appreciation of the work of biblical redactors is overly rigid, there clearly has been an improvement in the reputation of redactors in recent scholarship.

In fact, this shift in the focus of redaction critics toward the role of redactors in creating the final form of texts represents an important tie between newer literary-oriented analyses and older historical-critical approaches. Redactors are seen as creative individuals shaping, combining and adding to the received tradition in order to create a new work. Thus the final redaction of a book is an area of overlap in the concerns of redaction criticism and literary analysis. There is also significant room for common concerns between form criticism as practiced by biblical scholars and recent developments in New Historicism. The traditional form-critical foci of genre, formal features of composition, and social setting are both literary and historical concerns. Genre is both a socio-historical and a literary phenomenon. The juxtaposition of a formal literary pattern and a typical setting in the life of the community is also rooted historically—that is, it occurs in a particular setting in time. New Historicism includes all of these aspects of form criticism but also moves beyond the primary focus on the typical and characteristic to consider the distinctive and particular; one unique text in one specific socio-historical context.

As is the case in any historical-critical reading, a reader-oriented interpretation of Hosea concerned with a particular historical context of reading will necessarily involve a critical reconstruction of the historical, social and political shape of the reading community. Of course, it is impossible to abrogate one's own socially constructed self completely and assume the reading conventions of a community from another culture and era. But a reader-oriented analysis that is broad enough to include concern for the historical and social setting in which Hosea was produced, read and re-read will result in a useful, critically informed interpretation of the book.[9] The value of this type of analysis lies in its ability to provide a locus for the intersection of literary, historical and sociological concerns.

Reading the Parts in Relation to the Whole?

An important factor to be considered in any reading of the final form of a large text is the impact of the whole on the interpretation of the parts. Does the inclusion of a unit within a larger context and its specific

---

9. See S. Mailloux's definition of interpretation as 'acceptable and approximating translation' in his *Interpretive Conventions: The Reader in the Study of American Fiction* (Ithaca, NY: Cornell University Press, 1982), p. 144.

location in that larger context alter the way the unit is read? Or, more specifically, does the arrangement of the various materials that were brought together to form the 'book of Hosea' affect the experience of reading the book? A central interpretive issue is whether the composite authorship of the book of Hosea (and other prophetic texts) has resulted in a document that can be read with a conception of the whole in mind while reading. One traditional approach to prophetic studies views the final forms of the prophetic traditions as collections of independent units lacking interrelationship and having no overarching unity and purpose. According to this approach, Hosea is a composite document pieced together from discrete units, more like the book of Psalms,[10] a sort of collection of the best sermons of Hosea. A recent example of this common model for understanding prophetic literature is found in J.J.M. Roberts's commentary on Nahum, Habakkuk and Zephaniah. He claims that a prophetic book is most like 'a collection of relatively short sermons' and that 'in most cases, it makes no difference in what order one reads the sermons [or oracles] because the individual sermon [or oracle] is primary, not its placement in the book'.[11] Focusing on the work as a whole raises the alternative possibility that, for some readers, there is significance in the arrangement, in the experience of reading the words one after another. From this perspective Hosea (and other prophetic books) has more in common with narrative texts than collections of discrete poems or sermons. The final form, according to this second model, can be perceived as continuous with interconnections between sections and development or movement from beginning to ending. As a part of a larger work, each individual unit is not read in isolation but is shaped by the reader's knowledge of what precedes and follows it.

A reading that is cognizant of the whole book of Hosea does not require a particular timeframe or limit, such as, in one sitting. Such a reading of Hosea, like the reading of a novel, might occur over the course of several separate readings. Nor does such a reading require that the book be read from beginning to end in any particular reading or series of readings. Any reading of any portion of the whole that is

---

10. This is not a claim that there is no detectable shape to the Psalms as a collection but simply recognizes the difference between a collection of distinct texts and a single, continuous text.

11. J.J.M. Roberts, *Nahum, Habakkuk, and Zephaniah: A Commentary* (OTL; Louisville, KY: Westminster/John Knox Press, 1991), p. 9.

cognizant of and interpreted in relation to the text that precedes and follows that particular portion would qualify. Having read a novel previously it is possible to reread only a portion of the book in relation to the whole. In fact, it is unlikely that the second reading would be unaffected by the reader's knowledge of the narrative that precedes and follows the portion that is read. The central point is that the reader's knowledge of the spatial relationship of the words on the page effects the experience of reading any particular portion of the text. For this analysis of the book of Hosea the issue is whether the text may have been read in this manner within the specific socio-historical context of Persian period Yehud. In other words, the key questions relate not to the intentional design of the final redactor/author of the text but to the contemporary conventions of reading and the ostensible knowledge of the text of a Persian period reader.

One source for reconstructing the reading conventions of ancient readers is the evidence provided by the ancient texts themselves. It is possible to ascertain some of the conventions of textual production by means of a careful analysis of the text. These conventions of production provide indirect evidence of the conventions of reading. Communication is possible in any particular social setting because the producers and consumers share common conventions related to the production and consumption of texts. Although there will naturally be some divergence between the conventions of production of a particular author and the conventions of reading of a particular reader, if these divergences become too great communication becomes impossible. For example, if the producer writes a text with right-to-left and top-to-bottom conventions but the reader attempts to read the text with left-to-right and bottom-to-top conventions then chaos is the result. There is, necessarily, a substantial correlation between the conventions of textual production and reception for any specific socio-historical setting.

The spatial relationship of the words is one indication of the conventions of textual production and reception. The text of Hosea was produced, preserved and transmitted in the form of a sequential text in which one word follows another in the physical presentation of the text on the page. In addition, there are certain formal features, such as the superscription and postscript, plot development and reversals, which indicate that the book of Hosea was produced as a unit with a perception of the book as a whole rather than a series of unrelated parts.

The superscription and postscript of Hosea demonstrate this

conception of the whole at its most basic level. Both of these elements suggest an understanding by a redactor(s) that the 'book of Hosea' functions at some level as a literary unit. The superscription establishes the historical setting within which the reader is to read the text which follows and also makes a claim to divine authority for the whole text.[12] The postscript completes the book with the claim that the text which precedes it is not only of historical interest but preserves a message of contemporary significance which the reader is warned not to ignore. The postscript leads the reader to reinterpret the preceding text in light of the reader's contemporary situation. Thus the postscript also subtly implies, if not unity, at least the understanding of the book as a single work communicating something for the reader to learn and integrate into life. The focus of these features of the text is not with isolated portions of the book but with the book as a whole.

Some might suggest that such formal features only exist as a result of the reading conventions of the modern critical community and that they tell us nothing about the way in which the book of Hosea was read in an ancient context. But this objection applies equally to all historical research. All critical study of the ancient world—cultural, historical, archaeological and textual—is dependent upon some degree of continuity of human experience and analogy between the modern and ancient contexts. The extent of continuity and analogy must constantly be shaped and monitored by progress in the discipline, but analogy is absolutely indispensable in any analysis of the past. The fact that these features of the book can be perceived by the reading conventions of one community of readers suggests the possibility that this might also be true for other communities, including Persian period Yehud.

Additional aspects of the text that indicate conventions of production (and reception) related to the book as a whole are characterization, dialogue, reversals,[13] and the creation and resolution of tension. These are

12. 'The basic concern of this language is the theological problem of authority and revelation. Thus the fundamental intention of the superscriptions is to identify the prophetic books as the word of God. What had originally been claimed by the prophets for their individual oral addresses is now claimed for words written down, to be copied, read and therefore to live in future generations' (Gene M. Tucker, 'Prophetic Superscriptions and the Growth of a Canon', in George W. Coats and Burke O. Long, *Canon and Authority: Essays in Old Testament Religion and Theology* [Philadelphia: Fortress Press, 1977], pp. 56-70 [68]).

13. Cf. Michael Lee Catlett, 'Reversals in Hosea: A Literary Analysis' (PhD dissertation, Emory University, 1988).

aspects of a text that in some measure depend on spatial organization, one word after another on the page, and temporal experience, one word after another through time in the reading process.[14] For example, the idea that a text could be written containing reversals without the expectation that the reversal would be read in relation to the element that it reverses is meaningless. The recognition of a reversal is dependent on the reader's recognition of its relationship to the (previous) element in the text which it reverses. The reversal does not even require that the two texts be read 'in the right order' temporally. It is possible that a reader could read the reversal first and then, later, read the element of the text that is being reversed. The only requirements for the reversal to function as such is the reader's recognition of: (1) the linguistic and thematic connections between them; and (2) the spatial relationship of the two units within the book as a whole. Whatever the actual conventions of reading in relation to time devoted to reading, the selection of units, or the sequentiality of the reading of units from a particular book, the production of texts with reversals in the neo-Babylonian and early Persian periods indicates the expectation that these texts would be read with a perception of the whole in mind.

Precisely how the book was read in the Persian period is unascertainable or, at most, can only be ascertained by inference. That the convention of producing and reading extended texts with significant development and substantial interconnections from beginning to ending existed, however, is clear from the significant amount of narrative material that originated in the neo-Babylonian and Persian periods. If a coherent, meaningful structure emerges from a reading of Hosea that is cognizant of the whole, that would suggest the possibility that this convention may have influenced the shape of the final redaction of the book of Hosea. As was indicated above, while the modes of production and consumption are not necessarily coterminus, evidence of one is a strong indication of the contemporaneous existence of the other. The congruity between the conventions of textual production and the conventions of textual interpretation in any particular time and social setting is a basic requirement for communication within that specific social sphere. If readers use different conventions for reading than the authors use for writing then miscommunication can be the only result. The evidence for the production of substantial narrative texts during this period indicates

---

14. Or, in the case of rereading a part of the whole, the imagination of the spatial and temporal relationship between the part and the whole.

that texts were produced and read in early Achaemenid Yehud with a perception of the interrelationship of the various parts to the whole in mind.

The various features of the book of Hosea which indicate that it was produced as a single, unified work rather than an anthology of disparate but, ultimately, unrelated parts also suggest the possibility that the text may have been read in this way in antiquity. This evident structuring contrasts with the book of Psalms, for example, which has been transmitted as a collection of discrete units, each with a clear beginning and ending, often including a superscription and postscript, that serve to distinguish it from those that precede and follow. An obvious exception to this perception of discrete units is found in Psalms 9 and 10. The acrostic structure and lack of demarcating features (such as a superscription to Ps. 10) indicate that they may originally have been read as a single, unified text.[15] While there are pericopes within the book of Hosea which exhibit formal characteristics that suggest that they could stand as independent, coherent units apart from the remainder of the book,[16] the final form of the book lacks the internal, formal dividing features—such as superscriptions, postscripts and doxologies—which separate the individual psalms from the surrounding members of the collection. The form of the text of Hosea is more like the individual psalms, having a clear beginning and ending enclosing the text as a whole (see below, 'Reading within the Lines: The Function of the Superscript and Postscript to the Book of Hosea'), rather than the book of Psalms which is preserved as a collection of smaller texts each with its own beginning and ending.[17]

Recent studies of the final redactions of other prophetic writings have also detected coherent structuring[18] of their final forms. R.E. Clements, for example, has argued that the final form of the book of Isaiah 'provides a literary context which must inevitably affect the interpretation

15. In fact, these 'two' psalms are preserved as a single psalm in the Septuagint.

16. And, in fact, many of them may well have existed independently before their incorporation into the book.

17. The smaller collections within the Psalms may share common themes, genre or attribution but none of them is presented as a continuous text across the formal boundaries of the individual psalms within the collection.

18. As indicated above, whether such features are the result of the intention of the final redactor may be illuminated by an analysis of this type but is not essential to the argument. It is sufficient to note that these features, intentional or otherwise, become apparent when the text is read with a knowledge of the shape of the whole.

of the several parts of the whole'.[19] In addition, he suggests that the book as a whole demonstrates a unity or wholeness on both thematic and structural levels. After describing the way in which the book has been structured, he states: 'All of these considerations are sufficient to indicate that the overall structure of the book shows signs of editorial planning and that, at some stage in its growth, attempts were made to read and interpret the book as a whole.'[20]

Ellen Davis suggests that an even more developed cohesiveness is evident in the book of Ezekiel. Several features contribute to the book's 'comprehensive design, which appears highly deliberate'.[21] This comprehensive design is indicated by the book's tripartite structure, an overall coherence of style and perspective evidenced in the first-person narrative frame, and unity of content demonstrated by the three divine visions (1.1–3.15; 8.1–11.25; 40.1–48.35). The high degree of coherence and design leads Davis to propose that the book of Ezekiel represents a transitional form from the predominantly oral forms of earlier prophets to predominantly written forms.

In a recent study of Zephaniah, Ehud Ben Zvi has noted that four prophetic books—Isaiah, Jeremiah (LXX), Ezekiel and Zephaniah—all exhibit a similar organization: a tripartite structure (message of judgment against Judah/Israel; oracles against the nations; and message of salvation) which he attributes to the composition of the books in the Persian period.[22] While there are differences in style, content and compositional history, he concludes:

> the fact that despite all these differences, four different books, in their final form, show a similar structure leads to the unavoidable conclusion that this form addressed itself to the kind of questions that troubled the

19. R.E. Clements, 'The Unity of the Book of Isaiah', in J.L. Mays and P.J. Achtemeier (eds.), *Interpreting the Prophets* (Philadelphia: Fortress Press, 1987), pp. 50-61 (50). Cf. R.E. Clements, 'Beyond Tradition-History: Deutero-Isaianic Development of First Isaiah's Themes', *JSOT* 31 (1985), pp. 95-113; Walter Brueggemann, 'Unity and Dynamic in the Isaiah Tradition', *JSOT* 29 (1984), pp. 89-107; and Christopher R. Seitz, 'Isaiah 1–66: Making Sense of the Whole', in *idem* (ed.), *Reading and Preaching the Book of Isaiah* (Philadelphia: Fortress Press, 1988), pp. 105-26.

20. Clements, 'The Unity', p. 53.

21. Ellen F. Davis, *Swallowing the Scroll: Textuality and the Dynamics of Discourse in Ezekiel's Prophecy* (JSOTSup, 78; Sheffield: Almond Press, 1989), p. 11.

22. Ehud Ben Zvi, *A Historical-Critical Study of the Book of Zephaniah* (BZAW, 198; Berlin: W. de Gruyter, 1991), pp. 325-27.

communities in which these books received their final form, namely, questions concerning their self-understanding, their understanding of the world and of Yhwh's will, and their longing for an ideal future.[23]

Ben Zvi's analysis suggests that this structure leads the postexilic reader from the situation of living in a post-punishment world in which other nations are prospering, through the punishment of these other nations by Yahweh, to an ideal future in which all nations, with Israel/ Judah at the head, will serve Yahweh. Thus he establishes that the compositional shaping of these books grows out of the situation of the producing community and is designed to elicit a particular effect in Persian period readers.

All of these examples indicate that many of the prophetic books are not the result of a haphazard or accidental gathering of prophetic speeches. According to these critics, these prophetic books demonstrate purposeful design. The structures into which the various prophetic materials have been edited reflect the influence of the socio-historical setting in which the books were produced and read. The work of Ben Zvi, in particular, suggests that reading certain prophetic books cognizant of their entire contents and structure within the socio-historical context of the Persian period will produce particular effects (i.e. lead the reader down the path from a non-ideal to an ideal state in relation to God).

All of this provides evidence of the way(s) in which texts were being written and read in the Persian period. At the very least, the reading of one portion of a longer work was shaped by the surrounding context of the work as a whole. Whether it was the intention of the final redactor of the book of Hosea that it be read in such a fashion, the evidence suggests that it is highly probable that the various parts of the book were read conscious of and in relation to one another in the Persian period.

Reading the Prophets and Literary Theory

As indicated above, in terms of literary-critical methodology, this study is most heavily indebted to reader-oriented approaches. Many critics in recent literary scholarship have moved away from positivistic claims to objective interpretation as a result of the recognition that the situation

---

23. Ben Zvi, *Zephaniah*, p. 346.

of the reader (whether defined socially, psychologically, or in some other manner) plays an important role in the production of meaning. Reader-response critics, in particular, have argued persuasively that meaning is not inherent within the text, as a product that can be extracted.[24] Rather, meaning is continually created during the activity of reading. Thus, in reader-oriented criticism, meaning is not an object to be mined from the text, but an event that occurs during the process of reading. This shift in the understanding of the locus of meaning has necessitated a shift in the focus of analysis from the text as an object containing meaning to the activities of the reader and reading as a process in which meaning is produced.

This focus on readers and the process of reading has taken a variety of forms.[25] The definitions of text and reader have been pivotal points of discussion between the different theoretical orientations. Readers have ranged from actual readers reading the text, the readers inscribed in the text by the author and discovered by the critic, and informed or competent readers, usually a shorthand for the critic as reader.

Common to all forms of reader-oriented analysis is the rejection of several important theoretical positions of New Criticism. The exclusive textual focus of New Criticism not only excluded the interpretation of texts in relation to their original setting and authorial intention but also rejected as illicit any consideration of the experiences of the reader. Anything beyond the close reading of the text and delineation of its formal features was regarded as extrinsic to the goal of interpretation (the affective fallacy). This singular focus on the text undoubtedly represented an important advance over earlier psychologizing inter-pretations of the author's mental state at the time of writing, but the exclusion of any consideration of extra-textual information and experi-ence has been rejected in recent reader-oriented approaches.[26]

---

24. Stanley Fish, *Is There a Text in This Class? The Authority of Interpretative Communities* (Cambridge, MA: Harvard University Press, 1980). Cf. Wolfgang Iser, *The Act of Reading: A Theory of Aesthetic Response* (Baltimore: The Johns Hopkins University Press, 1978), pp. 4-7.

25. Cf. Jane Tompkins (ed.), *Reader-Response Criticism: From Formalism to Post-Structuralism* (Baltimore: The Johns Hopkins University Press, 1980).

26. The classic statement of this argument to which everyone refers is W.K. Wimsatt and M.C. Beardsley, 'The Affective Fallacy', *Sewanee Review* 57 (1949), pp. 31-55. The argument as presented in this article only excludes consideration of emotional responses (and only in the case of poetry) but has resulted in the neglect of the reader's involvement in the creation of meaning. One of the great weaknesses

Jonathan Culler refers to the exclusion from critical consideration of the activities of the reader and the effects generated by the reading process as the impossible fiction of New Criticism; 'that the reader, be he innocent or subtly trained in forgetting, should approach the poem wholly without preconceptions and, treating it as an autonomous artifact, read "the words on the page"'.[27] Reader-response criticism's inclusion of the reader's experiences[28] in critical inquiry results in the transformation of meaning from a product extracted from the text to meaning being intrinsic to the temporal process itself.[29] 'A temporal model of reading makes available for description a wide range of reading activities, which include making and revising judgments, solving mysteries and puzzles, discovering sequential structures of similarity and contrast, formulating questions and answers, making and correcting mistakes'.[30] By examining the reading process, reader-oriented criticism provides access to significant aspects of the techniques and intention of the author of a literary text that would otherwise be unavailable.

A second cardinal doctrine of New Criticism that has been rejected in reader-oriented approaches to literary analysis is the intentional fallacy, the precursor to Wimsatt's and Beardsley's affective fallacy.[31] As in the case of the affective fallacy, the intentional fallacy has been far more broadly applied than was intended by the authors of this programmatic essay. Wimsatt and Beardsley expressly limit their objections regarding intention to poetry.

> Poetry succeeds because all or most of what is said or implied is relevant; what is irrelevant has been excluded, like lumps from pudding and 'bugs' from machinery. In this respect poetry differs from practical

of this extreme form of the affective fallacy, which locates meaning solely in the text, is its inability to explain why so many different readings of a single text are produced by comparably trained readers.

27. Jonathan Culler, 'Reading and Misreading', *The Yale Review* 65 (1975), pp. 88-95 (88).

28. The term 'experience' is used here to indicate not only (or primarily) emotions or feelings that might occur during the reading process but the judgments, questions, alterations in judgments, etc. that occur while reading a text.

29. Fish, *Is There a Text in This Class?*, p. 158; cf. Mailloux, *Interpretive Conventions*, p. 68.

30. Mailloux, *Interpretive Conventions*, pp. 70-71.

31. W.K. Wimsatt and M.C. Beardsley, 'The Intentional Fallacy', *Sewanee Review* 54 (1946), pp. 468-88.

messages, which are successful if and only if we correctly infer the intention. They are more abstract.[32]

Perhaps as a result of the difficulty of separating 'practical messages' from works of 'literary art', this distinction was ignored. In any case, intention became a 'four-letter' word in literary-critical circles (and others, like biblical studies, that were affected by literary criticism).

Early versions of reader-oriented criticism rejected the affective fallacy as a necessary precondition to their development but the intentional fallacy continued to act as a constraint in this new approach to literature. More recently, however, the intentional fallacy has come under attack in the theoretical writings of reader-response critics. S. Mailloux has broached this subject from the perspective of textual criticism in American fiction. He argues that text-critical decisions are impossible without inferring the author's intention.[33] At about the same time M.L. Pratt argued that the intentional fallacy fell to the same arguments as the affective fallacy and pressed for the legitimacy of historical concerns in reader-oriented approaches to texts.

> The intentional fallacy is no longer a sufficient excuse for failing to treat literary works as historically determined human productions, any more than the affective fallacy is sufficient grounds for failing to treat literary interpretations as historical human productions. In other words, you have to be willing to read or receive or respond to texts as historical productions. This is not the only way they may be received, but it is one, and it is one to which the current theory of aesthetic reception and response must give a place if it is to avoid serious self-contradiction.[34]

Intention, however, is not simply the peculiar thoughts and feelings of the author at the time of writing. In Pratt's analysis both reception and intention are not the inscrutable activities of isolated individuals but are the acts of socially constituted beings. These acts grow out of the shared conventions of the interpretive and/or productive communities of which the reader and author are members. Thus both writing and reading, intention and interpretation, are not primarily individual, idiosyncratic activities but socially constructed activities performed according to communal conventions.

32. Wimsatt and Beardsley, 'The Intentional Fallacy', pp. 469-70.
33. Mailloux, *Interpretive Conventions*, pp. 93-125.
34. Mary Louise Pratt, 'Interpretive Strategies/Strategic Interpretations: On Anglo-American Reader Response Criticism', *Boundary 2* 11 (1982–83), pp. 201-31 (206).

S. Fish has offered a similar argument for the role of intention in both the production and interpretation of texts.[35] In response to the suggestions of R. Dworkin that the individual nature of intention makes it both difficult to ascertain and nothing but useless psychological data even when ascertained, Fish posits the social nature of intention. For Fish, intention in the production and interpretation of texts is constrained by the enterprise in which one is engaged. Intentions are forms of conventional behavior that are to be read conventionally.

> The crucial point is that one cannot read or reread independently of intention, independently, that is, of the assumption that one is dealing with marks or sounds produced by an intentional being, a being situated in some enterprise in relation to which he has a purpose or a point of view.[36]

He later modifies this statement slightly by admitting that one could conceivably read a text in a way in which it was not intended but that such a reading would not be an interpretation of the text.[37]

The recognition that readers constitute texts according to the interpretive strategies or conventions of their communities is a key to understanding the process of reading, at least as formulated by these anti-formalist theorists. In addition to this communal aspect of reading, however, there are an infinite number of idiosyncratic factors that may contribute to a particular reading and which can be traced to the personality and individual experience of the individual reader. Some of these factors may represent overlap and/or conflict between the strategies and conventions of the different interpretive communities a particular reader may inhabit simultaneously. Also, each individual is a unique combination of ethnicity, gender and life experiences.[38] Every act of interpretation is inevitably shaped by both the social forces of the individual's interpretive community(ies) and by a variety of idiosyncratic factors unique to that person.

In this combination of communal conventions and idiosyncratic personal factors many have seen the much feared victory of what I term

---

35. Cf. Fish, 'Working on the Chain Gang', pp. 87-102; and *idem*, 'Wrong Again', in his *Doing What Comes Naturally*, pp. 103-119.

36. Fish, 'Working on the Chain Gang', pp. 99-100.

37. Fish, 'Wrong Again', p. 119.

38. The lack of a detailed discussion of personal idiosyncrasies and the complicated reality of membership in various, overlapping, interpretive communities is a significant weakness in the theoretical writings of Fish.

'licentious reading', that is, that any text can mean absolutely anything to anyone. This fear has caused some to retreat into the apparently safe-haven of determinate meaning which they argue is somehow objectively 'in the text'. The truth, however, is that texts have always been read according to the reading conventions and idiosyncrasies of the interpreter. Objectified texts have never constrained the way in which readers have constituted them. This should be quite clear to professional biblical interpreters who are constantly confronted with an ever-growing variety of interpretations of the biblical texts and the vastly different interpretations of those same texts by those outside the guild operating with very different interpretive conventions.

Rather than being a liability, the inclusion of idiosyncratic factors in reading (and they never can be excluded) is a valuable asset to the scholarly community's efforts to understand these texts. The value of these idiosyncratic factors is discussed by Michael Steig.[39] In a summary of his model of reading, Steig declares, 'Because of personality and experience, some readers are capable of more original and deeper understanding of emotionally puzzling aspects of particular literary works than are others'.[40] Thus rather than representing an unfortunate aspect of our humanity that we should attempt to suppress, the individuality of each member of our interpretive community should be valued as a unique treasure. The fullest value of this diversity of experience lies in sharing the readings that result from each individual's unique interpretive perspective. As Steig states in the fifth premise of his summary:

> Such seemingly idiosyncratic understanding can be communicated to other readers of the "same" text so that those readers may absorb the account of that individual experience and make it part of their own understanding, thereby reducing the degree of what may previously have been a feeling of the text's opacity, as well as initial reactions of confusion and incredulity at another's reading of it. Thus the subjective state

39. Michael Steig, *Stories of Reading: Subjectivity and Literary Understanding* (Baltimore: The Johns Hopkins University Press, 1989).

40. Steig, *Stories of Reading*, p. xiv. A similar argument specifically in relation to biblical interpretation was made in L.E. Keck and G.M. Tucker, 'Exegesis', in *IDBSup*, pp. 296-303: conclusions may differ due to 'varying sensibilities and insights' (p. 297); and 'Some exegeses are better than others, not simply because some exegetes are more knowledgeable, but also because some are more attuned to the subject matter' (p. 298).

of understanding may, under the right conditions for communicating it, be made intersubjective.[41]

Thus the personal experience and background of the reader is a potential boon to interpretation.

But, if even the idiosyncratic experiences of the interpreter play a role in the interpretation of texts, what does prevent the licentious reading of texts so feared by some? The answer: reading has always been and will always only be constrained by the interpretive conventions of the reader. We cannot choose to be unconstrained nor are there objective controls to which we can submit our interpretive work. As Fish has stated recently,

> constraints are not something one can either embrace or throw off because they are constitutive of the self and of its possible actions. On the one hand, the condition of being without constraints is quite literally unimaginable and therefore need not be feared; but on the other, the constraints that are always in place are not fixed but interpretive—forever being altered by the actions they make possible—and there is no danger that they will forever hold us in the same position.[42]

Antifoundationalists like Fish are not arguing for the removal of constraints on interpretation but rather that *objective* constraints have never existed.

If we push a little further in this area we may find that the issue is really one of intention and not constraint. Objections to the anti-formalist position often take the form of questions such as, 'So, if I choose to read Amos 7.10-17 as a recipe for cookies, nothing in the text constrains me from doing so?' The answer, of course, is 'Yes, it can be read that way.' The lack of objective, external constraints explains the plethora of readings produced by a plethora of readers. We share meaning not because we have arrived at the obvious, objectively-there meaning of the text but because we share reading conventions. The ultimate criterion for determining whether a reading represents a valid interpretation of the text is not whether it can be conclusively demonstrated to be an accurate construal of the author's intended meaning but whether such a reading accurately reflects the interpretive constraints of the interpretive community.

41. Steig, *Stories of Reading*, p. xiv.
42. Stanley Fish, 'Introduction: Going Down the Anti-Formalist Road', in *idem*, *Doing What Comes Naturally*, pp. 1-33 (27).

Most, probably all, modern biblical interpreters would object to reading Amos 7.10-17 as a cookie recipe. The objection does not make such a reading impossible. The primary reason for objecting to such a reading would be that it does not accurately reflect the author's intention. The real issue for many is not whether such a reading is possible but whether such a reading represents an accurate construal of authorial intentions. The very use of the term construal, however, indicates the subjective, conventionally shaped nature of textual interpretation. Recent theoretical discussions of authorial intention have indicated the interpretive quality of this aspect of reading. Authorial intention cannot function as an objective standard to constrain the interpretation of texts. Quite the contrary, intention, like everything else, is an interpretive fact that must be construed by the interpreter.[43] The recent focus on authorial intention in the theoretical literature is a recognition of the fact that, as Knapp and Michaels have argued in 'Against Theory', the making of meaning *is* the construing of intention; they are one and the same.[44] Rather than providing a means for guaranteeing objectivity in interpretation, Knapp and Michaels have demonstrated that objectivity is impossible since the object of interpretation, authorial intention, is construed by the interpreter. As Fish notes,

> It is only if meaning is embedded in texts—is a *formal* fact—that one could devise a method for 'reading it off'; but if meaning is a matter of what a speaker situated in a particular situation has in mind (precisely the thesis of speaker-relative presupposition), one can only determine it by going behind the words to the intentional circumstances of production in the light of which they acquire significance.[45]

An example may be helpful at this point. Responding to Dworkin's suggestion that one could read *Hamlet* psychodynamically without

---

43. Fish, 'Working on the Chain Gang', p. 100.

44. Steven Knapp and Walter Benn Michaels, 'Against Theory', in W.J.T. Mitchell (ed.), *Against Theory: Literary Studies and the New Pragmatism* (Chicago: University of Chicago Press, 1985), pp. 11-30.

45. Fish, 'Introduction', p. 7. Fish also correctly indicates that this is the nature of all acts of communication: 'That is, communications of every kind are characterized by the same conditions—the necessity of interpretive work, the unavoidability of perspective, and the construction by acts of interpretation of that which supposedly grounds interpretation, intentions, characters, and pieces of the world' ('With the Compliments of the Author: Reflections on Austin and Derrida', in his *Doing What Comes Naturally*, pp. 37-67 [44]).

supposing that Shakespeare did or that he intended that we do so, Fish states:

> If we are convinced that the meaning of *Hamlet* is psychodynamic but that Shakespeare intended no such meaning, then we are attributing the meaning to an intentional agent other than Shakespeare, perhaps to the spirit of the age, to some transhistorical truth about human nature, or to the intentional structure of language. And if we are convinced both that Shakespeare intended no psychodynamic meaning and that the play displays no such meaning, but decide nevertheless to read it psycho-dynamically, then we have simply set aside what we know to be the play's meaning and Shakespeare's intention for something else. In neither case, however, will we have sundered meaning or interpretation from intention.[46]

Historical Readers

Who is the reader? After 25 years of reader oriented criticism it is generally acknowledged that reading is a process, an experience through time, that in various ways involves both words on a page and a reader. While this recognition has shifted the focus of critical inquiry away from the text as artifact and toward responses generated during the event of reading, the effect and significance of this shift depends on how one answers the most fundamental question: who is the reader?

Mailloux has suggested that very divergent forms of critical analysis have been thrown together because they share a reader vocabulary that distinguishes them from a text-centered formalism. The striking differences become obvious, however, when examining the various names given to the reader. 'Readers were actual, ideal, implied, intended, educated, informed, competent, inscribed; there were mock readers, super-readers, narratees, implied audiences, interpretive communities, literary competencies, reading conventions.'[47] Omitting those methodologies that focused on actual readers reading in the present, each of these varieties of reader-response criticism privileged the responses of the critic. The readers in the text—implied, intended, etc.—were those 'found' in the text by the critic. The competent, informed, ideal readers

46. Fish, 'Wrong Again', p. 119.

47. Steven Mailloux, 'Misreading as a Historical Act: Cultural Rhetoric, Bible Politics, and Fuller's 1845 Review of Douglass's *Narrative*', in James L. Machor (ed.), *Readers in History: Nineteenth-Century American Literature and the Contexts of Response* (Baltimore: The Johns Hopkins University Press, 1993), pp. 3-31 (4).

tended to be mirror images of the critic as reader. There was little or no talk of historical readers reading.[48] The reception aesthetics of Hans Robert Jauss was an exception to this dehistoricizing tendency of early reader-oriented criticism.[49] Jauss's methodology focused on historical readers and their horizons of expectation. This focus on the horizons of expectations of historical readers opens every particular reading to the influence of a multitude of elements. As S. Mailloux notes:

> Such talk could develop critical analyses and stories of reading open to a range of factors usually ignored in most reader-oriented criticism, factors constituted by social, political, and economic categories including race, age, gender, ethnicity, nationality, religion, sexuality, and class.[50]

This emphasis on the value of investigating reception within specific socio-historical settings has been developed in a number of ways. Mailloux has called for a rhetorical hermeneutics that focuses on 'the cultural rhetoric in which readings are presented, circulated, adopted, and contested.'[51] He rejects generalizing theories of interpretation for 'rhetorical histories of specific interpretive acts'.[52] Readings of texts are rhetorical transactions shaped by particular social and historical factors.

James Machor has offered a different version of historicized reader-oriented criticism that he calls 'historical hermeneutics'. Like Mailloux, Machor criticizes the moves of reader-response critics to either privilege their own readings by positing themselves as the ideal audience or to make the historical readers a formalistic function of the text. 'Both

---

48. The competent reader of Fish may have included knowledge of the historical situation in which the document was written. In one of his earlier writings Fish noted, 'In its operation, my method will obviously be radically historical. The critic has the responsibility of becoming not one but a number of informed readers, each of whom will be identified by a matrix of political, cultural, and literary determinants. The informed reader of Milton will not be the informed reader of Whitman, although the latter will necessarily comprehend the former' ('Literature in the Reader: Affective Stylistics', in Jane Tompkins [ed.], *Reader-Response Criticism: From Formalism to Post-Structuralism* [Baltimore: The John Hopkins University Press, 1980], pp. 70-100 [87]).

49. Hans Robert Jauss, *Aesthetic Experience and Literary Hermeneutics* (Minneapolis: University of Minnesota Press, 1982); *idem*, *Towards an Aesthetic of Reception* (Minneapolis: University of Minnesota Press, 1982).

50. Mailloux, 'Misreading as a Historical Act', p. 5.

51. Mailloux, 'Misreading as a Historical Act', p. 5. Cf. *idem*, *Rhetorical Power* (Ithaca, NY: Cornell University Press, 1989).

52. Mailloux, 'Misreading as a Historical Act', p. 8.

practices thus succumb to a temporal solipsism that fixes reading within a single set of interpretive conventions while ignoring the historically constituted conditions of response, including those informing the critics' own activities'.[53] As a corrective to this temporal solipsism Machor suggests a hybrid created from response theory and reception theory.

> Such a reorientation needs to integrate response theory, which concentrates on the stages of hermeneutical processing, and the contextual emphasis of reception theory to create a historical hermeneutics that identifies specific reading practices and explores the role of interpretive communities in the way texts were constructed and made meaningful in a given era. For an era other than our own, such a turn would necessitate a close analysis of interpretive traces preserved in the archive, but in doing so, a historical hermeneutics would have to go beyond Jonathan Culler's call for a history of reception that merely surveys the legacy of responses to a particular text to reconstruct the codes that produced its various interpretations. Instead, such an approach would reconstruct the shared patterns of interpretation for a specific historical era to define the reading strategies of particular interpretive communities and to examine the impact of those strategies on the production and consumption of literary texts.[54]

These historicized reader-oriented approaches are now grouped by some under the broad heading of New Historicism. This theoretical orientation not only opens the possibility for detente between the 'new' literary- and 'old' historical-critical approaches to the biblical texts but also invites active cooperation and integration. While these perspectives on reading present a wealth of theoretical possibilities for the reading of biblical texts, they raise significant methodological questions. The combination of response and reception perspectives presents the possibility of readings of the biblical texts that result from a fruitful cooperation between affective analyses and historical-critical analyses. Is it really possible, however, to talk about the reading strategies of particular historical communities in specific historical eras? Both Mailloux and Machor have the apparent advantage of working with nineteenth-century literary works which were the subject of many critical reviews

---

53. James L. Machor, 'Historical Hermeneutics and Antebellum Fiction: Gender, Response Theory, and Interpretive Contexts', in *idem* (ed.), *Readers in History: Nineteenth-Century American Literature and the Contexts of Response* (Baltimore: The Johns Hopkins University Press, 1993), pp. 54-84 (55).
   54. Machor, 'Historical Hermeneutics', p. 60.

near the time of writing. This is certainly a luxury not afforded the reader of the texts of the Hebrew Bible. Are their methodological proposals at all relevant to the interpretation of literature that has no concurrent critical reviews?

Perhaps the extent of their advantage is illusory. Although there is certainly an advantage to having interpretations of a work that are contemporary with its production, these interpretations do not give the critic unmediated access to the interpretive conventions of a particular community in a specific historical era. That is, the critic's reading of a review of a primary work is shaped by historical distance and the reading conventions of the critic in the same way that the reading of the primary work is shaped. In other words, the existence of reviews of a literary work do not magically implant the reading conventions of historical readers into the mind of the critic. Access to all of reality is always mediated through the interpretive conventions of the interpreter. Both Mailloux and Machor recognize this inherent subjectivity. Machor is quite clear on the subjectivity of interpretation in summarizing the goal of historical hermeneutics:

> Because reader-oriented criticism, as Tompkins has argued, 'attack[s] the very foundations of positivism' and its privileging of objectivity by maintaining that 'all language…is constitutive of the reality it purports to describe', the goal of that criticism is not to reach a transcendent objectivity outside a historical context of interpretive acts. Similarly, the purpose of a historically based reader-response criticism is not to restore the subjective/objective dichotomy but to collapse it by grounding the reading experience of fiction in an awareness of historical conditions, including the critic's own. In its interplay between the historical experience (re)constructed from the archive and the critic's own self-conscious enactment of interpretation, a historical hermeneutics would provide not an objective description of historicized reading so much as a Gadamerian 'fusion of horizons' that is always partial, provisional, speculative, and thus open to the flux characterizing interpretation as an intertextual, historical, and gender-based activity.[55]

While the biblical critic's archive for (re)constructing the socio-historical setting in which the documents were produced and read may be less extensive than that for nineteenth-century American fiction, there are still textual and artifactual remains from which the historical experience can be constructed. The interpretation of these textual and

---

55. Machor, 'Historical Hermeneutics', p. 63.

artifactual remains will always be partial, provisional and speculative, but the only alternative is to abandon the enterprise altogether. With a document like the book of Hosea the difficulty is also magnified by the problem of determining the precise date of production of the final form. However, the proposed reading in early Achaemenid Yehud, although perhaps not reflective of the final redactor's *Sitz im Leben*, can provide valuable insight into an early phase of the book's history of inter-pretation.[56] It will undoubtedly have more to do with the book as an object of interpretation and the Persian period Yehudite community than with the intentions of the prophet or the many redactors of earlier periods. The hope is that this fusion of the horizons of literary criticism and historical investigation will facilitate the fusion of the horizons of ancient and modern readers and provide insight into the life of both the text and this particular ancient community of readers.

The Sociology of Imperial Control

Sociological theory is often a useful tool in the reconstruction and analysis of historical situations and entities. Awareness of general patterns of social organization, for example, patterns of imperial organ-ization and control, can provide valuable insight into the nature of ancient empires. This happens on at least two levels. First, the recog-nition of general patterns of social organization can provide the basis for interpreting some historical evidence which may otherwise be inscrutable. Sociological analysis can aid in the understanding of less well-known historical empires through comparative studies of the common forms of imperial organization. Second, when used cautiously in relation to the available historical data, these same sociological theories can also highlight unique aspects of a particular implement-ation of a social system. Knowledge of typical patterns not only allows for the identification of those patterns but also deviations from and alterations to them.

S.N. Eisenstadt's analysis of historical empires as bureaucratic systems centered around the emperor has been influential in later his-torical treatments of various ancient empires. Eisenstadt believed that

---

56. See the discussion below, 'The Date of the Book of Hosea', where it is suggested that the final form of Hosea, with the possible exception of some minor editorial changes, would have been fixed by the early Persian period.

the various arms of imperial administration were designed primarily for the purpose of resource extraction. While they might provide some social services to benefit some members of the society, these services were only provided to maintain stability. The chief goal of the imperial bureaucracy was to take rather than to provide.[57]

The sociological analysis of ancient Near Eastern empires has been further developed as a result of the influence of the concepts of center and periphery drawn from the world-systems theory of Immanuel Wallerstein.[58] Wallerstein's analysis describes the relations between the core nations and non-core nations of the modern world economy in terms of a center (the core nations) which extracts resources from the periphery (the non-core nations). Although Wallerstein did not apply his theory to historical world empires, he did recognize similarities between his understanding of the modern world in terms of core–periphery and the social forms of empires: 'It is the social achievement of the modern world, if you will, to have invented the technology that makes it possible to increase the flow of the surplus from the lower strata to the upper strata, from the periphery to the center, from the majority to the minority, by eliminating the 'waste' of too cumbersome a political superstructure'.[59] In other words, Wallerstein saw similarities between world empires and the modern world economy but he believed the latter represented a more efficient form of resource extraction by the center from its periphery. Thus, this form of analysis can also be a useful means for considering the dynamics of the relationship between a centralized imperial government and its outlying imperial colonies.

While the theories of both Eisenstadt and Wallerstein have been very influential in the analysis of ancient Near Eastern empires, their use must be modified as a result of two substantial critiques of Michael

---

57. S.N. Eisenstadt, *The Political Systems of Empires* (Glencoe: Free Press, 1963), p. 16.

58. Immanuel Wallerstein, *The Modern World System*. I. *Capitalist Agriculture and the Origins of the European World-Economy in the Sixteenth Century* (New York: Academic Press, 1974).

59. Wallerstein, *The Modern World System*, I, pp. 15-16. Later he states: 'It is further argued that thus far there have only existed two varieties of such world-systems: world-empires, in which there is a single political system over most of the area, however attenuated the degree of its effective control; and those systems in which such a single political system does not exist over all, we are using the term "world-economy" to describe the latter' (p. 348).

Mann.[60] First, Mann has criticized sociological analyses in general for defining 'society' too narrowly. He argues that societies are not closed and distinct, unitary totalities, but rather are 'constituted of multiple overlapping and intersecting sociospatial networks of power'.[61] The extent of these various networks of power vary both within and across the boundaries of the society. Mann regards the highly centralized, unitary preindustrial societies of Eisenstadt and others as a myth. Rather, he believes that the historical empires were 'essentially federal' in nature.[62] Thus, although the center–periphery relationship is a useful frame for understanding many aspects of an empire and its colonies, it is important to remember that this is not the totality of the power relationships in such a situation. Power networks differ in their expanse, intersect and overlap. They exist both within and across the defined borders of an empire. Human social interactions are always multivalent.

Second, Mann has criticized center–periphery analyses for their typical depiction of the imperial center merely as a parasite on the economic production of the periphery. He counters these parasitic depictions with a modified version of Herbert Spencer's notion of 'compulsory cooperation'. Rather than being solely a consumer of surplus, Mann argues that empires could also be the creators of accumulation.[63] He cites five processes of compulsory cooperation which could lead to economic development: (1) Military pacification: by providing protection which created the opportunity for the expansion of agriculture further outside the existing city walls than was previously possible, military pacification provided the means for increased production and increased surpluses. In addition, the protection of trade routes within the empire and the regulation and protection of trade with states outside the empire created the conditions for substantial economic growth. (2) The military multiplier: although the military's needs for a wide variety of staples, both food stuffs and various equipment, could be a parasitic drain on the economy, the building of roads, the improvement in communications and the increase in production that could result from corvee labor would all have a beneficial impact on the production of these core items. 'It is impossible to separate "economic"

---

60. Michael Mann, *The Sources of Social Power*, I (Cambridge: Cambridge University Press, 1986).
61. Mann, *The Sources of Social Power*, I, p. 1.
62. Mann, *The Sources of Social Power*, I, p. 10.
63. Mann, *The Sources of Social Power*, I, p. 148.

and "military" motives, because the pacification needs were similar to supply needs. The economic spinoff to most of society was considerable.'[64] (3) Authority and economic value: by establishing fixed exchange values for a wide variety of products over a large geographical area, the state could turn items of exchange into commodities that could achieve a monetary status. In addition, the provision of guaranteed weights and measures, the official recording of contracts and property rights were all means of producing economic value. (4) The intensification of labor: both corvee labor for the construction of imperial infrastructure and an increase in slave labor could benefit the economy by increasing production. (5) Coerced diffusion:

> The four aspects of compulsory cooperation discussed so far have involved authoritative power, a highly organized, logistical base providing a bridge between local particularisms. But much of this organization would be unnecessary if similar ways of life and similar culture could be *diffused* throughout a population, breaking down local particularisms, forcing local identities into a broader one.[65]

In this regard Mann cites the impact on literacy created by the fusion of the Akkadian language with Sumerian literacy, creating a syllabic script which boosted literacy. By increasing literacy, bureaucracy, trade, diplomacy and social knowledge were all increased. 'Thus Akkadian conquest could lead to an extension of culture, of an ideological power capable of providing further diffused power supports to empire.'[66]

This last point is particularly pertinent to the analysis of imperial-colonial relationships. The territorial expansions of empires are never solely predicated on the simple goal of having a larger territory over which to rule. Territorial expansion means greater responsibility, greater expense of finite resources, and the potential for greater instability. Although increasing the territorial holdings of the empire may serve the purpose of increasing the glory and honor ascribed to the emperor by the citizens of the empire, this increase does not invariably result from territorial conquest but is constructed from the socially perceived worth of the territory. Stated baldly, increases in the territory controlled by the empire should mean, from the perspective of the imperial center, increased resources. Territorial expansion serves the needs and goals of

---

64. Mann, *The Sources of Social Power*, I, p. 150.
65. Mann, *The Sources of Social Power*, I, p. 152 (emphasis original).
66. Mann, *The Sources of Social Power*, I, p. 152.

the empire through the extraction of resources—material, animal and human. These extracted resources can then be deployed in a variety of ways by the imperial administration. Ultimately, the expense of territorial conquest is justified by the benefits that accrue from the empire's exploitation of the resources of the resulting colony(ies).

Military coercion is far too expensive to function as the sole means of maintaining imperial domination of a colonial possession. If the means of control are more costly than the material and rhetorical benefits deriving from the possession of a specific colony, then the implicit goal of territorial expansion is not met. Similar to the assessment of Mann noted above, Michael Rowlands suggests that imperial exploitation must rely on military coercion in times of crisis. 'But in more stable circumstances, repression may be more securely based through establishing a hegemony of shared interests and beliefs in the benefits of maintaining the established order'.[67] As a result, there are a variety of strategies that have been employed by empires as a means of establishing and maintaining their control over colonies that insure that the balance of expenses to income remains in favor of the imperial center. The sociology of imperial control coupled with an analysis of the particularities of the unique historical situation provides a firmer basis than either alone for understanding the situation of colonial Yehud and its relation to the Persian imperial center.[68]

Reading Hosea in the Early Persian Period: A Preview

The production and reproduction of texts in Yehud of the sixth and fifth centuries BCE is evidence of a high degree of literacy, at least in a portion of the population. Such activities are also suggestive regarding the social setting for the reading of texts. Texts are written to be read.[69]

---

67. Michael Rowlands, 'Preface', in Michael Rowlands, Mogens Larsen, and Kristian Kristiansen (eds.), *Centre and Periphery in the Ancient World* (Cambridge: Cambridge University Press, 1987), p. viii.

68. Two statements of Mann are appropriate: 'Sociological theory cannot develop without knowledge of history.' 'If historians eschew theory of how societies operate, they imprison themselves in the common sense notions of their own society' (*The Sources of Social Power*, I, p. vii).

69. There may be certain exceptions such as incantations, curses, and the like that may be written down for ritual purposes but never intended to be read (cf. Num. 5.23).

As Ben Zvi states, 'It seems obvious that written texts were produced and copied for people who could read for themselves, and to others'.[70] This section will attempt to define as specifically as possible the readers and situations of reading in early Persian period Yehud, from the beginning of Persian control (539 BCE) to the completion of the second temple (c. 516 BCE). This will involve an evaluation of evidence regarding the degree of literacy; socio-economic constraints pertaining to literacy, text production, and reading; and political, social and ideological factors relating to the reading of texts during this period.

The Date of the Book of Hosea
A detailed analysis of the compositional history of the book of Hosea leading to the determination of the date for the production of the final form of the book of Hosea is beyond the scope of this study. However, in light of the proposal to read the book in the Persian period it is appropriate to indicate the general scholarly consensus that a reasonable *terminus ad quem* for the existence of the final form of the book permits such a reading. If the book did not exist during the period in which the reading is being proposed then it obviously could not have been the subject of interpretation.

Modern redactional analysis of the book of Hosea has generated very diverse proposals for the composition history of the book. A variety of suggestions have been made with regard to what material is original to the prophet Hosea and what represents later redactional additions. There have also been a multitude of suggestions regarding the date and socio-historical location of the various redactional layers that have been 'discovered'. In spite of this multiplicity of competing theories regarding the details of the process of redaction, there is a surprising degree of unanimity regarding the period in which this process came to an end. For the most part, scholars have concluded that the last redactional activity that can be detected in the book of Hosea comes from the late neo-Babylonian or early Persian period. For example, Gale Yee suggests a two-phase redactional process similar to those proposed for the Deuteronomistic History. She finds many similarities between her first redactional layer (R1) and a Josianic redaction of the DtrH and posits a second Deuteronomistic-style redaction (R2) in the neo-Babylonian

---

70. Ehud Ben Zvi, *A Historical-Critical Study of the Book of Obadiah* (BZAW, 242; Berlin: W. de Gruyter, 1996), p. 4.

period.[71] Although not all agree with these two stages of redaction, there is general agreement that the process was completed before the end of the sixth century.[72] This general scholarly consensus regarding the date of the completion of the book of Hosea suggests that the proposed reading of the text within the framework provided by the socio-historical setting of the early Persian period is reasonable.

Literacy in the Ancient World

Readers undoubtedly would have represented a very small percentage of a very small population in Achaemenid Jerusalem. Recent demographic studies have suggested that the population of Persian period Yehud was probably no more than 20,000 (see below 'The Population of Achaemenid Yehud'). The number of literate individuals in such a small population would likely be very low. The ability to read is normally more widespread in a society, and sometimes much more widespread, than the ability to write.[73] William Harris has suggested that discussions and assumptions about literacy in the ancient world have not always differentiated the various shades of literacy. He posits three gradations of literacy (each representing points along a continuum): professional literacy, such as one would expect of scribes; craftsman's literacy, the level of literacy of those involved in crafts; and mass literacy, ranging from the illiterate to semi-literate.[74]

The increasing number of inscriptions coming to light through archaeological investigation may suggest that a significant proportion of ancient populations could read at a very minimal level. The ability

---

71. Gale Yee, *Composition and Tradition in the Book of Hosea* (SBLDS, 102; Atlanta: Scholars Press, 1987), pp. 120-22, 129-30.

72. Graham I. Davies, *Hosea* (NCB; London: Marshall Pickering, 1992), pp. 36-37; James Luther Mays, *Hosea* (OTL; Philadelphia: Westminster Press, 1969), pp. 16-17; Hans Walter Wolff, *Hosea*, (Hermeneia; Philadelphia: Fortress Press, 1974), p. xxxii; cf. Ina Willi-Plein, *Vorformen der Schriftexegese innerhalb des Alten Testaments: Untersuchungen zum literarischen Werden der auf Amos, Hosea und Micha zurückgehenden Bücher im hebräischen Zwölfprophetenbuch* (BZAW, 123; Berlin: W. de Gruyter, 1971), pp. 241-53. This does not exclude the possibility of minor additions that are of such a character that they are not obvious to redactional analyses, nor does it exclude the textual variations that undoubtedly arose during the long history of textual transmission.

73. William V. Harris, *Ancient Literacy* (Cambridge, MA: Harvard University Press, 1989), p. 4.

74. Harris, *Ancient Literacy*, pp. 7-8.

necessary to read an inscription or function as a craftsperson, however, is far removed from reading and writing even simple literary compositions. Indeed, although inscriptions may indicate a limited level of literacy in some proportion of the general population, the impressive iconography of kingdoms and empires coupled with (unreadable) inscriptions may have functioned even more effectively as propaganda for the largely illiterate portion of the population. The inability to read the inscriptions may have had the effect of heightening the self-aggrandizing potential of the monuments. The limited number of highly literate individuals would create an association of literacy with power and authority, especially since most highly literate individuals functioned within the spheres of government and religion.

Harris suggests that literacy can extend beyond a very small percentage of the population only with the support of large-scale changes supporting literacy, for example, the invention of the printing press, the Protestant emphasis on the value of private Bible reading, the need for a more literate workforce as a result of the industrial revolution, the instigation of political leaders who hold positive beliefs about the value of a literate population, etc. Widespread literacy requires, as a necessary precondition, large-scale production of low cost texts. 'But no historical culture is known to have achieved more than a rather low level of craftsman's literacy without the printing press.'[75] Also, although an alphabet can be learned without formal education, a system of schools providing educational opportunities for the majority of the population is essential to widespread literacy.[76]

This analysis suggests that the production and reading of the biblical texts would have been the province of a very small number of social elites. Only highly educated professionals, composed predominantly of the male children of aristocratic families, would have had the opportunities to learn and practice the skills necessary to produce or read such complex literary productions. This literati is unlikely to have represented more than 1 per cent of the total population.[77] Given the

---

75. Harris, *Ancient Literacy*, pp. 12-15.

76. Harris, *Ancient Literacy*, p. 16.

77. Compare John Baines, 'Literacy and Ancient Egyptian Society', *Man* NS 18 (1983), pp. 572-99; J. Ray, 'Literacy in Egypt in the Late and Persian Periods', in A.K. Bowman and Greg Woolf (eds.), *Literacy and Power in the Ancient World* (Cambridge: Cambridge University Press, 1994), pp. 51-66. Philip Davies suggests that even in modern societies with high levels of literacy fewer than 1% write books

relatively small population of Persian period Yehud and the minuscule percentage of the population possessing the literary skills necessary for the writing and reading the biblical texts, it is most likely that these texts were written, edited and copied by the same small group (circle? school?), not a variety of different and\or competing 'schools'.[78] The production, reproduction, reading and rereading of texts would have been in the control of a group numbering, perhaps, between 50 and 200.

Depictions of Reading in the Biblical Texts
The biblical literature is replete with various accounts of the entire community of Israel listening to the reading or explanation of a text. The entire text of Deuteronomy is presented as an explanation (באר) of the Torah by Moses to all the Israelites in the plains of Moab (Deut. 1.5). On completing this explanation of the law, Moses produces a written copy that is placed in the keeping of the priests, the sons of Levi, and instructs that it should be read to the entire community every seventh year during Sukkoth (Deut. 31.9-13). Joshua is depicted as reading the entire 'law, blessings and curses, according to all that is written in the book of the law' to כל קהל ישׂראל ('the entire assembly of Israel', Josh. 8.33-35). In the account of Josiah's reform, first the book discovered during the Temple renovations is read to the king (2 Kgs 22.10), then the king reads the book to all the people, and they respond by committing themselves to this covenant (23.1-3). All of these accounts occur in texts that are clearly Deuteronomistic in language and perspective. Their historical veracity is, to say the least, highly suspect. However, even though these accounts may not accurately reflect the social situation of their literary setting in the monarchic period, they do

---

(*In Search of 'Ancient Israel': A Study in Biblical Origins* [JSOTSup, 148; Sheffield: JSOT Press, 1992], p. 102).

78. This insight was suggested in Ehud Ben Zvi, 'The Urban Center of Jerusalem and the Development of the Old Testament/Hebrew Bible Literature', unpublished paper delivered at the conference on 'Urbanism in the Ancient Near East', Lethbridge, January 1996. My thanks to the author for making a copy of this paper available. This understanding of the social situation of the early Persian period Yehudite community corresponds with Eric Meyers's suggestion that there was a spirit of cooperation between priests and prophets in this period ('The Use of *tora* in Haggai 2:11 and the Role of the Prophet in the Restoration Community', in Carol L. Meyers and M. O'Connor [eds.], *The Word of the Lord Shall Go Forth: Essays in Honor of David Noel Freedman in Celebration of his Sixtieth Birthday* [Winona Lake, IN: Eisenbrauns, 1983], pp. 69-76).

indicate that the social situation in which the DtrH was produced was one in which the entire community, that is males and females of all social strata (including children and resident aliens), participated in readings of the religious traditions of the community. Significantly, in every instance the reading of the text is mediated to the community by one or more members of the divinely authorized, ruling elite.

The importance of written texts to the rhetoric of the books of Ezra and Nehemiah has been indicated by Tamara Eskenazi. She highlights three specific examples of the power attributed to written texts. First, messages from God come through the medium of the written text in the form of public reading from the book of the Torah (Neh. 8). Second, the function of written texts for providing authority is demonstrated by the references to official correspondence (Ezra 4–5). Third, the covenant in the book of Nehemiah is presented as a written document to which the leading figures in the community attach their signatures (Neh. 10.1-27). In each of these examples, the written text plays a substantial and authoritative role within the life of the community.[79]

The narrative of the reading of the book of the Torah of Moses by Ezra on Rosh Hashanah and during the celebration of Sukkoth (Neh. 8) is particularly relevant for this study. As with the accounts of similar events in the DtrH, Ezra reads to the entire assembly (קהל), both men and women and all who could hear with understanding (וכל מבין לשמע), each day of the festival (Neh. 8.2-3, 18). There may be grounds to question the likelihood that the entire Yehudite community gathered for communal reading and instruction, but the rhetoric of the text is clear: the whole community gathers to hear and be instructed.[80] While Eskenazi asserts the important function of the people in initiating the reading of the Torah (Neh. 8.1; 9.1-3), these texts function to indicate the eagerness of the people to hear the words of the Torah, not their control over them. There are two clearly defined groups represented in Nehemiah 8–9: the ruling elites, who read and interpret the texts, and the people (עם) or assembly (קהל), who listen to and obey the words of the texts. While the people are represented as eager consumers of the written texts, their consumption is wholly mediated by the literate elites

---

79. Tamara Cohn Eskenazi, *In an Age of Prose: A Literary Approach to Ezra–Nehemiah* (SBLMS, 36; Atlanta: Scholars Press, 1988), p. 5.

80. There is a definite stress on the participation of the entire community. There are 13 references to the people (עם) in these verses, of which eight refer to 'all the people'. Cf. Eskenazi, *In an Age of Prose*, p. 97.

of the colony. The readings not only proceed from the mouth of a divinely authorized agent, but the Levites, as representatives of the political and religious authorities, are on hand to provide an interpretation of the reading for the gathered assembly (8.7-8).

Also prominently highlighted in this text is the gathering of the ruling class of the society, the heads of ancestral houses, priests, Levites and Ezra (the scribe!). They join together to gain insight (hiphil of שׂכל) into the words of the Torah (8.13). Their interpretation of these written words is then communicated to the people (8.14-15), who willingly implement the instructions (8.16-18). Clearly, this text illustrates a situation in which the written word functions as a societal standard and the educated, economically privileged function as the arbiters of the interpretation of that text.[81]

The intermediary function of the educated, ruling class is also evident in the Chronicler's depiction of priests, Levites, and other royal officials as instructors authorized by Jehoshaphat travelling through Judah teaching from the book of the law (2 Chron. 17.7-9). As with the texts from the DtrH previously discussed, this narrative is unlikely to reflect an actual historical occurrence in the ninth century but it does indicate something about the social matrix in which the text was produced; it reflects 'a post-exilic reality, anachronistically projected back to the age of the monarchy'.[82] Japhet indicates that the function of the Levites as teachers of the Law is a purely Second Temple phenomenon and that the attribution of the initiative for instruction of the people to a monarch is only paralleled in Persian period practice. Curiously, she also highlights the unusual nature of the itinerant teaching, paralleled only in the circuit of Samuel, and asks whether this may be modelled on the image of Samuel rather than reflective of Persian period reality. However, the proximity of the composition of the DtrH to the Persian period (rather than to the early Iron Age) and the more literary than historical nature of the Samuel character in the DtrH raises the possibility that his teaching circuit is not an accurate historical depiction of events in the early Iron Age but a reading of later practice into the depiction of that period.

---

81. Joseph Blenkinsopp suggests that the inconsistency between the practice depicted in this text and the Pentateuchal law indicates that this narrative precedes the final form of the Pentateuch. Joseph Blenkinsopp, *Ezra–Nehemiah* (OTL; Philadelphia: Westminster Press, 1988), p. 291.

82. Sara Japhet, *I & II Chronicles* (OTL; Louisville, KY: Westminster/John Knox Press, 1993), p. 749.

In any case, although it is possible that 2 Chron. 17.7-9 may be a reflection of the literary depiction of Samuel, it is more likely that both Samuel's itinerant teaching and Jehoshaphat's itinerant teachers reflect Persian period practice. Certainly the account of Jehoshaphat's officials performing itinerant teaching in the monarchic period is a retrojection of Persian period practice.

The Social Function of Reading in Yehud

The neo-Babylonian and early Persian periods have been recognized as significant periods in the production and development of a substantial portion of the biblical literature. The final edition of the DtrH is generally considered to be a product of the neo-Babylonian period. The editing of most of the eighth-century prophetic collections is also generally assigned to this period. This apparent intensity in textual production and preoccupation with the preservation of national traditions can be explained by several factors. The need to account for the national disaster of 587/586 BCE, especially in relation to the preservation of communal identity after the loss of many of the social institutions that had previously served this function, created an ideal climate in which the contemporary situation would have been linked to and explained by the ancestral traditions of the community. This can be seen most clearly in the DtrH and Lamentations. It should also be noted that the ethnic Judahite community in Mesopotamia, living close to the political and religious heart of the neo-Babylonian empire, was immersed in a culture deeply concerned with the collection and preservation of its own ancient traditions at this time.[83] Finally, the transition to life under Persian rule with the resulting altered social structures would have stimulated the need to find validation of the new social institutions in the traditions of the past. The community in the Persian province of Yehud (or at least the elites who produced the texts which originate with this community) clearly believed (and\or wanted others to believe) that their society was a renewal or continuation of monarchic period Israel and Judah. Such a link could only be established and maintained by a recontextualization of the traditions of monarchic Israel to the altered setting of the Persian period community.

---

83. Bustenay Oded, 'Judah and the Exile', in John H. Hayes and J. Maxwell Miller (eds.), *Israelite and Judean History* (Philadelphia: Trinity Press International; London: SCM Press, 1977), p. 438.

The social situation of Persian period Yehud in which the reintro-
duced 'community of the exile' (בני הגלה), with imperial support,
needed and wanted to impose their rule on the existing inhabitants of
Yehud would require some form of religious sanction in shared
tradition and a setting in which that sanction could be communicated.
As the texts examined above reveal in every instance, access to the text
is mediated to the vast majority of the society through the reading and
interpretive practices of the small layer of educated social elites.[84] As
indicated above, this educated class was probably not a large, diverse
population divided into competing 'schools' or 'circles' but a relatively
monolithic social group with common goals and ideology. By establishing their control on the basis of the production and interpretation of
'divinely authorized' texts (see below), they established themselves and
their policies as representative of the divine will. 'Significantly, the
more the text is considered a gate towards divine knowledge—as all
prophetic books claim to be—the more the educated readers and interpreters (and indirectly those who support them) play the social role
of 'brokers of the divine' for the rest of the population, and for
themselves'.[85]

The production, reproduction and official interpretation of the biblical literature would require, as an absolute necessity, a scribal school
for both the execution of these activities and the training of the next
generation of practitioners. At issue is not a minimal ability to read and
write but highly developed literary skills combined with the time, economic means and access to archives necessary for the production,
preservation, study and teaching of complex literary texts of a wide
variety of genres and styles. Such could only be the product of trained,
professional scribes who were both part of and supported by the secular
and religious ruling class. Generally, temples and palaces were both the
setting for scribal activities and the depositories for scribal products in
the ancient Near East. In Persian period Yehud this would certainly
have been the provincial administrative center of the Persian colony
and, after its construction, the Jerusalem temple. These scribal activities

84. Cf. the statement of Davies, *In Search*, p. 101: 'This literature is neither the
product of a total ancient agrarian society (95% of it illiterate) nor of isolated individuals but of a class or body, and arises from ideological, economic, and political
preconditions.'

85. Ben Zvi, *Obadiah*, p. 5.

would have provided a variety of benefits to the governing elite. As Davies notes, 'these scrolls will have existed for the purposes of the temple—either as an archive, or for temple liturgy, or for recourse in legal disputes, or other economic or diplomatic purposes'.[86]

Both the production and reading of texts by this professional literati would, on the whole, have reflected the values, beliefs and social and political goals of the ruling class that functioned as both their patrons and peers. There can be little doubt that they read their own beliefs and practices in(to) the texts they were writing and reading. The result was the retrojection of their own social situation into their accounts of the past (as was suggested above with regard to the reports of communal reading). As with all socially rooted interpretations (which includes all interpretations), their communal conventions acted as constraints on the interpretation of the texts they read. This is not to suggest that much, if any, of this process occurred at the conscious level. Rather, the shape of their reading of these texts would have been the result of the way in which they had themselves been shaped by their socio-historical setting and the conventions of textual production and interpretation that were then current. It is inconceivable that their social setting and the belief/ desire that they represented a continuation of the monarchic Judean society would not have colored their perception of the texts they were both reading and writing.[87]

Reading Prophetic Texts in Yehud
The dramatically altered social structures and transformed relationship to ancestral traditions resulting from the defeat of Jerusalem and the transition to life as a Persian imperial province are evident in the institution of prophecy. William Schniedewind suggests that what has variously been described as the death or decline of classical prophecy in the Persian period is, rather, a transformation in the conception of prophecy.[88] He demonstrates that in the Persian period the phrase, 'the

---

86. Davies, *In Search*, pp. 105-106.

87 'Certainly, the literature was not commissioned and then written to order! But it is conceivable that the task of constructing a history of the society in which the cult, laws and ethos of the ruling caste would be authorized was undertaken deliberately and conscientiously by scribes serving the ruling caste, partly at their behest, partly from self-interest, and partly from sheer creative enjoyment' (Davies, *In Search*, p. 115).

88. William M. Schniedewind, *The Word of God in Transition: From Prophet*

word of Yahweh' (דבר יהוה), which had been used exclusively as a designator of the prophetic word in the monarchic period, is extended to cover both prophetic traditions and the Mosaic legal texts. The Deuteronomic depiction of Moses as both lawgiver and prototypical prophet provided a foundation for this confluence of prophetic and legal texts under the single, broad designation, 'word of Yahweh'.[89] The focus shifted in the Persian period from divinely authorized individuals to authoritative texts. Schniedewind is too limiting, however, when he states, 'Torah replaced prophecy and the prophetic office became unnecessary'.[90] Undoubtedly the Torah eventually assumed the central position in this textually oriented religion. But, it appears more correct to say that 'word of Yahweh' became the common designation for authoritative texts (legal and prophetic) and that these authoritative texts assumed the function of classical prophecy in the Persian period.

Rex Mason suggests that it was not the failure of prophecy that led to the decline of classical prophecy in the Persian period but its success. Since the prophetic oracles of the prophets of preceding generations were proven correct, they were collected and became written texts. These written texts became the focus of authority that had previously been invested in the prophetic office. Prophecy was replaced by the interpretation of prophetic texts.[91] The analyses of both Mason and Schniedewind stress that a transition occurred between the monarchic and early Persian periods from the primacy of the oral proclamation of prophetic individuals in the monarchic period to the primacy of written texts and their authoritative interpretation in the Achaemenid period.

In relation to the monarchic period prophetic traditions, Zechariah 1 demonstrates an exegetical interest in the words of the 'former prophets' and their relevance to life in the Persian period Yehudite community. The opening oracle of Zechariah calls on the Yehudites, unlike their ancestors, to be faithful to Yahweh. The words of the former prophets spoken to the ancestors are summarized, 'Thus says the LORD of hosts, Return from your evil ways and from your evil deeds'.

---

to Exegete in the Second Temple Period (JSOTSup, 197; Sheffield: Sheffield Academic Press, 1995).

89. Schniedewind, *The Word of God in Transition*, pp. 130-38.

90. Schniedewind, *The Word of God in Transition*, p. 137.

91. Rex Mason, 'The Prophets of the Restoration', in R. Coggins, A. Phillips and M. Knibb (eds.), *Israel's Prophetic Tradition: Essays in Honour of Peter Ackroyd* (Cambridge: Cambridge University Press, 1982), pp. 137-54.

But, Zechariah notes, the ancestors did not listen to the warnings of the former prophets (Zech. 1.4). The community is reminded that even though both the ancestors and the former prophets are now dead, the words of Yahweh through the former prophets overtook their ancestors. Both the prophets and their audience are no longer present but the words of the prophets remain. The result of Zechariah's historically grounded exegesis of the former prophets are reported in the concluding summary, 'So they repented and said, "The LORD of hosts has dealt with us according to our ways and deeds, just as he planned to do"' (1.6). A question concerning ritual fasts that had begun during the period of exile is answered by reference to 'the words that the LORD proclaimed by the former prophets' (Zech. 7.7). This is immediately followed by a warning to live justly based on the desolation of the land that resulted because of the unwillingness of the ancestors to 'hear the law and the words that the LORD of hosts had sent by his spirit through the former prophets' (7.8-14).

Other texts indicate a comparable understanding of the earlier prophets as messengers who brought a warning to the ancestors. In Neh. 9.30, a text from Ezra's sermon surveying the nation's history and relationship with Yahweh, the earlier prophets are recalled as the source of a warning from Yahweh. Both 2 Chron. 24.19, from the account of the reign of Joash, and 2 Chron. 36.15-16, from the account of the reign of Zedekiah and the fall of Jerusalem, stress the function of the prophets as messengers to the ancestors, the refusal of the ancestors to listen to the prophets, and the disastrous consequences which ensued as a result of their refusal to listen. All of these texts demonstrate that the interpretation of the past in the light of the prophetic traditions was important to the Yehudites of the Persian period. This understanding of the earlier prophets functioned as both a lens for making sense of the past and a foundation for the relationship of the community with Yahweh in the present.

A similar attitude is also evident in Trito-Isaiah. In a catalog of the multiple cultic sins of a portion of the population, the contemporary sins and their eventual outcome are paralleled with the sins of the ancestors (Isa. 65.1-13, esp. v. 12). Many of these texts also demonstrate an interest in the nation's history as a context that is useful for making sense of the community's present.[92]

---

92. Although the date of Trito-Isaiah is less easily established, many of the prophecies have been dated in the early Persian period in examinations of the

Significantly, these texts suggest that during the early Persian period the prophetic traditions of preceding generations were being read with some recognition of the historical setting of the prophet and the original audience.[93] In fact, they indicate a belief that the current generation could learn from a historical reading of their traditions and avoid the disasters that had overtaken their ancestors.[94] There are indications of a similar understanding of the texts of Isaiah and Jeremiah. At one point the prophet is told to write down an oracle 'so that it may be for the time to come as a witness forever' (Isa. 30.8). The prophetic word functions not only in the time in which it was given but for all generations. The prose sections of the book of Jeremiah also reflect a perception that the words of the prophet continue to have significance for succeeding generations. The devastation of Babylon after 70 years have been completed is said to be according to 'everything written in this book, which Jeremiah prophesied against the nations' (Jer. 25.13). In Jer. 30.2-3 the purpose for writing the oracles in a book is explicitly related to the restoration of the Judahite community and their return to the land. Finally, in the narrative of Daniel 9, Daniel is depicted as interpreting the words of Jeremiah in relation to the length of exile (9.2). Here we have a Hellenistic period text creating a character in a narrated world in the early Persian period, who then reads an even 'earlier' text as a past word with continuing significance for later situations. These texts indicate an abiding belief in the continuing significance of earlier prophetic texts for new and different situations, a belief that is further demonstrated by the preservation and dissemination of these texts over many centuries and in many different contexts.

This textual evidence from the Persian period[95] suggests interpretive practices quite different from some later communities, such as the Qumran community and early Christian communities, which often read

---

question. The foundational study for an early Persian period date is Karl Elliger, *Die Einheit des Tritojesaia (Jesaia 56–66)* (BWANT, 9; 3rd series; Stuttgart: W. Kohlhammer, 1928), pp. 75-122. Cf. Claus Westermann, *Isaiah 40–66* (OTL; London: SCM Press, 1969), p. 296; and Paul Hanson, *The Dawn of Apocalyptic: The Historical and Sociological Roots of Jewish Apocalyptic Eschatology* (Philadelphia: Fortress Press, rev. edn, 1979).

93. The summary of the former prophets given by Zechariah suggests access to a written collection of earlier prophetic traditions in some form. David L. Petersen, *Haggai and Zechariah 1–8* (OTL; London: SCM Press, 1985), p. 133.

94. Cf. Petersen, *Haggai and Zechariah 1–8*, p. 135.

95. And in the case of Daniel, the Hellenistic period.

the words of the prophetic traditions as if they were spoken directly to their own situations without concern for the ancient historical context in which the words were first spoken and heard. The examples cited above certainly do not mean that the prophetic texts were being read critically in Persian period Yehud, nor do they provide detailed evidence of Persian period interpretive practice. But they do provide the only available evidence of the interpretive use of earlier texts in this period. They reveal that the prophetic traditions were understood and read as words given in particular historical settings. Although the texts were believed to have continuing relevance in the new situation in which the Yehudite community found itself, the historical gap between the situation of the prophet and the situation in the Persian province of Yehud was clearly recognized by these readers.

Chapter 2

READING HOSEA AND PERSIAN PERIOD POLITICS

This chapter will primarily examine Achaemenid imperial structures, including their precursors, and, in particular, aspects of those structures related to the province of Yehud in the sixth and fifth centuries BCE. This imperial setting provides the broad context for understanding life in the Achaemenid province of Yehud and, specifically, how the book of Hosea may have been read in that context. Many have observed that specificity with regard to the analysis of the social structures and history of Yehud in the Persian period is difficult to obtain. The sources, both archaeological and textual, are limited in quantity and disputed in quality. As Hoglund notes, 'By necessity, any general assessment must be provisional until further analysis can be undertaken'.[1] But the situation is not entirely hopeless. Weinberg divides the available textual evidence for historical reconstruction of the Achaemenid period in Yehud into the following categories: texts from the Achaemenid period containing information about the period, texts from this period about earlier periods, and later texts containing information about this period.

> A survey of this material leads to the conclusion that the 'obscure period' is not as obscure as assumed and that it is provided with sources similar in scope to all Near Eastern history as well as other periods of ancient Jewish history.[2]

1. Kenneth G. Hoglund, 'The Achaemenid Context', in Philip R. Davies (ed.), *Second Temple Studies 1: Persian Period* (JSOTSup, 117; Sheffield: JSOT Press, 1991), pp. 54-72 (56). Commenting on the limited amount of reliable information available from the texts of the Hebrew Bible, Hayes suggests that 'any reconstruction of the history of Palestinian Judaism for this period is at the mercy of the narrow documentation that has survived' (J. Maxwell Miller and John H. Hayes, *A History of Ancient Israel and Judah* [OTL; Philadelphia: Westminster Press, 1986], p. 437).

2. Joel Weinberg, *The Citizen–Temple Community* (JSOTSup, 151; Sheffield: JSOT Press, 1992), p. 128.

Precursors to Achaemenid Yehud

The situation of the early Persian period cannot be viewed in isolation from the preceding neo-Babylonian context. The final century of the Judahite monarchy was played out within the perimeters defined by its relations with the great powers of the ancient Near East. Judah had existed not as an independent state but as a vassal (or, at best, minor ally) of the great powers of the ancient Near East from the late eighth century BCE. Although the Judahite kingdom (unlike the Israelite kingdom) continued to exist as a monarchic state until the Babylonian destruction of Jerusalem in 586 BCE, Judah was continuously dominated by the geopolitical machinations of the Assyrians, Egyptians and Babylonians during this period. With the exception of the disastrous revolt of Hezekiah that was crushed in 701 BCE, Judah was dominated by and paid tribute to the Assyrians from the late eighth century to the late seventh century. Josiah's confrontation with Necho II at Megiddo may indicate an attempt by the Judahite king to establish an independent (perhaps pro-Babylonian) foreign policy. In this period all of the small kingdoms of the Levant were caught up in the struggle between the Egyptians and the Babylonians for domination of the region.[3] Following Josiah's death, Egyptian dominance of Judahite affairs is indicated by the fact that Necho was able to determine the succession to the throne in Judah, replacing Jehoahaz with Jehoiakim (2 Kgs 23.31-35). It was during the reign of Jehoiakim that Judah was transferred from the realm of Egyptian control to Babylonian domination (2 Kgs 24.1). Judahite kings throughout this period ruled only by the good will of the emperor of the power that was dominant in the region at the time. Any analysis of life in Judah during the sixth and fifth centuries BCE must take this larger, imperial context into account as an essential ingredient.

From Judah to Yehud

The period between the end of the Judahite monarchy and the imposition of Persian imperial rule (586–539 BCE) has often been depicted as a time of major social breakdown. Berquist, for example, suggests that this period was a time of 'retribalization' in which there was little if

---

3.   See the discussion of the period in Amélie Kuhrt, *The Ancient Near East c. 3000–330 BC* (2 vols.; London: Routledge, 1995), II, pp. 590-91.

any social organization beyond the level of family or tribe in the geographical territory of the old Judahite kingdom.[4] On the basis of the biblical texts that claim that all the fairest and brightest of the land were exiled and that only the poorest people remained (2 Kgs 24.14-15; 25.11-12; Jer. 39.10; 40.7; 52.15-16), it has been easy to assume that Judah was devastated and that the local economy was severely depressed during the last half century of the neo-Babylonian empire.[5] It is certainly true that the deportations to Mesopotamia (2 Kgs 24.14-16; 25.11; Jer. 52.28-30), the dislocation of a portion of the population as refugees to surrounding areas (Jer. 40.11-12; 43.1-7; 44.1), and the deaths resulting from warfare and the associated diseases and famine would have resulted in a substantial decrease in the population of the province.

It is highly implausible, however, that the population of the region was left by the Babylonians without an integrated social structure. Babylonian rule of this region would certainly have been maintained by the imposition of imperial governors or some similar form of local administration. Imperial conquest and rule required some form of local administration to watch over the interests of the empire, including the maintenance of order and the collection of taxes. It is inconceivable that the Babylonians would have expended the massive amount of resources necessary for the siege and conquest of Jerusalem only to leave the region in total anarchy, or so minimally structured as to make the extraction of resources by the empire virtually impossible. The loss of tribute was the trigger for imperial military intervention in the first place. The restoration of the empire's extraction of resources from this holding must have been the primary goal of the operation and this would have required the creation of a reliable colonial administration.

---

4.   Jon L. Berquist, *Judaism in Persia's Shadow: A Social and Historical Approach* (Minneapolis: Fortress Press, 1995), pp. 131-33.

5.   W.F. Albright, *From the Stone Age to Christianity: Monotheism and the Historical Process* (Garden City, NY: Doubleday, 2nd edn, 1957), pp. 264-68; Kathleen Kenyon, *Archaeology in the Holy Land* (London: Ernest Benn, 1960), pp. 291, 296-97. Note the summary of Bustenay Oded: 'There is no clear, explicit information concerning the situation of this population, but it seems that in the absence of civilian and military leadership and the destruction of the strongholds on the one hand, and the persecution and strict control of the Babylonians on the other (Lam. 5), the Jewish population which remained in the country was in a state of depression, lack of confidence, economic poverty, and political and national inactivity' ('Judah and the Exile', p. 479).

In fact, the texts of the Hebrew Bible indicate that immediately after suppressing the Judahite rebellion the Babylonians instituted a local administration to look after the affairs of the empire in the area (2 Kgs 25.22-24; Jer. 40.5-12). This is consistent with other regions dominated by the Babylonians. An inscription listing officials in the imperial administration of Nebuchadrezzar II indicates the use of client rulers in some of the provinces of the empire.[6] As in the late monarchic period, the governance of the province of Judah during the neo-Babylonian period may have been in the hands of local Judahites but the key aspects of that rule were determined from Babylon for the benefit of the empire.[7]

So the significant political change from the Judahite monarchy to life as the Persian province of Yehud was not the imposition of foreign domination, since this had been a fact of life for many years, but rather the fundamental alteration of the local administrative structures and accompanying ideology. Jerusalem and its surrounds were no longer under the rule of a local hereditary monarch but existed as a small administrative region in a world-dominant empire with local administrators who were appointed by the imperial center. But even this difference is somewhat illusory. As indicated above, during the final 150 years of the Judahite kingdom the members of the Davidic dynasty had ruled solely at the discretion of the monarch of one of the great powers of the ancient Near East (2 Kgs 23.33-34; 24.1, 7, 17; 25.22). Indeed, the fundamental transformation of the local political structure in the neo-Babylonian and Achaemenid periods was primarily rhetorical and ideological. Judah was no longer an 'independent' nation with a royal

---

6.   *ANET*, pp. 307-308. Although this text is treated as a list of court officials in *ANET* (see p. 308 n. 11), Kuhrt regards the list of kings at the end of the extant text as a list of client rulers. This latter interpretation seems more likely given the location of this list following lists of regional and city officials (Kuhrt, *The Ancient Near East*, II, p. 607).

7.   See Kuhrt, *The Ancient Near East*, II, pp. 592-93; Ehud Ben Zvi, 'Inclusion in and Exclusion from Israel as Conveyed by the Use of the Term 'Israel' in Post-Monarchic Biblical Texts', in Steven W. Holloway and Lowell K. Handy (eds.), *The Pitcher is Broken: Memorial Essays for Gösta W. Ahlström* (JSOTSup, 190; Sheffield: Sheffield Academic Press, 1995), pp. 95-149 (103); Miller and Hayes, *History*, pp. 421-25; Gösta W. Ahlström, *The History of Ancient Palestine* (Minneapolis: Fortress Press, 1993), pp. 799-800, 806-807; Kenneth G. Hoglund, *Achaemenid Imperial Administration in Syria-Palestine and the Missions of Ezra and Nehemiah* (SBLDS, 125; Atlanta: Scholars Press, 1992), pp. 21-22.

house and associated ideology/theology. The nation had become a minor administrative district within a world empire and the monarch had been exchanged for a minor imperial official.

Immediately following the Babylonian campaign the seat of government in the region was transferred from Jerusalem to Mizpah. This shift in location partially resulted from the fact that the area around Mizpah had been spared from the destructive effects of the warfare. As indicated below, the main area of destruction was limited primarily to Jerusalem and its immediate vicinity.

More important in the selection of Mizpah as the regional seat of government, however, was the recognition that this area was the heart of pro-Babylonian sentiments in Judah. Weinberg suggests that at the end of the monarchic period the Judahite elite in Jerusalem was pro-Egyptian while the Benjaminites were disposed to prefer the neo-Babylonians. In addition to the lack of artifactual evidence for substantial destruction in Benjamin during the Babylonian campaign, he notes that material remains indicate economic ties between southern Judah and Egypt, while the primary economic ties in Benjaminite territory were with Ephraim, which was part of the neo-Babylonian empire. Some of the textual evidence indicates that the pro-Egyptian and pro-Babylonian factions were both represented at the royal court. In addition to the indications in the book of Jeremiah that some at the royal court supported Jeremiah's pro-Babylonian position while others violently opposed it, Weinberg notes that the pro-Egyptian Achborites are associated with the murder of other pro-Babylonian prophets (Jer. 26.20-23).[8] Weinberg also suggests that the pro-Babylonian sympathies of Jeremiah, a prophet from a priestly clan from Anathoth, are indicative of the connection of priests dislocated by the Josianic reforms with Benjamin and that these dislocated priests had pro-Babylonian sympathies. Finally, Weinberg notes the connections between the Shephanides, Mizpah and Jeremiah, and the choice of Gedaliah, a Shephanide, to rule as Babylonian governor from Mizpah.[9] The evidence suggests that Benjaminites, in particular, among the Judahite elite

---

8.   Cf. the possible participation of an Achborite in the murder of a pro-Babylonian prophet according to the Lachish letters 3.15-18; 6.5-7 in Harry Torczyner, Lankester Harding, Alkin Lewis and J.L. Strakey, *Lachish I: The Lachish Letters* (London: Oxford University Press, 1938). Note particularly the commentary on 6.5-7, pp. 112-15.

9.   Weinberg, *The Citizen Temple–Community*, pp. 37-39.

were favorably disposed toward the Babylonians. These regional sympathies provide a likely explanation for the choice of Mizpah (and Gedaliah) for the administration of the Judahite province by the Babylonians.

The almost apocalyptic descriptions of social and economic upheaval commonly found in reconstructions of the fall of Jerusalem have been contradicted by recent analyses of the archaeological evidence. The material remains suggest that Jerusalem and the region immediately to the south were the only areas substantially affected by the Babylonian military operation. Many settlement sites in Judah, particularly in Benjamin and the area south of Jerusalem but beyond the immediate outskirts of the city, remained inhabited before, during and after the neo-Babylonian military campaign that resulted in the destruction of the capital.[10]

On the basis of the excavated material remains, both Barkay and Stern have suggested a continuity of culture in Judah from the late monarchic period through the neo-Babylonian period.[11] This continuity is indicated by both the form and quality of the primary manufactured goods. In fact, the material remains indicate a similar standard of economic prosperity throughout the neo-Babylonian period. Barkay notes that finds in tombs from the period, particularly jewelry and prestige items, indicate considerable wealth rather than severe poverty in sixth-century Judah.[12] The primary trend during the course of the sixth century is a gradual increase in Persian influences detectable in the excavated pottery. By the end of the sixth century this Persian-type pottery constitutes the majority of vessels found.[13]

The ethnic composition of the population of Judah during this period also reflects continuity with earlier periods. Unlike Assyrian practices

10. Gabriel Barkay, 'The Iron Age II–III', in Amnon Ben-Tor (ed.), *The Archaeology of Ancient Israel* (New Haven: Yale University Press), pp. 302-73 (372); cf. Ephraim Stern, *Material Culture of the Land of the Bible in the Persian Period, 538–332 BC* (Israel Exploration Series; Warminster, England: Aris & Phillips, 1982), p. 229.

11 'Continuity is the main characteristic of the culture of the period' (Barkay, 'Iron Age II–III', p. 372). 'Close scrutiny of the archaeological record shows that the real turning point in terms of material culture came only at the end of the sixth century, when Persian authority was established, new pottery types appeared, and Attic ware was imported from Greece' (Stern, *Material Culture*, p. 229).

12. Barkay, 'Iron II–III', p. 372.

13. Stern, *Material Culture*, p. 229.

in Israel after the fall of Samaria, there is no evidence to suggest that the Babylonians employed a policy of forced settlements of ethnically diverse populations from other parts of their empire into Judah, nor would the economic incentives have been sufficient to encourage large-scale immigration to Judah during the neo-Babylonian period.[14] Thus the population of the province of Judah under neo-Babylonian rule was almost entirely composed of descendants of the monarchic period population.

While life changed dramatically for those who were deported to Mesopotamia, the changes in the day-to-day existence of the majority of the population who remained in the province of Judah were much less dramatic. As J. Berquist notes:

> Family life, cultural traditions, modes of economic productivity, behavioral norms and values, ideological assumptions, and local religious rituals probably were among these cultural constants. The removal of the elite meant the end of national ideology, military conscription, obligatory temple worship, and other elements of social centralization, but it is difficult to assess the degree to which these social institutions had ever penetrated rural Judah. Their cessation during the exile may have affected the rural population very little indeed.[15]

Life in Judah—economically, religiously and politically—was modified, but it did not end with the arrival of the Babylonians. Although those who found themselves directly in the path of the Babylonian suppression of the Judahite uprising would have suffered during and after the war, this would not have been true of the whole population. A large portion of the pre-586 BCE population undoubtedly continued their existence much as they always had done. The evidence points predominantly to continuity rather than discontinuity in the material and social life of most inhabitants of Judah during the so-called 'exilic period'.[16]

The situation regarding life in Jerusalem and the cult of Yahweh in Jerusalem in the decades immediately following the Babylonian destruction of the city is uncertain. The later Yehudite shapers of the

---

14. Ben Zvi, 'Inclusion', p. 103; Miller and Hayes, *History*, p. 421; Ahlström, *History*, p. 799.

15. Berquist, *Judaism in Persia's Shadow*, p. 17.

16. Stern states: 'Firstly, we can conclude that in the Babylonian period, despite the destruction of the Temple, the culture of the Israelite period continued' (*Material Culture*, p. 229).

biblical traditions have left behind texts which indicate the total devastation of Jerusalem and the end of the worship of Yahweh in the Jerusalem temple. Indeed, many biblical texts suggest that the entire land of Judah was uninhabited prior to the arrival of descendants of the Judahites deported by the Babylonians. There are hints, however, which suggest that life did not cease entirely in Jerusalem. The description of the burning and looting of Jerusalem in 2 Kings 25 lists the temple of Yahweh, the palace of the king, and all the houses of Jerusalem (v. 9). This seems quite complete but the last item in the list, all the houses of Jerusalem, is qualified by the phrase: וְאֶת־כָּל־בֵּית גָּדוֹל שָׂרַף בָּאֵשׁ ('every large house he burned with fire'). This final, explanatory clause functions to define more precisely the referent of the preceding general statement.[17] The implication of 2 Kgs 25.9 is not that all the dwellings of Jerusalem were destroyed but that all of the great houses (בֵּית גָּדוֹל) were destroyed along with the royal palace and the central sanctuary. So this verse indicates that the specific target of the Babylonian attack was the national seat of religion and government, that is, the temple-palace complex and surrounding houses of royal officials. The following verse then adds the breaking down of the city walls to remove the primary defensive capabilities (v. 10). This reading is far more plausible than the suggestion that the Babylonians literally destroyed the entire city. It also suggests that the city may have continued to be inhabited, undoubtedly on a much smaller scale, after the destruction of 586 BCE. The continuation of Jerusalem as an inhabited city also lends support to the interpretation of the Babylonians' choice of Mizpah as their administrative seat as a reflection of pro-Babylonian sentiments in the region of Benjamin.

The suggestion that Jerusalem may have continued to be inhabited is further strengthened by the description of those who were taken into exile. The text indicates that the remaining inhabitants of Jerusalem and those who had deserted to the Babylonians were taken captive (2 Kgs 25.11). This is then qualified by the following verse which notes that not all of the inhabitants were deported, some were left behind to perform agricultural labor (v. 12).[18] In other words, this text is only

17. Compare 1 Chron. 5.26 where the similar grammatical construction, אֶת־רוּחַ פּוּל מֶלֶךְ־אַשּׁוּר וְאֶת־רוּחַ תִּלְּגַת פִּלְנֶסֶר מֶלֶךְ אַשּׁוּר, is used with singular verbs following indicating only one king, the second clause functioning to more clearly define the first (cf. Japhet, *I & II Chronicles*, p. 142).

18. Compare the parallel account in Jer. 52.15-16 which adds to the two groups

concerned with the treatment of a portion of the population of Jerusalem by the Babylonians and should not be considered definitive of the
disposition of the population of the entire territory of Judah.

The evidence is ambiguous regarding the status of the cult of Yahweh
following the Babylonian destruction and looting of the Jerusalem
temple. The account of 80 men from Shechem, Shiloh and Samaria
coming south, performing rituals of mourning and making offerings at
the temple of Yahweh (יהוה להביא בית), appears to indicate ongoing
cultic activity at the site of the Jerusalem temple (Jer. 41.4-5).[19] Alternatively, this text may indicate the continuation of the cult of Yahweh
at a temple in Mizpah, the seat of Babylonian regional administration,
after the destruction of the Jerusalem temple.[20] In either case the
worship of Yahweh continued in neo-Babylonian Judah after 586 BCE.
Given the continuation of life in Jerusalem during the period of neo-
Babylonian rule, it is likely that some form of cultic activity continued
on the site of the temple. The book of Lamentations adds further weight
to the argument for a continuation of the Yahwistic cult in Jerusalem.
These cultic poems of lamentation reflect rituals of communal mourning that would most likely have occurred at the site of the destroyed
temple.[21]

The Rise of the Achaemenid Empire[22]

In the period leading to the invasion and conquest of the neo-Babylonian empire by Cyrus II, some elements within Babylonian society were
highly disgruntled and many may even have welcomed the defeat of
Nabonidus. This period of social unrest preceding the Persian defeat of
Nabonidus may be the setting for the oracles concerning Babylon in

of deportees given in 2 Kgs 25: 'some of the poorest of the people' and 'the rest of
the artisans'. This suggests even more strongly that some of the inhabitants of Jerusalem were left in the city by the Babylonians.

19. So William L. Holladay, *Jeremiah*, II (Hermeneia; Minneapolis: Fortress
Press, 1989), p. 297.

20. Cf. Miller and Hayes, *History*, p. 426.

21. This brief discussion is only intended to highlight some of the central issues
just prior to the Achaemenid period. A fuller discussion of religion and cult is given
in Chapter 4.

22. It is beyond the scope of this study to present a detailed, critical history of
the Achaemenid empire. The following discussion highlights aspects of the social
history of the empire that impinge upon the central focus of this study.

Jeremiah 50–51. Dandamaev has suggested the period of tension between Babylonia and Media earlier in the sixth century as the backdrop for these oracles but the later setting seems a more likely candidate.[23]

The apparently rapid fall of Babylon to the Persian invasion has often been attributed to the failings of Nabonidus as a ruler and the internal dissensions within the neo-Babylonian empire, particularly dissensions related to the religious policies of Nabonidus. According to Dandamaev, the neo-Babylonian empire was deeply divided in the period following the death of Nebuchadrezzar (562 BCE). Primary among the sources of division according to Dandamaev were conflict between (1) ethnic Chaldeans and ethnic Arameans, and (2) priests and military.[24] Nabonidus was of Aramean descent not Chaldean like most Babylonian kings. Although he also worshiped the traditional Babylonian deities, Nabonidus was primarily a worshiper of Sin.

> It is also possible that Nabonidus was planning to change the Babylonian temple of Marduk, the supreme god of the land, into a temple of Sin. These reforms brought Nabonidus into conflict with the priesthood and the population of various ancient cities, such as Babylon, Borsippa, Nippur, Larsa, Uruk, and Ur.[25]

Dandamaev suggests that three groups in particular were willing to work with the invading Persians. First, the dissatisfaction among the priesthood of Marduk related to the religious reforms of Nabonidus resulted in their complicity with the Persians. Second, the merchants, whose trade routes were controlled by the Persians, were keen to see broader markets and the safe passage of goods, which a large territorial empire could provide. Third, foreign communities hoping for return to their homelands were prepared to see the Persians as saviors.[26] 'When Cyrus attacked Mesopotamia, the priests welcomed him as the appointed of Marduk; the Jewish prophets declared that he was the saviour of their people, while the other foreigners regarded him as their liberator.'[27] There are various reports in later accounts (Herodotus, etc.) which depict the battle for Babylon as long and bloody but these appear to be

---

23. M.A. Dandamaev, *A Political History of the Achaemenid Empire* (Leiden: E.J. Brill, 1989), p. 14.

24. Dandamaev, *Political History*, p. 39.

25. Dandamaev, *Political History*, p. 40; cf. J.M. Cook, *The Persian Empire* (New York: Schocken Books, 1983), p. 28.

26. Dandamaev, *Political History*, pp. 41-42.

27. Dandamaev, *Political History*, p. 42.

dramatic fictions. The contemporary Babylonian Chronicle reports the peaceful surrender of the city and a joyous reception of Cyrus by the local population.[28] This reconstruction indicates a social situation in which Persian rule was desired by substantial segments of Babylonian society.

There is a small possibility that the perfect fit between the Judahite aspirations represented by Deutero-Isaiah and Persian political aspirations was the result of an orchestrated propaganda campaign. Dandamaev theorizes the possibility of an organized propaganda campaign arranged between Cyrus and the Marduk priesthood. Perhaps Cyrus had hired Babylonian priests to produce propagandistic religious texts in opposition to Nabonidus which had similar themes to those of Deutero-Isaiah.[29] The similarity in themes may indicate that the Judahites represented by Deutero-Isaiah were also working for the Persians. In the end, it is impossible to determine with any certainty whether such an arrangement may have existed between Cyrus and Judahite groups. Deutero-Isaiah may simply represent a self-interested, religious reading of the contemporary political situation.[30] In any case, it is likely that many in the Judahite community in Mesopotamia, as well as many of the native Babylonians, were strong supporters of Persian rule even prior to its arrival.

In contrast, Amélie Kuhrt has argued that these supposed divisions within Babylonian society and the opposition to Nabonidus are the result of misreadings of the available evidence. Kuhrt suggests that the only textual evidence that clearly indicates a negative judgment on Nabonidus, the Verse Account of Nabonidus, is obviously a Persian era

---

28. See Dandamaev, *Political History*, pp. 47-49. Dandamaev's summary of the events is similar to and develops the earlier analysis of Sidney Smith, *Babylonian Historical Texts Relating to the Capture and Downfall of Babylon* (London: Methuen, 1924).

29. 'The Verse Account of Nabonidus', *ANET*, pp. 312-15. Cf. Dandamaev, *Political History*, p. 53; M. Boyce, *A History of Zoroastrianism.* II. *Under the Achaemenians* (Handbuch der Orientalistik; Leiden: E.J. Brill, 1982), pp. 43-47. Cf. the confident assertion of Cook: 'He [Cyrus] had no doubt been in touch with Babylonian priests, to whom Nabunaid had caused grave offence; and his propaganda showed him as the elect of Marduk... It is astonishing too how he was hailed in Jerusalem as nothing short of the Messiah; possibly he had used the Jews of Mesopotamia as a fifth column' (Cook, *The Persian Empire*, p. 31).

30. See Berquist, *Judaism in Persia's Shadow*, pp. 30-32, who argues for the self-interested interpretation.

propagandistic text intended to legitimate the reign of Cyrus.[31] Kuhrt's analysis of the unreliability of the Verse Account's portrayal of Nabonidus is probably correct. Thus the only textual support for the supposed social unrest in Babylon at the end of the reign of Nabonidus is clearly propagandistic. Kuhrt suggests that the internal opposition and, particularly, the conflict between the religious and secular realms, which she assigns to the modern, Western expectations of church–state conflicts, have been overstated in some analyses. However, the quick defeat of the Babylonian army and the surrender of Nabonidus and the city of Babylon to Cyrus following a single military defeat do lend some support to the suggestions of internal opposition to the reign of Nabonidus.[32] Ultimately, it is impossible to determine whether Cyrus actively encouraged this opposition before the invasion. The portrayal of Nabonidus in the Verse Account may accurately reflect the views of some segments of the local population, but it is ultimately impossible to separate completely fact from Persian-inspired propaganda.

The fact remains, however, that the pro-Cyrus, propagandistic nature of Deutero-Isaiah is paralleled in native Babylonian documents from the period. For purposes of understanding the Babylonian Judahite community it is clear that this community, either before or after the fact, offered unambiguous support for the imposition of Persian rule and that evidence of similar support can also be found within other segments of Babylonian society. There were many, including many within the Babylonian Judahite community, who were willing to cooperate extensively with Achaemenid rule.

Imperial Mechanisms for Control
The establishment and maintenance of mechanisms by which new territories could be integrated into the social, political and economic life of the empire were primary objectives of an imperial administration. For the rapidly expanding Achaemenid empire in the third quarter of the

---

31. Amélie Kuhrt, 'Nabonidus and the Babylonian Priesthood', in Mary Beard and John North (eds.), *Pagan Priests: Religion and Power in the Ancient World* (London: Gerald Duckworth, 1990), pp. 141-46.

32. Contra Kuhrt's suggestion in 'Nabonidus and the Babylonian Priesthood', p. 134, that Cyrus had fought a prolonged campaign against Babylonia beginning immediately after his defeat of Astyages in 550 BCE. Indications of an occasional border skirmish do not prove the existence of an 11-year campaign by Cyrus against the Babylonians.

sixth century these objectives must have been absolutely vital.

One key feature of the social analysis of imperial systems is the recognition that exclusively coercive relationships are inherently unstable. As a result, successful imperial governments seek to integrate conquered territories into the empire by means of a complex set of interrelated mechanisms that create mutually beneficial relations with the center.[33] For the Achaemenid empire in this early period, attempting to integrate territories from the Indus to the Greek city-states of Anatolia, the exercise of force alone would have been insufficient for the maintenance of their far-flung imperial holdings over time.[34] The inherent difficulties and prohibitive costs of maintaining order and exerting control solely by means of imperial military forces required more creative, though not necessarily less oppressive, means of integration.

Hoglund identifies three of the common mechanisms exploited by imperial systems to accomplish the integration of new conquests into the empire: 'the dissolution of self-sufficient economic structures, the incorporation of traditional territorial aristocracies into the imperial governing structure, and the development of new and efficient means of communication between the imperial center and the outlying imperial territories.'[35] To this analysis of Hoglund can be added Jon Berquist's list of strategies employed by the Achaemenids: 'At a minimum, a list of Persian strategies should include the common language of Imperial Aramaic, the construction of provincial bureaucracies, the appointment of Persians to roles within colonial governmental structures, military control of vast regions, taxation and other redistribution of resources, and conscription of various persons into imperial service, whether at

33. Hoglund, *Achaemenid Imperial Administration*, p. 56. This is what M. Rowlands calls 'a hegemony of shared interests and beliefs in the benefits of maintaining the established order' ('Preface', in Rowlands, Larsen and Kristiansen [eds.], *Center and Periphery in the Ancient World*, p. viii). See also the discussion in Chapter 1 above, 'The Sociology of Imperial Control'.

34. Hoglund states the point clearly: 'While it is possible for an individual ruler to amass the necessary military and political resources to impose governance over a spatially and ethnically diverse region, the reproduction of that rule by successors requires the utilization of those techniques and administrative structures normally associated with the term "empire"' (Hoglund, *Achaemenid Imperial Administration*, p. 95.

35. Hoglund, *Achaemenid Imperial Administration*, p. 167; Hoglund is drawing from Eisenstadt, *Political Systems*, pp. 33-34.

local levels or within the imperial core.'[36] The Achaemenid administration made use of all these vehicles, as well as others, in varying degrees.

Where appropriate, the Achaemenids made use of local, hereditary rulers as their representatives to the subject populations. Dandamaev notes that both Cyrus and Cambyses generally retained local administrative structures in the areas of their imperial expansions.[37] As long as the local officials involved cooperated with the imperial system, this offered a much less risky option than the alternative of using a charismatic, leadership figure from within the subject population but outside the previous ruling structure.[38]

The continuation of previous economic structures is also a common feature of early Achaemenid policy.[39] Evidence from both Elam and Babylon suggest a continuation of life under Achaemenid administration much as it had been prior to the Persian conquest.[40] Economic activity in Babylon continued almost entirely unchanged immediately following the arrival of Cyrus and the Achaemenid military. 'Not more than twelve days, at the most, elapsed after the death of Nabu-naid before commercial documents were being dated by the accession year of Cyrus.'[41] The key alteration was at the macro-economic level. The various local economic structures continued to operate as they had prior to the arrival of the Achaemenids but they were incorporated into a centralized imperial system operated from the imperial treasury.[42] An

36. Jon Berquist, 'Postcolonialism and Imperial Motives for Canonization', *Semeia* 75 (1996), pp. 15-35.

37. M.A. Dandamaev and V.G. Lukonin, *The Culture and Social Institutions of Ancient Iran* (Cambridge: Cambridge University Press, 1989), p. 97.

38. Cf. Ben Zvi, 'Inclusion', pp. 105, 126.

39. Dandamaev and Lukonin summarize Achaemenid policy as follows: 'The Achaemenids tried to create normal conditions in the conquered countries for the development of the economy and transit trade' (*Culture and Social Institutions*, p. 95).

40. See A.T. Olmstead, *History of the Persian Empire* (Chicago: University of Chicago Press, 1948), pp. 68-85.

41. Olmstead, *History*, p. 77. Cf. Hoglund's summary: 'There is ample evidence to conclude that at its inception the new Achaemenid administration of Babylon sought to retain the same economic, political, and social conditions that had prevailed under the Babylonian kingship' (*Achaemenid Imperial Administration*, p. 5.

42. The main imperial treasury was in Persepolis. In addition, each satrapy had its own treasury and districts or regions had local treasuries. See Dandamaev and Lukonin, *Culture and Social Institutions*, pp. 206-209.

obvious result of this incorporation into the imperial economic structure was the extraction of surplus by the imperial center, but the embedding of these local economies within the imperial economy also had other significant effects. Incorporation into the Achaemenid imperial structure created new opportunities for trade for many regions of the ancient Near East.[43] This expansion of trade not only created prosperity locally and increased the available surpluses for the empire, but also trade between various localities and regions within the empire created important economic ties that functioned to reduce the self-sufficiency of the localities and bind them more firmly to the empire.

Interregional trade also had the effect of developing common cultural links throughout the governed territories without the need for coercion from the center. The excavations at Tell Deir 'Alla, for example, demonstrate that the introduction of cultural features common to other parts of the Persian empire during this period resulted mainly from trade. No evidence was discovered for the forced imposition of a foreign culture on the region by the imperial center.[44] This suggests that even in peripheral areas of the empire economic links served the function of creating cultural and social cohesion. All of this could be accomplished at little or no additional expense to the imperial administration.

The legitimation of imperial rule often took the form of claims that the Achaemenid rulers had been chosen to rule by the local deity(ies). Such claims were often reinforced by participation in the historic kingship rituals and/or adoption of the royal titles of a newly conquered area. Such techniques functioned as vital tools in the legitimation of Achaemenid rule in the eyes of local populations. These practices are evident in Achaemenid imperial propaganda in Babylon, Media, Egypt and Yehud.

Another means of legitimating the imposition of new practices was their depiction as the restoration of previously abandoned traditions. Restoration and reform were typical elements of imperial propaganda.

---

43. As indicated above this may have been a key factor in the support for Achaemenid rule among Babylonian merchants who had seen their markets restricted as a result of the decline of the neo-Babylonian empire.

44. G. van der Kooij, 'Tell Deir 'Alla (East Jordan Valley) during the Achaemenid Period', in Heleen Sancisi-Weerdenburg (ed.), *Achaemenid History*. I. *Sources, Structures and Synthesis* (Proceedings of the Groningen 1983 Achaemenid History Workshop; Leiden: Nederlands Instituut voor het Nabije Oosten, 1987), pp. 97-102 (101).

By portraying innovations as the restoration of an older, previously abandoned practice the emperor could be depicted as a defender of the traditional values of the society over against the previous ruler(s) who had instituted the changes that made the reforms necessary. This was as true of the Achaemenids as any other ancient Near Eastern power. Such practices provided an important medium for creating administrative stability by insinuating the imperial center into local traditions.[45]

This brief survey indicates some of the imperial structures employed by the Achaemenids as a means of integrating newly conquered territories into the empire and maintaining their rule over subject populations. Many of these elements will be examined in more detail in relation to Yehud below.

The Achaemenids and the Return of Deportees

One of the earliest and most significant developments in the life of Yehud after the imposition of Achaemenid rule was the migration of the descendants of Judahites who had been deported to Mesopotamia. The arrival of these Mesopotamian Yahwists and their participation in the local administration made a significant impact on life in the province and left an indelible mark on the traditions of the Hebrew Bible.

The return of Mesopotamian Yehudites should be examined within the wider imperial social context in which it occurred. Allowing displaced ethnic populations to return to their homeland was one aspect of Achaemenid imperial policy.[46] In addition to the well-known example of Yehud, there is some evidence of the return to ethnic homelands by other population groups. The Neirab tablets (discovered in the 1920s southeast of Aleppo) contain information about an ethnic group living in Babylonia who returned to their Syrian homeland around the time of Zerubbabel's return to Palestine.[47] Diodorus reveals that Cyrus encouraged Phoenicians and Elamites as well as Jews to return to their homelands.[48]

There is at least one example of a forcibly deported population

45. Cf. Ben Zvi, 'Inclusion', pp. 145-48.

46. For example, the claim on the Cyrus Cylinder, 'I (also) gathered all their (former) inhabitants and returned (to them) their habitations' (*ANET*, p. 316).

47. Hoglund, *Achaemenid Imperial Administration*, p. 27; following Israel Eph'al, 'The Western Minorities in Babylonia in the 6th–5th Centuries B.C.: Maintenance and Cohesion', *Or* NS 47 (1978), pp. 84-87.

48. Diodorus 13.22.3; cf. Berquist, *Judaism in Persia's Shadow*, p. 25.

returning home without imperial permission. In 499 BCE the Ionian rebels aided the Paeonians, who had been deported from their homeland in Thrace 20 years earlier, in returning to their ancestral lands. The effect of this unauthorized benevolence by the Ionians was to irritate the Persians further. It is significant, however, because it provides an additional example of deported peoples maintaining their ethnic identity and ties to their homeland until the opportunity to return arose.[49]

The Achaemenid policy of permitting the return of deported peoples was not an innovation in the history of the ancient Near East but followed precedents established by the Assyrians.[50] Neither should Cyrus's policy of returning ethnic populations to their homelands be seen as some great humanitarian act. Rather, it was a pragmatic political policy designed to strengthen connections between the provinces and the imperial center.[51] Berquist suggests that one of the functions of the policies permitting the return of displaced populations and the rebuilding of ancient cult sites was the strengthening of the periphery of the empire. Not only would the increase in loyal population groups in border areas reduce the dangers of rebellion or invasion but it would also help to sustain imperial military movements and provide staging grounds for possible territorial expansion.[52]

As with the Assyrians and Babylonians before them, the Persians were willing to use deportations when such practices suited their purposes. After ending the five-year-long Ionian rebellion in 494 BCE they deported many of the survivors of the defeated city of Miletus to Mesopotamia and they resettled Carians in the area around Miletus.[53] Similarly, the Eretrians were deported from their homeland off the Greek mainland to Elam in 490 BCE.[54] Both of these policies, return and deportation, are pragmatic decisions based on the needs and goals of the empire, and not the expression of some deeply held humanitarian sentiments.

49. See Dandamaev, *Political History*, p. 160.
50. Hoglund, *Achaemenid Imperial Administration*, p. 23; cf. Amélie Kuhrt, 'The Cyrus Cylinder and Achaemenid Imperial Policy', *JSOT* 25 (1983), pp. 83-97; R.J. van der Spek, 'Did Cyrus the Great Introduce a New Policy towards Subdued Nations? Cyrus in Assyrian Perspective', *Persica* 10 (1982), pp. 278-83.
51. See Dandamaev and Lukonin, *Culture and Social Institutions*, p. 349.
52. Berquist, *Judaism in Persia's Shadow*, pp. 25-26; cf. Weinberg, *The Citizen–Temple Community*, pp. 110-11, 131.
53. Dandamaev, *Political History*, p. 165.
54. Dandamaev, *Political History*, pp. 171-72.

The two versions of the decree of Cyrus authorizing or commanding the return of the descendants of the Judahite deportees (Ezra 1.1-4; 6.1-6) contain elements that reflect later, Yehudite theological perspectives.[55] Certainly these later perspectives have influenced the language of the texts and their use in Ezra, but these elements should not lead to a complete rejection of the historical value of these decrees.[56] In some cases it is possible to distinguish between later interpretations and earlier traditions. For example, Hoglund has attributed the religious motivation given for the Cyrus edict in Ezra 1.1, that Yahweh stirred up the spirit of King Cyrus of Persia, to the theocentric understanding of the redactor.[57] While this may be true, such ties between imperial policies and local deities also fit the needs of imperial propaganda.[58] Although the versions of Cyrus's decree preserved in Ezra may reflect some Yehudite interpretation of the original imperial decree, the core instructions are consistent with Achaemenid imperial policies and goals and with the historical situation as far as it can be reconstructed.

As previously indicated, Palestine, in particular, would have been central to imperial preparations for the incorporation of Egypt into the Achaemenid realm (a move already planned during the reign of Cyrus). The increase in population and consequent increase in land under cultivation resulting from Mesopotamian returnees to Yehud would have been of strategic importance, providing for the production of larger agricultural surpluses to supply the military while it was in the region. In addition, a local administration composed of Achaemenid-sponsored returnees would have been more reliable in the eyes of the imperial administration.[59]

The Population of Achaemenid Yehud

Before proceeding to further consideration of issues concerning the migration of ethnic Judahites from Mesopotamia to Yehud, a brief

55. See, e.g., the analysis of Blenkinsopp, *Ezra–Nehemiah*, pp. 74-76.

56. See Hayes and Miller, *History*, pp. 443-45.

57. Hoglund, *Achaemenid Imperial Administration*, p. 23.

58. This issue will be explored in more detail in 'Achaemenid Adaptation of Local Kingship Traditions', in Chapter 3.

59. 'These preparations, therefore, could include the foundation of a community of Jewish returnees from Mesopotamia, initiated and supported by the Persian king and therefore grateful and loyal to him' (Weinberg, *The Citizen–Temple Community*, p. 131).

examination of population density is appropriate. The estimates have varied dramatically, ranging from c. 250,000 down to fewer than 20,000. The range is so wide, in fact, that a decision regarding population figures will substantially alter one's reading of the social situation. Unfortunately, demographic studies have often been little more than speculation informed by an uncritical reading of the biblical texts. The higher estimates, in particular, tend to rely on a combination of uncritical use of the biblical texts and guesswork.[60] For example, in support of the claim that the late monarchic population of Judah was 220,000-250,000, Weinberg combines the data from Tufnell[61] on population density of settlements with the lists of settlements from Josh. 15.21-62 and 18.21-28, which (following Alt and Aharoni) he takes to be monarchic administrative documents.[62] He also combines the deportation figures from 2 Kings and Jeremiah, arguing that they represent those deported from Jerusalem and Judah respectively (following Mowinckel),[63] to arrive at a total of 12,000-14,000 exiles. To this figure he adds those who fled to other countries to reach a total population loss of approximately 20,000 or about 10 per cent of the late Iron II population.[64] Thus he concludes that the deportations did not result in a massive reduction in population and that the population in the Achaemenid period was similar to the late monarchic period (c. 200,000).

In contrast, W.F. Albright reached a figure of 20,000. Albright based his estimate on the assumption that many settlements in late monarchic Judah were abandoned after 586 BCE resulting in a significant population reduction from the monarchic period. In addition, he argued that the list preserved in Ezra 2 and Nehemiah 7 was a census list from c. 440 BCE and indicates a natural population growth, supplemented by

60. See Charles E. Carter, 'The Province of Yehud in the Post-exilic Period: Soundings in Site Distribution and Demography', in Tamara C. Eskenazi and Kent H. Richards (eds.), *Second Temple Studies 2: Temple and Community in the Persian Period* (JSOTSup, 175; Sheffield: JSOT Press, 1994), pp. 106-45 (107-108).

61. O. Tufnell, *Lachish III (Tel ed-Duweir): The Iron Age* (London: Oxford University Press, 1953), p. 34.

62. Weinberg, *The Citizen–Temple Community*, p. 35.

63. Kreissig also follows Mowinckel's arguments but arrives at a post-586 population of perhaps 60,000 (Heinz Kreissig, *Die Sozialökonomische Situation in Juda zur Achämenidenzeit* [Berlin: Akademie Verlag, 1973], p. 34).

64. Weinberg, *The Citizen–Temple Community*, pp. 34-48 (esp. 36-37).

returnees from Mesopotamia, to about 50,000 over three generations.[65]

The estimates of both Weinberg and Albright are based on doubtful biblical and archaeological assumptions. The difficulties in arriving at an estimate are further compounded by the lack of clarity regarding the geographic region being analyzed. Since borders change over time it is difficult to compare estimates diachronically unless the geographic area is clearly defined and consistently maintained. On the other hand, while precision is elusive, the determination of population figures as accurately as is currently possible is an important aspect of reconstructing the socio-historical setting.[66] The recent population estimate of Carter based on modern archaeological surveys and current methods of demographic analysis addresses many of the weaknesses of previous estimates. Carter's analysis suggests that the population of the province of Yehud in the early Persian period would have been smaller than proposed by either Weinberg or Albright (though much closer to Albright). Carter has suggested a range from 11,000 in the early Achaemenid period to 17,000 in the late fifth to early fourth centuries.[67] These estimates, based on the most recent archaeological survey data available for the Judah/Yehud and Benjamin regions,[68] provide the most reliable indication of the population for this period.

Although the variations in population of Yehud during the period of Achaemenid rule and the possibility of establishing precise estimates should be handled cautiously, this survey of previous demographic analyses indicates that the lower estimates offer a more accurate interpretation of the available evidence. In relation to the empire, Yehud was a very small regional center. In relation to the migration of Judahite descendants from Mesopotamia, the best estimates suggest that the number of migrants would have been relatively small but that their impact as a percentage of the total population of the province may have been quite large. Just a few thousand well-educated migrants with

65. W.F. Albright, *The Biblical Period from Abraham to Ezra: An Historical Survey* (New York: Harper & Row, rev. edn, 1960), p. 87 n. 180.

66. Although Blenkinsopp's sentiment has some merit, 'There would appear to be too many imponderables here to make even an approximate guess worthwhile', the data from this period cannot be analyzed without some kind of working hypothesis regarding the population of the province. An informed guess is preferable to an uninformed assumption (Blenkinsopp, *Ezra–Nehemiah*, p. 66).

67. Carter, 'The Province of Yehud', pp. 106-45.

68. Carter had access to the unpublished survey data of A. Ofer on Judah and I. Finkelstein, N. Feig, A. Feldstein and Y. Kameisky on Benjamin.

imperial support could have dramatically transformed the provincial society.

Propaganda for Return

There is very little evidence, biblical or non-biblical, regarding the early response of ethnic Yehudites in Babylon to Achaemenid encourage-ment for return to their homeland. There are a few brief references to Sheshbazzar but little information can be gleaned from these references. The text indicates that Sheshbazzar was accompanied on his return by the articles that had been removed from the Jerusalem temple by Nebuchadrezzar and a group of exiles (הגולה; Ezra 1.11). In Ezra 5.14-16 he is connected not only with the return of the vessels from the first temple but also the laying of the foundations for the new temple. This text also indicates that he was appointed governor (Aramaic פחה) by Cyrus.

Most analyses of the list of provincial citizens who returned from exile (בני המדינה; Ezra 2; Neh. 7; 1 Esd. 5) suggest that, in its many forms, it may preserve some historically reliable evidence of the popu-lation, or some segment of the population, of the province of Yehud. There are, however, discrepancies between the three extant versions and the appropriate chronological setting for the list is also disputed. The placement of the list in the book of Ezra immediately following the account of the journey of Sheshbazzar, the temple vessels, and some unnamed exiles (Ezra 1.5-11) creates the impression that those named in the list comprise the company of those who migrated with Shesh-bazzar (cf. the parallel in Neh. 7 where the list is introduced as a record of those who first returned, v. 5). The contents of the list, however, suggest that it originates from a later period. Blenkinsopp argues that the heading of the list collapses history by providing a catalogue of community leaders from various times during the Persian period (Zerubbabel, Jeshua, Nehemiah, etc.).[69] The historical discrepancies reveal the dangers of assuming that this list accurately reflects the population who immigrated from Babylon to Yehud in the early Achaemenid period.

---

69. Blenkinsopp, *Ezra–Nehemiah*, p. 84. Cf. the analysis of Kurt Galling, *Studien zur Geschichte Israels im persischen Zeitalter* (Tübingen: J.C.B. Mohr, 1964), pp. 89-108.

The length of the period of settlement in Mesopotamia combined with the apparent prosperity of some of the descendants of the Judahite deportees to Babylon would have discouraged many from migrating to Yehud in the early years of Achaemenid rule. It is unlikely that many Babylonian Judahites would have been willing to exchange an established and, in some cases, prosperous life in Babylonia for an uncertain existence in Yehud. The early returnees would have been comprised mainly of those with strong religious or nationalistic motives. Later in the Persian period, when issues regarding the ownership of ancestral lands had been resolved in favor of returnees and a stable, pro-Achaemenid administration was firmly established, more members of the Mesopotamian community might have been likely to migrate. Migration may have become particularly appealing during the early years of the reign of Darius I. Darius came to power as a result of a conspiracy that assassinated Bardiya/Gaumata who had seized the throne in a coup while Cambyses was in Egypt. The instability in the empire did not cease immediately after Darius took the throne. Widespread revolts occurred throughout the empire during the first two years of his reign. In Babylon there were two rebellions in successive years, late 522 and late 521. This continuing period of instability, particularly in Babylon, could have made the security and stability of Yehud more inviting than had previously been the case.[70]

The instability created by the widespread rebellions nearly led to the complete disintegration of the empire. Darius, however, managed to subdued most areas and restore imperial control within the first year or 18 months after his accession. The last region to be subdued and reincorporated was Egypt.[71] Encouraging a further influx of population into Palestine, particularly Yehudites from Mesopotamia with religious and ethnic ties to the region, would have been advantageous both to the ruling class in Jerusalem and the imperial administration. If the suggestion by Berquist connecting the rebuilding of the temple with preparations for the invasion of Egypt during the reign of Darius I is correct,

70. Cf. Ephraim Stern, 'The Persian Empire and the Political and Social History of Palestine in the Persian Period', in W.D. Davies and Louis Finkelstein (eds.), *The Cambridge History of Judaism* (Cambridge: Cambridge University Press, 1984), I, pp. 70-87 (72); cf. Miller and Hayes, *History*, p. 447.

71. Egypt had only been added to the Persian holdings at the end of the reign of Cambyses. In fact, Cambyses was still in Egypt when word came about the rebellion of Bardiya/Guamata.

it would provide a coherent explanation for the timing of the temple construction and imperial interest in both the project and the migration of ethnic Yehudites from Mesopotamia to Yehud.[72] The passage of the Persian army through the Levant on the way to Egypt under Darius would have created the need for substantial increases in agricultural surpluses. The local population would be required to provide a significant proportion of the food needed to feed the troops. Berquist suggests that the rebuilding of the temple and reinstitution of the temple cult could have been, in part, payment from the empire for Yehud's participation in the provisioning of the army. In addition, the presence of the temple in Jerusalem would have provided a valuable administrative center for the Persian colonial administration. In other words, the construction of the second temple under the direction of the Persians was not motivated by a humanitarian concern for the religious traditions of a subject people, but by the military and administrative interests of the empire.[73]

In preparation for a campaign of this magnitude long-term advance planning was necessary. This could explain the arrival of Zerubbabel and the accompanying returnees. The necessary increase in agricultural production, the construction of storage facilities for the surplus[74] and the implementation of administrative structures to ensure success would have required capable and loyal administrative personnel. Given the vital administrative and economic functions of temples in the ancient Near East it is probable that the Jerusalem temple was considered a necessary administrative center in a region bordering on Egypt. In the eyes of the Achaemenids, rebuilding the temple in Jerusalem is likely to have been an action directed toward securing the fringes of the empire, particularly in light of the ongoing difficulties with Egypt throughout the Persian period.

The infusion of additional population and financial resources, both from the migrants and the imperial treasury, would have provided a substantial boost to the economy and the means necessary to begin reconstruction of the temple under the leadership of the Achaemenid administration led by Zerubbabel. The administrative program of the provincial leadership would have needed the support of officially

---

72. Berquist, *Judaism in Persia's Shadow*, pp. 60-63.
73. Berquist, *Judaism in Persia's Shadow*, pp. 62-63.
74. Berquist refers to the article by Lawrence E. Stager, 'Climatic Conditions and Grain Storage in the Persian Period', *HTR* 64 (1971), pp. 448-540 (450).

sponsored interpretations of the theological traditions of the people. The old prophetic traditions of the Yahwistic faith read within the ideological framework of the new Yehudite community would have played a vital role in the effort to (re)construct the community, including encouraging ethnic Yehudites to immigrate from Mesopotamia, and (re)construct the Yahwistic temple and cult.

Writing and Reading as Social Control

The interpretation of earlier prophetic texts would have functioned as one of the tools used by those returning from Mesopotamia as the means of establishing control over the local population and, eventually, achieving the integration of this pre-existing local population of the province and the new immigrants. Among the other tools used by the provincial ruling class would have been: imperial sanction and support; management of the rebuilding of the temple; control of religious and political appointments and the ideological support of each by the other; and dominance of the regional economy. The prophetic texts would have functioned in this system to provide theological justification for the newly established system (or, put more crassly, propaganda for the establishment and maintenance of the new system). The depiction of unfaithfulness to Yahweh by the ancestors as the cause of the disaster of 586 BCE combined with the implication that those who 'returned from exile' were fulfilling the plan of Yahweh given through the prophets would be a powerful tool for control.[75] The combination of imperial support and the use of local religious traditions as the foundation for the dominance of the newly established provincial elite provided substantial mechanisms for fostering a smooth transition to the new administration.

In a recent controversial suggestion, Davies has argued that many of the central biblical traditions were produced during this period as the ideological justification for the rule of the newly arrived 'immigrant' community. He suggests that the Mesopotamian population which moved into Yehud at the direction of the Persians was not necessarily,

---

75. Note the references in Zech. 1–8 (First Zechariah) to the words of the earlier prophets (1.2-6; 7.7-14). These references function as appeals to an authoritative tradition to encourage acceptance of the position being argued in this early Persian period text. See the further discussion in Chapter 1 above, 'Reading Prophetic Texts in Yehud'.

or even likely, composed of descendants of the people who were deported from the area by the Babylonians. According to Davies this new
society incorporated a few traditional elements from the local population,[76] but the history by which they established their own identity was
predominantly a new creation generated by them in the Persian period.[77]
The depiction of the origin of the original 'Israel' as immigrants suited
the purposes of the new elite who were also immigrants. They adapted
their Mesopotamian high god beliefs to the name of an indigenous
deity, Yahweh. Finally, by making cultic holiness a defining concept
they strengthened the authority of the priesthood and provided a basis
for denying land rights to those who would not conform to the new
social structure. 'The ideological triumph of the biblical story is to
convince that what is new is actually old.'[78]

Davies's reconstruction of Israelite history is undoubtedly overly
skeptical. The correlation of many of the traditions of Iron Age Israel
with evidence from extrabiblical sources confirms that there is a significant proportion of earlier traditions incorporated into the final forms of
the biblical texts. Davies's rejection of correlations between 'biblical
Israel' and the Iron Age society that can be known from archaeological
excavations is entirely untenable.[79] Although his total reconstruction is
unconvincing, the recognition that many of the biblical texts have been
shaped by the ruling class of Achaemenid Yehud is correct.[80] Further,
the socio-historical context of Achaemenid Yehud not only shaped the
texts which the ruling elites of the province edited and produced but also
shaped their reading of the textual traditions which already existed.[81] As

---

76. Davies, *In Search*, p. 75.

77. Davies, *In Search*, p. 112. In fact, Davies places the creation of much of the
biblical literature in the Hellenistic period but this seems unlikely.

78. Davies, *In Search*, p. 114.

79. See, e.g., the sharp critique of William G. Dever, '"Will the Real Israel
Please Stand Up?" Part I: Archaeology and Israelite Historiography', *BASOR* 297
(1995), pp. 61-80 (67-69). On the value and necessity of integrating biblical and
archaeological evidence in reconstructing Israelite and Judahite history, see
J. Maxwell Miller, 'Is it Possible to Write a History of Israel without Relying on the
Hebrew Bible?', in D.V. Edelman (eds.), *The Fabric of History: Text, Artifact and
Israel's Past* (JSOTSup, 127; Sheffield: JSOT Press, 1991), pp. 93-102.

80. Cf. Ahlström, *History*, p. 822.

81. For example, Ackroyd correctly notes that the DtrH could not be read in the
same way after the destruction of Jerusalem as before, even if the editorial changes
were minor. 'To the sensitive reader, and more still to the exponent of a religious

was argued in Chapter 1, reading is a function of the reading conventions of any particular reading community. The socio-historical setting of Achaemenid Yehud and, primarily, the ruling elites who dominated textual production and interpretation, is central to the task of reconstructing this particular slice of the history of interpretation.

The administrative and scribal practices of the elite in early Achaemenid Yehud should be understood within the framework established by the administrative and legal reforms of Darius I. Berquist notes that Darius gained the reputation as a lawgiver but that this resulted not from the production of a single, uniform imperial law code but from the establishment of an administrative system in which various local legal traditions could be codified.[82] This reform of the legal system and law codes in use throughout the empire was a significant aspect of Darius's assertion of control over the recently subdued colonies.[83] Given the recent turmoil in relations between the provinces and the imperial center, the reform of administrative and legal codes represented the institution of new mechanisms to establish a mutually beneficial relationship between the center and the periphery. The primary objective of the relationship resulting from these mechanisms was the reassertion of imperial control and, thereby, stability.

The mission of Udjahorresnet in Egypt is an excellent example of these imperial mechanisms of control in action. By sending Udjahorresnet back to Egypt in 520 BCE with support to restore the school at Sais and codify the last native law code, Darius laid the foundation for Egyptian acceptance of Persian rule without the need for a military conquest. This incident is reflective of Darius's policy of using propaganda, building projects and the support of local religious practices in combination with military intervention to incorporate the outlying regions into a cooperative relationship with the imperial center.[84] Hoglund notes the ideological function of the report of the mission of Udjahorresnet. It legitimizes the reign of Darius over Egypt by

---

interpretation of Israel's experience, the whole of this wealth of earlier material took on a new meaning' (Peter Ackroyd, 'The Jewish Community in Palestine in the Persian Period', in W.D. Davies and L. Finkelstein [eds.], *The Cambridge History of Judaism* [4 vols.; Cambridge: Cambridge University Press, 1984], I, pp. 130-61 [131]).

82. Berquist, *Judaism in Persia's Shadow*, p. 55.
83. Already Olmstead, *History*, pp. 119-28.
84. Berquist, *Judaism in Persia's Shadow*, pp. 56-57, 61.

highlighting his restoration of an Egyptian cult and the codification of the laws of the last native Egyptian pharaoh. The connection with the last ruling native Egyptian pharaoh rather than his Persian predecessor and the reform of Egyptian cultic practices rather than the imposition of a foreign cult served the vital role of connecting the rule of Darius with key local political and religious traditions.[85]

The close temporal relationship between the mission of Udjahorres-net and the restoration of the Jerusalem temple under Zerubbabel adds further support to the suggestion that the rebuilding of the Jerusalem temple was part of a wider imperial policy to strengthen its grip on the western fringes. The parallels are substantial: restoration of a traditional cult; recruiting someone from the local ethnic population as the imperial representative; the institution of administrative and legal reforms; and the depiction of the actions as reforms rather than innovations.[86]

In light of the preceding summary, it is not surprising to find Achaemenid appointees in Yehud restoring the temple and cult of Yah-weh, codifying the traditional legal codes and loyally administering the province for the empire. Berquist suggests that the control of literary production by the elites of the province would explain why there is no extant evidence of opposition to Persian rule. These elites were dependent upon the empire for their position and therefore any opposition to the empire would have originated outside the circles of the ruling class.[87] The limitation of literacy and, therefore, the production and interpretation of complex texts to the very small population of the ruling class was a key to the success of Achaemenid rule in Yehud. In effect, by creating and sustaining a mutually beneficial relationship with these elites who held a monopoly on literary skills, the Achaemenids could be assured that transmission and interpretation of the local religious, historical and legal traditions would support rather than undermine their rule.

---

85. Hoglund, *Achaemenid Imperial Administration*, p. 28. See the similar analysis by J. Blenkinsopp comparing the mission of Udjahorresnet with those of Ezra and Nehemiah in 'The Mission of Udjahorresnet and Those of Ezra and Nehemiah', *JBL* 106 (1987), pp. 409-21.

86. On the significance of this last point see above: 'Imperial Mechanisms of Control'.

87. Berquist, *Judaism in Persia's Shadow*, p. 145 n. 20.

Exile, Return and the Desolate Land

Two interrelated elements of the ideology of the Achaemenid-sponsored ruling class are central to issues surrounding migration and community identity. First, the identification of 'Israel', that is, the community representing the continuation of the pre-586 BCE Yahwistic states and the Yahwistic faith, with the 'exilic community' and its heirs who returned to Yehud. Second, the concept of the empty land, that is, that the territory of Judah was unoccupied during the period between the fall of Jerusalem to Nebuchadrezzar and the return authorized by Cyrus. These two elements are vital to reconstructing how prophetic texts may have been read in Achaemenid Yehud.

Ehud Ben Zvi has provided a full and detailed analysis of the ubiquitous connection between 'Israel' and 'Exiled Israel' in the late biblical texts. He demonstrates that the use of the term 'Israel' in late biblical literature refers to those exiled and/or returned to the exclusion of those who remained in the land during the neo-Babylonian occupation. 'Israel' in this literature is the designation of a particular community rather than, or perhaps in addition to, a geographical location. In addition to the motif of the empty land, he notes the presentation of the return from Babylon as a second exodus (Ezra 1; Deutero-Isaiah) or as a new conquest of the land (Ezra 2).[88] Ezra 2 clearly makes the connection between returnees (vv. 1, 68) and 'Israel', that is, the ethnic and/or religious community (vv. 2, 70). In addition, note the reported exclusion from this 'Israel' of those who returned but lacked proof of their genealogical descent. The use of both of these images, exodus and conquest, has the effect of excluding all non-returnees from this post-exilic 'Israel'.[89]

Many texts in the Hebrew Bible depict a situation in which the territory of Judah was completely depopulated either by the exile to Mesopotamia in 586 or by other means soon after. The Chronicler clearly indicates a belief that the land lay dormant, making up for its sabbaths, from the exile 'until the establishment of the kingdom of Persia' (2 Chron. 36.20-21). The DtrH may depict an uninhabited land by indicating that the remaining population (כל־העם) of Judah departed for Egypt after the assassination of Gedaliah (2 Kgs 25.26; cf. Jer. 43.5).

88. Cf. Blenkinsopp, *Ezra–Nehemiah*, pp. 83-84.
89. Ben Zvi, 'Inclusion', pp. 95-100.

Similarly, the account of the Babylonian destruction of Jerusalem and the exile in Jeremiah concludes with the statement: 'So Judah went into exile out of its land' (52.27). So all three major narrations of the end of the kingdom of Judah depict a complete depopulation of the land.

Several other texts in Jeremiah also indicate that the land would be desolate as punishment from Yahweh. Jeremiah 4.23-31 depicts the future of the land resulting from the foolishness and sin of the people (v. 22). This text paints a picture of near apocalyptic desolation in which the fruitful land has become a desert and the cities lie in ruins (v. 26; cf. 9.9-10 [Eng. vv. 10-11]). In promising future buying and selling of land, Jer. 32.43 summarizes the attitude toward the land of Judah during the period of exile: 'It is a desolation, without human beings or animals.' The total annihilation of all the remaining inhabitants of the land is predicted in Jer. 24.10. Ezekiel 33.24-29 lists multiple accusations against the remaining inhabitants of the land and describes a series of judgments against them. The conclusion of these judgments is the total desolation of the land so that it becomes a waste (Ezek. 33.29; cf. Jer. 24.8-10). Finally, add to these depictions of the total desolation of the land the fact that the common ending of both Jeremiah and 2 Kings focuses exclusively on the Babylonian (exilic) community.[90] These texts clearly reflect an ideology of the producing community that emphasized the legitimacy of the exiled community to the exclusion of anyone who had remained in the land.

These texts provide a stark contrast to the evidence presented above for a continuity of life throughout the neo-Babylonian period.[91] The disparity between the evidence for continuity of habitation and culture in Judah/Yehud and the claims of these texts that the land was a desolate waste require an explanation. This disparity may, in fact, reflect changing social discourse with regard to the composition of the Yehudite community over the course of the first 75-100 years of Achaemenid rule. It is commonly assumed in reconstructions of early Persian period Yehud that conflict developed between returnees and remainees almost immediately.[92] Although this is clearly the perspective of Ezra–Nehemiah, particularly Ezra 1–6, such conflict is not reflected in Haggai or Zechariah 1–8.[93] This discrepancy between the earlier prophetic sources

90. See Ben Zvi, 'Inclusion', p. 95 n. 2.
91. See above: 'Precursors to Achaemenid Yehud'.
92. Ahlström, *History*, pp. 844-47.
93. For example, compare the use of הארץ עם or הארצות עם as a designation of

and the later historiographic sources substantiates the suggestion that
social conditions changed over time.

Ezra 1–6 is a composite of sources from different periods edited to
reflect the ideology of the redactor. The first hint of opposition to the
returnees appears in Ezra 3.3. This text simply indicates, in passing, that
there was some fear among those restoring the altar of opposition from
foreign populations (עמי הארצות), whether within Yehud or the surrounding localities is unclear. The lack of integration with the
surrounding narrative may indicate that Ezra 3.3 functions literarily as a
forewarning of the opposition to come later in the narrative. Ezra 4
provides a primary piece of the evidence for the supposed conflict in the
time of Zerubbabel and Joshua, but the composite character of this text
suggests great caution in its use as historical evidence.[94] Verses 6-24, a
letter objecting to the reconstruction of the walls of Jerusalem from the
time of Artaxerxes, have been inserted into the present context as
though they represent the efforts of those opposed to the reconstruction
of the temple in vv. 1-5. Additionally, the preceding verses contain
several anomalies. Those who wish to help with the rebuilding are
variously termed 'adversaries' (v. 1), Samarians (by implication in v.
2), and 'the people of the land' (v. 4). Whatever the identity of this
group, they request participation in the rebuilding during the early years
of Darius I but their opposition is summarized by noting that they
frustrated the rebuilding of the temple from the time of Cyrus to that of
Darius (v. 5). Ezra 4 ends with the halting of the rebuilding of the
temple (v. 24) even though the letter had concerned the walls of the
city.

The chronology and activities in the early Persian period are further
confused in Ezra 5–6. Here the governor of the satrapy, Beyond the
River, raises questions about the reconstruction of the temple (5.3) but
the text explicitly states that the work on the temple did not cease while
the matter was investigated (5.5). The response of Darius is to issue a
decree commanding support for the temple rebuilding project (6.6-12).
The response of the satrapal officials is to comply with the decree and
help the rebuilding effort (aid that was apparently accepted by the community!). These events are then summarized with the statement: 'They

---

the adversaries of Israel in Ezra (e.g. 3.3; 4.4) with the threefold address to Zerubbabel, Joshua and all the people of the land (כל־עם הארץ) in Hag. 2.4. The Ezra
texts reflect a later development in the usage of the phrase.

94.   Contra Blenkinsopp, *Ezra–Nehemiah*, pp. 105-106.

finished their building by command of the God of Israel and by decree of Cyrus, Darius, and King Artaxerxes of Persia; and this house was finished on the third day of the month of Adar, in the sixth year of the reign of King Darius' (6.14b-15).

The most likely explanation for the existence of these contradictory narratives of the reconstruction of the temple is that later elements have been introduced by a redactor to reflect the situation of conflict that developed in a subsequent age. These later elements, which consistently reflect opposition to the work of reconstruction by those outside the community, have been inserted into an earlier account of the reconstruction which contained no references to opposition.[95] This suggests that the separation between 'the returnees' and 'the people of the land' was a later development in the life of the community. This division, however, does not reflect the historical situation of the community in the late sixth century.

In discussing the ubiquity of the correlation between Israel of the exile and Israel from the Persian period onward, Ben Zvi notes that the significance of this correlation is that it communicates the post-judgment condition of the Yehudite population.

> Thus to claim that 'EI = I' [Exiled Israel = Israel] within the matrix of these discourses is to claim that Israel has already paid its penalty (cf. Isa. 40.2), and therefore is ready for a new beginning; conversely, to deny the exilic (or post-exilic) character of Israel would be tantamount to associating oneself with those who are still unpunished.[96]

One possible implication of this theological argument is to place those who remained in the land outside the group that had been punished and, therefore, outside the new 'Israel'. If Yahweh's judgment on 'Israel' is co-terminus with exile then the identification of those who had been exiled with 'Israel' is inevitable.[97] But rather than interpreting this theological position as exclusive, Ben Zvi argues on the basis of the fluidity of ethnic boundaries and genealogies and the composite nature of the population lists of Ezra 2 and Nehemiah 7 (following Weinberg) that an integration of returnees and remainees probably took place.[98] This integration of the community in the early Achaemenid period

95. Contra Blenkinsopp, *Ezra–Nehemiah*, p. 106.
96. Ben Zvi, 'Inclusion', p. 135.
97. Ben Zvi, 'Inclusion', p. 135.
98. Ben Zvi, 'Inclusion', pp. 111-12.

provided the basis for all members to be included within the identification 'Exiled Israel = Israel'.

Hosea on Exile and Return

As indicated in the previous chapter, the recontextualization of the prophetic traditions from the monarchic period had already begun by the sixth century. Jeremiah (25.13; 30.2-3) and First Zechariah (1.2-6; 7.7) both refer to the significance of the words of the earlier prophets for understanding the past and present situations of Judah/Yehud. These appropriations of the words of earlier prophets indicate the importance placed upon the interpretation of the earlier prophetic traditions by these communities. First Zechariah provides clear evidence that the prophetic traditions of earlier generations were being read in the early Persian period as authoritative texts that would provide understanding and guidance for the Yehudite community. This evidence provides an important insight into the reading of early prophetic texts, including Hosea, in this period. These earlier texts would have been read according to the prevailing interpretive conventions of the community in relation to their contemporary situation.

The pervasiveness of the message of the complete depopulation of the land during the neo-Babylonian period, demonstrated above, would have significantly shaped the reading of certain texts in the book of Hosea during the early Persian period.[99] Several texts in the book of Hosea depict the judgment of Yahweh on monarchic Israel (and eventually Judah; see Chapter 5) as removal from the land. The reading of these texts within a context in which the extant texts demonstrate a discourse which stressed the desolation of the land during the neo-Babylonian period would be drastically different from a reading within an interpretive community that believed the experience of exile to have been limited to a small percentage of the total population. As a result of this prevalent discourse about the desolation of the land, those who had remained continuously in Judah/Yehud (or their descendants) would have potentially found themselves in a dramatically different rhetorical context in relation to these prophetic texts concerning punishment.

99. The relationship between social discourse and the reading of specific texts is circular. While the reading is shaped by the socio-historical setting in which it occurs, the reading event also shapes, in a variety of ways, the setting (or, at the least, the reader's perception of the setting).

Perhaps even more significant, they would also potentially stand in a very different relationship to the texts which depict the salvation of Yahweh for the future in terms of a return to the land. If punishment is primarily depicted as removal from the land and salvation is primarily depicted as return to the land, then those who remained in the land may be rhetorically excluded from both. Alternatively, they could be included in both, punishment and salvation, but such an inclusion would require them to identify with a history that was not actually their own. The available evidence does not permit a conclusion regarding the existence of an alternative story for the inhabitants whose ancestors had remained in the land. However, the lack of an extant alternative account suggests that an integration of the two communities, those who were exiled and those who remained, under the common identification 'Exiled Israel = Israel' occurred during the Persian period.

The creation of common community identity in early Achaemenid Yehud would have been important to the imperial center and the provincial administration. Both would benefit substantially from the peaceful integration of the two populations. As indicated above, such an integration would have required the continuous inhabitants of the land to identify with and be incorporated into the prevailing story of exile and restoration. This integration of the population within the context of a single story would have been a central goal of the ruling elite in their efforts to establish order and maintain control over the whole population of the province. The pervasiveness of the equation, 'Exiled Israel = Israel', in the post-monarchic biblical literature suggests that the inclusion of the whole population within this discourse was the goal of the Yehudite elite. The reading of the texts from the book of Hosea relating to punishment and salvation would have been shaped by and contributed to this pervasive discourse in the early Persian period context.

There is an important interrelationship between the prevailing discourse of the Persian period and the earlier prophetic texts. The depiction of punishment and suffering in relation to the desolation and restoration of the land in the earlier prophetic texts provides the foundation upon which the later discourse is built. The prophetic texts of earlier generations were vital to the self-understanding of the Persian period community.

Hosea 9.17 provides a summary of the message of the prophet: because the people have failed to be obedient to Hosea's God they will be rejected. This experience of divine rejection is expanded in the following clause, 'they will be fugitives among the nations'. נדד is often used to refer to the act of fleeing from imminent danger or, in participial form, as a designation of those who flee (Isa. 10.31; 16.3; 21.14-15; 22.3; 33.3; Jer. 49.5). The act of fleeing from disaster in search of safety in many of these texts has become a state of existence. Those who have fled become either fugitives in a juridical context or refugees in a context of warfare; though the two are not unrelated. In commenting on Hos. 9.17 Wolff suggests a parallel with Cain who is condemned to be a fugitive and a wanderer (נע ונד; Gen. 4.12) when rejected by God.[100] There is a temporal sequence in Hos. 9.17: the people fail to obey God; God rejects the people; the people become refugees among the nations (בגוים).

> The use of בגוים to denote the location of their wandering emphasizes the removal from the land. This is substantially different from the accusation in 7.8 that Ephraim is mixed (בלל) with the peoples (בעמים), an indication of a blurring of ethnic boundaries rather than a change of location.

In 9.17 בגוים indicates that the punishment which is a consequence of their disobedience results in removal from the land and status as refugees.

A similar fate is indicated by Hos. 8.8, 10. This text asserts a departure from the homeland as the result of their iniquity. Israel is depicted as swallowed up and like a useless vessel among the nations (בגוים; v. 8). Although this text could be read as the threat of foreigners intermingling with and overwhelming the people (cf. 7.8), the context points in the other direction. The threat, 'I will gather them up' (v. 10a), that results in domination by foreign rulers (v. 10b) is suggestive of prisoners being gathered to go into exile. The depiction of the punishment for their sins as a reversal of the Exodus, 'they shall return to Egypt' (v. 13) strongly supports reading בגוים as a reference to departure from the land. Indeed, regardless of their interpretation by earlier audiences, these images would be strongly suggestive of exile to an Achaemenid period reader.

The same image is used in 9.3 where the Exodus reversal is introduced by the ruthless statement: 'they shall not remain in the land of Yahweh'. The consequence of departing from their God (9.1) is

---

100. Wolff, *Hosea*, p. 168.

removal from that God's land and return to their condition prior to Yahweh's saving activity, namely, back to Egypt. The dramatic nature of this reversal of the Exodus becomes clearer with the recognition that this is the only biblical text in which Palestine (or some portion thereof) is designated as ארץ־יהוה.[101] The ownership of the land is emphasized in this text in a way that is unique in the Hebrew Bible. A similar phrase, 'my land' (ארצי), occurs in Jeremiah in contexts depicting the desecration of the land by its inhabitants (2.7) and a threat by Yahweh to remove them from the land because of their abominations which have polluted the '(my) land' (16.16-18; cf. v. 13). In fact, the conception that Yahweh was the owner of the land and the inhabitants were simply tenants of Yahweh became a cornerstone of legal traditions regarding the land in the Achaemenid period (Lev. 25.23). Ownership of the land means that Yahweh has sole discretion in determining its tenancy. For the Persian period reader of the book of Hosea (and Jeremiah) their ancestors' pollution of the land had been the catalyst for the owner's anger which resulted in their eviction.

According to Hosea 9 the eviction of the ancestors also had ritual and cultic significance. Their expulsion from the land resulted in the consumption of unclean food (v. 3). The following verse (v. 4) connects this expulsion from the land with the end of the (legitimate) sacrificial cult. According to these verses ritual purity and sacrificial worship were both inherently dependent on their tenancy in Yahweh's land. This same theological view underlies the argument in Hag. 2.10-19. The failure to restore the sanctuary and cult resulted in the uncleanness of the people and, therefore, agricultural failure. The foundation of the temple (v. 18) is the turning point which results in agricultural surplus. In Haggai it is only the nexus of land, people and temple/cult that could create ideal conditions. In the early Persian period, Hosea 9 could provide important, authoritative support for the theological perspective represented in Hag. 2.10-19.

This same perception of the land as the possession of Yahweh and the interdependence of the land and its inhabitants both lie behind and would shape a Persian period reading of Hos. 4.1-3. The text opens with a two-part indictment against the inhabitants of the land (יושבי הארץ; v. 1b); in relation to God the attributes on which the covenant relationship is based are missing from the *land* (v. 1c) and all the ethical

---

101. Wolff, *Hosea*, p. 155.

norms have broken down within the society (v. 2). The result of these crimes by the inhabitants of the land and the absence of the appropriate social norms from the land causes the land itself to mourn (v. 3a). Subsequently, all creatures that depend upon the land for existence, both the human inhabitants of the land and the animals, languish and die (v. 3). This portrayal of the relationship between the land, its inhabitants and their behavior provides a much more subtle account of the connection between the sins of the ancestors and their expulsion from the land than the threats to reverse the exodus. In fact, the ill effects that infect the land and all its inhabitants, human and wildlife, seem to result 'naturally' from the failures of the human inhabitants.[102] Most significant for the Yehudite readers is this intimate connection between human conduct and human tenancy in the land. Just as in Hag. 2.10-19, there is a direct relationship between human activity and the health of the land. The ancestors' inappropriate actions brought mourning and death to the land. According to Haggai, the failure of the Yehudite population in relation to temple and cult also had disastrous consequences for the land and its inhabitants.

In Hos. 11.5 the reversal of the exodus occurs again. Israel, depicted in this text as the son of Yahweh, 'will return to the land of Egypt' for failing to return to Yahweh. The use and reversal of the exodus tradition is heightened in this text by the specific reference to Israel's 'Egyptian' origins, 'since Egypt I have called (him) my son' (11.1). In this instance the political ramifications for the eighth-century audience (from the perspective of the later reader) of this threatened exodus reversal are spelled out, 'Assyria shall be his king' (11.5). In the context of Achaemenid Yehud the use of language regarding a reversal of the exodus would strongly suggest deportation and exile from Yahweh's land. The connection in Hos. 11.5 with the Assyrian domination and deportation of monarchic Israel would function to strengthen that identification, particularly in light of the tradition of the complete deportation of all Israelites and subsequent resettlement of foreign populations in the north (2 Kgs 17.22-41; note especially that Israel was exiled from their land until this day [v. 23] and that the descendants of

---

102. See Gene M. Tucker, 'Sin and "Judgment" in the Prophets', in Henry T.C. Sun and Keith L. Eades (eds.) with James M. Robinson and Garth I. Moller, *Problems in Biblical Theology: Essays in Honor of Rolf Knierim* (Grand Rapids: Eerdmans, 1997), pp. 373-88. Tucker argues that Hos. 4, among other prophetic texts, reflects a dynamistic relationship between sin and its consequences.

the foreign populations continue their inappropriate worship 'to this day' [v. 41]). Another text, suggestive of the wilderness tradition, threatens the people with a return to living in tents (12.10 [Eng. 9]). Yahweh, their God since Egypt, threatens to make the festival reenactment a reality.[103] For the Persian period reader of the prophetic traditions, these texts are significant because they all connect the punishment of the ancestors with removal from the land. The interpretation of this interconnection between punishment of the ancestors and absence from the land would be shaped by and provide authoritative substantiation for the dominant discourse equating exiled Israel and contemporary Israel.

Several texts in the book of Hosea depict the salvation of Yahweh in terms of the repopulation of the land. As the texts relating to depopulation would have been read in relation to the exile in the Persian period (as suggested above), these texts relating to repopulation would have been read in relation to the return from exile. In 2.1-2 [Eng. 1.10-11] the reversal of the narrative of judgment in 1.2-9 depicts a time when the fortunes of the people have been restored. Both the people of Judah and the people of Israel will be gathered together under a single head and they will take possession of the land. This promised salvation is cast in terms of the promises to the patriarchs. As Wolff observes:

> The new message Hosea proclaims is always related to the ancient traditions. This message is new in that it proclaims a complete transformation of Yahweh's judgment, which Hosea himself had announced in 4:3, 10; 9:12a, 16b; 14:1 as a catastrophic decimation of the population... Hence, with these words of the prophet, the promise to the patriarchs has become a new eschatological promise of salvation.[104]

This text indicates that even deportation cannot negate the promises to the patriarchs contained in the community's traditions. The promises of Yahweh cannot be frustrated.

Hosea 14.8 [Eng. 7] depicts a future for the restored community in lush agricultural imagery. Similarly, Hos. 2.23-25 [Eng. 21-23] represents Yahweh's salvation in terms of the fertility of the land (vv. 23-24). This image of fertility is then extended from the produce of the land to the renewal of the divine–human relationship. The restoration of Israel's relationship to God is depicted as a sowing in the land. As

---

103. Mays, *Hosea*, pp. 167-68.
104. Wolff, *Hosea*, p. 26.

indicated above, Hag. 2.10-19 connects the land and its inhabitants, and the welfare of both, with proper relationship to Yahweh. In the Achaemenid period this metaphor would likely have been read in relation to the return of the exiled community and the restoration of the cult of Yahweh. This image of sowing in the land is particularly interesting in relation to the suggestion above that the first major return of exiles during the reign of Darius I may have been connected with the imperial need to increase agricultural surpluses in advance of the anticipated Egyptian campaign.

This connection between return from exile, the fertility of the land and the restoration of the relationship of the community with Yahweh could have been easily exploited by the administration of Yehud in its efforts to increase land under cultivation and collect surplus crops. As noted above, Haggai connected the failure of agricultural activities with the failure to begin the temple rebuilding project (1.7-11). Indeed, the parallels between Hos. 2.23-25 and Hag. 1.7-11 are quite striking. The lack of rebuilding activity has caused the heavens to withhold moisture (Hag. 1.10) as Yahweh promised that the new era of salvation would see the heavens answer the earth (Hos. 2.23). The withholding of moisture has resulted in crop failure, specifically, grain, wine and oil (דגן, תירוש and יצהר; Hag. 1.11; exactly the same list, in the same order as Hos. 2.24). It may well be that the fulfillment of this promise in the book of Hosea was connected by Haggai with the beginning of the rebuilding of the temple.

Hosea 11.10-11 depicts the salvation of Yahweh as a return from Egypt and Assyria. The use of this imagery functions as a reversal of the various texts which portray the punishment of the ancestors as a return to Egypt, that is, a reversal of the exodus. Whether this text would have been read as a characterization of the return of the exiles as a new exodus or simply as a reversal of the reversal is unclear. Possibly of more significance to the early Achaemenid period setting is the promise to return them to their homes (והושבתים על־בתיהם; v. 11b). Although it is unlikely that the disposition of family lands was a source of substantial social conflict in the early Achaemenid period, there were certainly some disputes between those occupying the land at the time of the 'return' and the descendants of the exiled owners of the land. This text could provide an important argument for the claims of the immigrants.

All of these texts would fit neatly within the framework of the 'Exilic

Israel = Israel' discourse so common in the late biblical literature. They would support a social discourse which connected the punishment of the ancestors with the exile and the focus of Yahweh's salvation with the return of the exiled community. In relation to these texts from Hosea the future community of 'Israel' is the one that has come through a period of expulsion from the land to be restored to both relationship with Yahweh and the land.

Chapter 3

YEHUDITE LOYALTY TO THE ACHAEMENIDS

The loyalty of the province of Yehud to the Persian imperial center was very constant. In spite of numerous opportunities to exploit situations of imperial instability, there is no evidence for Yehudite participation in rebellion against Achaemenid rule at any time during the first century of Persian rule over Jerusalem.[1] This scrupulous loyalty to an imperial power is a substantial shift from the last century of the Judahite monarchy during which the king and court were constantly shifting alliances and playing the various powers off against one another in an effort to re-establish or maintain some measure of independent self-rule. This loyalty is also outstanding in the history of the relations of the Achaemenid empire with its colonies. Even at times when most of the imperial holdings were in revolt, Yehud remained a center of loyal Achaemenid support.[2]

This chapter will examine significant periods of rebellion in the early Achaemenid empire in which Yehudite participation has been proposed. After examining these proposals and establishing the constant loyalty of the province, the focus will shift to two theological issues which are

1.   Given the variety of possible interpretations of the evidence regarding Yehudite participation in the Tennes rebellion it is possible that there was never a period of Yehudite revolt against the Achaemenids. The later periods, however, are outside the scope of this study.

2.   'The Hebrews in Palestine, on the contrary, were usually loyal supporters of the Achaemenids even in times of trouble when Egypt or Syria was in revolt, and the Old Testament books of Esther, Ezra and Nehemiah, though not to be treated as history, indicate a closeness of the two. The diaspora of Jews throughout the empire, from a military garrison in Elephantine, an island on the upper Nile, to exiles in Hyrcania, probably aided their standing with the Persian overlords.' Richard N. Frye, *The History of Ancient Iran* (Handbuch der Altertumswissenschaft; Munich: C.H. Beck, 1984), p. 114; cf. Berquist, *Judaism in Persia's Shadow*, p. 144.

significant for understanding Yehudite loyalty to a foreign imperial power: possible hopes for the restoration of the Davidic monarchy; and the ideology surrounding the appropriate relationship to foreign powers. A central focus of the analysis of these issues will be the potential contribution to the social discourse concerning these issues from a Yehudite reading of the book of Hosea.

Instability in the Empire

The early years of the Achaemenid empire were dominated by constant territorial expansion under the leadership of Cyrus II. Between 559 and 539 BCE Cyrus transformed his kingdom from a small Median vassal to the most expansive empire known up to that time in the ancient Near East. After his death, the kingdom passed peacefully to his son, Cambyses. Like that of his father, Cambyses's reign was predominantly focused on expansion of the imperial holdings. Most of Cambyses's final years were spent in Egypt and Ethiopia seeking further conquests.

The internal coherence of the empire was shattered near the end of Cambyses's reign by the rebellion of Bardiya or Gaumata in the Persian homeland. According to the Behistun inscription of Darius I, the official imperial version of the events surrounding the rebellion, Bardiya, the brother of Cambyses, had long been dead. He had been killed by Cambyses to prevent a possible rebellion, and the revolt was really led by an impostor named Gaumata.[3] Berquist suggests that there was an ethnic component to the revolt, that Gaumata, a Median, was attempting to assert Median dominance within the empire. As support for this position he argues that the revolts in the provinces began during the reign of Gaumata, not after the counter-revolution of Darius.[4] If this argument were correct it would indicate that the assumption of power by Bardiya/ Gaumata was predominantly seen as illegitimate within the empire.

Dandamaev denies the theory that the rebellion of Bardiya was an attempt to shift the balance of power to Media. He notes that there were

---

3. For the best translation and textual analysis of the Old Persian version of the inscription see Rüdiger Schmitt, *The Bisitun Inscriptions of Darius the Great: Old Persian Text* (Corpus Inscriptionum Iranicarum, Part I, Vol. I; London: School of Oriental and African Studies, 1991). See also his briefer analysis in Rüdiger Schmitt, 'BISOTUN, Part iii', in *Encyclopaedia Iranica*, IV (London: Routledge, 1990).

4. Berquist, *Judaism in Persia's Shadow*, pp. 52-53.

seven Persian noble families who had been granted special privileges
by Cyrus in the (rapid) transition from a tribal society to an empire and
suggests that Cambyses had angered these families when he moved to
consolidate his royal powers at their expense. By removing the privileged position of these seven noble families Cambyses created an
atmosphere in which they were happy to see Bardiya take control. This
scenario is supported by the peace and stability that followed Bardiya's
coup (contra Berquist) and the widespread rebellion, even within Persia
itself, at the accession of Darius.[5] There appears to have been support
for the coup of Bardiya among the ruling class of the Persian empire
which would suggest that he was not considered an outsider by the
ethnic Persian nobles.

Though generally providing valuable historical information regarding
the early years of the reign of Darius I, the veracity of the Behistun
inscription regarding the identity of Gaumata/Bardiya must be questioned. While this version of events may preserve the true identity of
the leader of the revolt, the depiction of the revolutionary leader as an
imposter (Gaumata) masquerading as Bardiya (Cambyses's brother)
does conveniently coincide with the propagandistic purposes of Darius
in the Behistun inscription.[6] The portrayal of Bardiya as the Median,
Gaumata, who took advantage of Cambyses's absence to assert Median
preeminence in the empire would certainly have been in the interests of
Darius as he attempted to restore order in the empire following his
counter-revolution. The effect is to portray Darius, who was an
Achaemenid but not from the ruling family line, as a restorer of the
Achaemenid dynasty which was threatened by a usurper. In fact, if
Bardiya was truly the brother of Cambyses then Darius was the usurper.

The importance of the Behistun inscription in legitimating the reign
of Darius is indicated by the fact that it was distributed not only in the
Persian heartland but was also spread throughout the empire. Its
function as a tool of propaganda for Darius within the geographical

---

5.   Dandamaev, *Political History*, pp. 95-102.

6.   Dandamaev favors the probability that Darius killed Bardiya, the younger
son of Cyrus, and lists many others who accept this opinion (*Political History*,
p. 91). Olmstead, *History*, pp. 107-10, also indicates a variety of reasons for believing Darius to be a usurper. Although the point is peripheral to this study, the identification of the revolutionary as Bardiya, the brother of Cambyses, seems most
probable. Compare also Frye, *History*, pp. 96-106; Cook, *The Persian Empire*,
pp. 49-55.

center of the empire is demonstrated by the monumental original, carved into the side of a cliff on the road from Babylon to Ecbatana. The inscription is carved into the rock face in three languages (Old Persian, Elamite [two versions] and Akkadian) along with depictions of the representatives of each of the subdued ethnic groups standing in a line with a rope tied around each of their necks joining them together in a chain. These representatives are depicted in a much smaller size than Darius and stand before him in a subservient position. Surely the form makes as much of a statement as the content.[7] The function of the inscription as a tool of propaganda throughout the empire is demonstrated by the discovery of fragments of a stone slab containing the Akkadian version which were found in the excavations of the palace of Nebuchadrezzar II and papyrus fragments of an Aramaic version for distribution in western parts of the empire which were found at Elephantine.[8] The widespread distribution of this text in a variety of languages establishes its propagandistic function and demonstrates that this text was a vital aspect in Darius's efforts to consolidate his power over the empire. The text, which attempts to legitimate and aggrandize Darius, would primarily function as a method of restoring the relationship of dominance and subordination between the imperial center (particularly as embodied in the emperor, Darius) and the colonies.

The revolt of Bardiya against the rule of his brother, Cambyses, resulted in a period of immense imperial instability. Cambyses, who heard of his brother's revolt while in Egypt, mysteriously died in Syria while returning to put down the rebellion. However, even with Cambyses conveniently removed from the scene the reign of Bardiya only lasted about six months. Darius and his co-conspirators successfully executed a plot to kill Bardiya and then made Darius emperor.[9] As a

---

7.   Schmitt suggests that the fact that the inscriptions cannot be read by those passing along the road below is an indication of the function of the carving to impress by its presence in an almost magical way (*The Bisitun Inscriptions*, p. 18).

8.   Dandamaev, *Political History*, p. 132; see the transcription and translation of the Aramaic papyri in Bazalel Porten and Ada Yardeni, *Textbook of Aramaic Documents from Egypt* (4 vols.; Jerusalem: Hebrew University, 1993), III, pp. 60-71; cf. A.E. Cowley, *Aramaic Papyri of the Fifth Century B.C.* (Oxford: Clarendon Press, 1923), pp. 248-71.

9.   See Dandamaev for a summary of and references to the accounts in the classical historians (*Political History*, p. 83). On the length of Bardiya's reign compare the Behistun inscription, which records three months, and Herodotus (*Hist.* 3.67) who has seven months. Bardiya's reign was quickly brought to an end

result of this prolonged period of instability in the imperial leadership, nationalistic rebellions arose throughout the empire. Darius spent much of the first two years of his reign putting down the rebellions and restoring stability to the empire.

The revolts during the early years of the reign of Darius included most of the empire. The Mediterranean coast was one of the few areas that remained loyal to the imperial center during this period. The Behistun Inscription provides most of our information regarding the events of this turbulent time. Directly in the heart of the empire there was a rebellion in Persia that engaged the forces of Darius on several occasions between c. October 522 and July 521 BCE. The rebellion spread beyond the Persian heartland to most other regions.[10] In the three vital areas of Elam, Media and Babylonia the difficulties for Darius were just as severe as in the Persian heartland. There were three rebellions against Darius in Elam during the period 522–520 BCE. The first two died quickly without popular support, but the third in 520 required the intervention of the army. In Media there was a bloody seven-month revolt that ended in May 521.

There were two successive revolts in Babylonia. Nidintu-bel, claiming to be a son of Nabonidus, was declared king by 3 October 522 BCE. After two battles in a military campaign led by Darius in December 522 the rebellion was ended. Beginning in August 521 Babylonian commercial documents are dated to the reign of Nebuchadrezzar IV, indicating the revolt led by Arakha. This revolt was crushed in battle on 27 November 521 BCE and led to the destruction of the city walls of Babylon (cf. Herodotus, *Hist.* 3.159).

Additionally, the Behistun inscription provides evidence of revolts in Sattagydia, Parthia and Hyrcania, Armenia and Margiana. All of these were ended by December 521 at the latest. The record of the defeat of the Saka tribes, attributed to Darius in 519 BCE, was apparently a new

by Darius and his co-conspirators. On the basis of the Behistun inscription and the classical historians, Danadamaev notes that the killing of Bardiya was the result of a conspiracy by seven men from noble families among the Persian tribes. The numerous revolts against the rule of Darius and the regular references in imperial inscriptions to the fact that he was the choice of Ahura Mazda both strongly indicate that Darius had difficulty in consolidating his claim to the throne (Dandamaev, *Political History*, pp. 103-14).

10. 'Vahyazdata not only managed to extend his control over Persia, but also over Carmania, Drangiana, Gedrosia, and certain parts of Media, Arachosia and Sattagydia' (Dandamaev, *Political History*, p. 118).

conquest, not the ending of a revolt, and was added to the Behistun Inscription secondarily.[11]

According to the Behistun inscription the Egyptians rebelled at the beginning of the reign of Darius. It is unclear, however, when the revolt ended. Specific evidence regarding the length and extent of the rebellion is unavailable, but it is known that Darius spent time in Egypt in 518 BCE.[12] Apparently the Egyptians revolted at the accession of Darius (or perhaps even as early as the departure of Cambyses?) and were not compelled to return to the imperial fold until the military visit of Darius after 520 BCE.

After quelling the various revolts early in his reign, Darius made use of the period of peace to institute an administrative reorganization of the empire (Herodotus, *Hist.* 3.89-97). This reorganization of the administrative districts and systems provided Darius with the means to consolidate his reign. The Persians did not face a revolt again until the uprising in Anatolia c. 499–493 BCE. Although order was eventually restored in the Anatolian holdings, they complicated Persian plans for expansion. Afterward the desired westward expansion was halted (at least temporarily) by the victory of the Athenian forces at the battle of Marathon in August 490 BCE.

The absolute lack of evidence for Yehudite rebellion or disloyalty to the empire during this tumultuous period is both remarkable and significant. The Yehudites' fidelity to the imperial center even in a period when the empire appeared to be on the verge of total collapse indicates the creation and maintenance of a strong relationship between the provincial administration and the Achaemenids.

Supposed Yehudite Rebellions

A variety of hypotheses suggesting the participation of the province of Yehud in rebellion against the Achaemenid empire have been proposed

---

11. Dandamaev, *Political History*, pp. 139-40. See also Olmstead, *History*, p. 141.

12. Dandamaev, *Political History*, pp. 141-43. Compare Frye, who seems to provide contradictory positions. 'Curiously nothing is said about rebellions in Egypt, Palestine or Anatolia in the inscription although they can hardly have remained completely loyal to Darius from the outset' (Frye, *History*, p. 98). But also: 'None of the revolts in the western possessions are mentioned in the Behistun inscription, although (II, 7) Egypt is recorded as a rebellious land' (Frye, *History*, p. 100).

over the years. Most significant for consideration of life in Yehud in the early period of Achaemenid rule are the widespread suggestions of a Yehudite uprising led by Zerubbabel.

The reconstruction of this supposed rebellion is based almost exclusively on a few texts from Haggai and Zechariah 1–8 combined with the 'disappearance' of Zerubbabel, which is attributed by some to Persian retribution for his leadership of the insurrection.[13] Even those who are more cautious about implicating Zerubbabel in the scheme find evidence in these prophetic texts for moves toward independence in this period.[14]

Julius Morgenstern not only argued for a rebellion under Zerubbabel during the reign of Darius I but also suggested that this was followed by a second revolt led by Menahem at the beginning of the reign of Xerxes. He proposed that Xerxes, as a result of the pressing need to put down a revolt in Babylonia, 'delegated' the task of bringing the Yehudite community back into line to the surrounding ethnic communities, including the Edomites. The resulting attack brought about the destruction of the second temple and the walls of Jerusalem. According to Morgenstern's reconstruction, the programs of Ezra and Nehemiah resulted in the building of a third temple and another restoration of the walls of the city.[15] This suggestion of a second Yehudite rebellion is

13. The account of Olmstead, *History*, pp. 135-43, is typical. Similarly, see Blenkinsopp, *Ezra–Nehemiah*, p. 63; Albright, *From the Stone Age to Christianity*, p. 324; J. Morgenstern, 'Jerusalem—485 BC', *HUCA* 27 (1956), pp. 101-79 (167-75); Ahlström, *History*, pp. 820-21; Rolf Rendtorff, *The Old Testament: An Introduction* (Philadelphia: Fortress Press, 1985), pp. 61-62.

14. Miller and Hayes, *History*, pp. 458-60; Niels Peter Lemche, *Ancient Israel: A New History of Israelite Society* (Biblical Seminar, 5; Sheffield: JSOT Press, 1988), pp. 190-91. Geo Widengren refers to 'wild expectations' created by the turmoil in the empire following the accession of Darius, but concludes that such messianic speculations did not stir up significant political unrest ('The Persian Period', in John H. Hayes and J. Maxwell Miller [eds.], *Israelite and Judean History* [Philadelphia: Westminster Press, 1977], pp. 489-538 [521]). See also the account of Weinberg, who accepts the historicity of the account of the collapse of the rebuilding of the temple and the refortification of the walls depicted in Ezra 4 (*The Citizen–Temple Community*, p. 112 [esp. n. 1]).

15. Julius Morgenstern, 'Further Light from the Book of Isaiah upon the Catastrophe of 485 B.C.', *HUCA* 27 (1956), pp. 1-28; *idem*, 'Jerusalem—485 B.C.', pp. 101-79; *idem*, 'Jerusalem—485 B.C. (continued)', *HUCA* 28 (1957), pp. 15-47; *idem*, 'Jerusalem—485 B.C. (concluded)', *HUCA* 31 (1960), pp. 11-29.

based on an extremely tendentious reading of the biblical texts and has not been widely accepted.[16]

Apart from the 'mysterious disappearance' of Zerubbabel and the supposed messianic expectations of the Yehudites in the early Persian period, there is no evidence for any animosity or lack of cooperation between the local administration in Yehud and the imperial center. Although there may have been those who opposed Persian rule, they have left no evidence of their opposition. In fact, there is no indication in any of the Achaemenid sources of an uprising in Yehud (in any period). The probability of a Yehudite rebellion is further reduced by two key factors: first, it is unlikely that the Yehudites would have rebelled in late 520 BCE *after* Darius had successfully suppressed rebellions in other parts of the empire; and, second, the coordination of an uprising with the planned arrival of the main military force of the empire on its way to Egypt is also highly improbable.[17]

The lack of further references to Zerubbabel should be treated with caution. It is certainly too much to assume that the silence can be equated with his execution by the Persians. He may have died of some other cause. Perhaps Berquist's suggestion is correct that the lack of references to Zerubbabel after the second temple was completed can be explained by the fact that his administrative role was directly related to that project and the provisioning of the army for the invasion of Egypt. Once these tasks were accomplished there would be little to report about his work.[18]

The absence of any record of Zerubbabel in the period after 520 BCE may have more to do with administrative and economic reforms of Darius than internal events in Yehud. These reforms began about 519 BCE but would have taken several years to implement fully. The reorganization was further complicated by the division of the province Abar Nahara c. 516 BCE. Dandamaev and Lukonin note that one aspect of these reforms was a preference for Persians in leading administrative posts as opposed to local hereditary monarchs.[19] This reorganization of provincial administration provides another possible explanation for the 'disappearance' of Zerubbabel that does not require his execution by

---

16. See the detailed summary and critique of Hoglund, *Achaemenid Imperial Administration*, pp. 51-61.

17. Berquist, *Judaism in Persia's Shadow*, pp. 62-64, 136.

18. Berquist, *Judaism in Persia's Shadow*, p. 64.

19. Dandamaev and Lukonin, *Culture and Social Institutions*, pp. 97-101.

the Persians. Perhaps Zerubbabel was a victim on the administrative chopping block (rather than a literal one) or, alternatively, perhaps his administrative skills were required in another part of the imperial system.

Restoration of Davidic Rule?

A central consideration in the speculations regarding the possibility of a Yehudite nationalistic rebellion against the Persians and the eventual status of Zerubbabel concerns the expectations of the community for the restoration of the Davidic monarchy. The analysis of these expectations must consider more than the simple question as to whether or not the Yehudites in the early Persian period expected the restoration of the monarchy. The restoration of the Davidic line may indicate hopes for the re-establishment of an independent monarchic state but this would not necessarily be the only understanding of a restoration of the Davidides. It is also possible that eschatological expectations related to a Davidic ruler may have their roots in this period. Alternatively, the selection of a Davidide as the provincial governor of Yehud within the Persian imperial system may have met the expectations of many Yehudites in the early Persian period. It is likely that diverse opinions existed within the community on the issue.

The release of Jehoiachin from prison in 560 BCE may have raised hopes that the Davidic line would be restored to power in Jerusalem. However, the report of this fact at the end of the DtrH (2 Kgs 25.27-30) does not necessarily indicate that the restoration of the Davidic line was where the compilers of the Deuteronomistic History saw the future hope of the community.[20] Rather than representing the future hope of the Deuteronomists, the account of the release of Jehoiachin functions to shift the focus of the reader's attention to the Judahite community in Babylonia, and highlights the centrality of that community for the neo-Babylonian and early Persian periods. Although there is a strong pro-Davidic element in the source material used in the composition of the

---

20. 'Under the circumstances Dtr. cannot mean the improvement in the deported Jehoiachin's personal fortunes (2 Kgs 25.27-30) to herald a new age. Apart from the fact that the subject matter of this event does not lend itself to such a comprehensive interpretation, in view of what we have said above, Dtr. would have no reason to take such a view' (Martin Noth, *The Deuteronomistic History* [JSOTSup, 15; Sheffield: JSOT Press, 2nd edn, 1981], p. 143).

Deuteronomistic History, there is little, if any, indication in the DtrH of an expectation of the restoration of the Davidic monarchy.

The situation regarding the Davidic line is similar in Chronicles. The Chronicler omits the reference to the situation of the Davidic descendants entirely, choosing instead to end the account with the decree of Cyrus announcing that God had charged him (Cyrus) with the rebuilding of the temple and encouraging the descendants of the exiles to return for that purpose (2 Chron. 36.22-23). The central focus of post-monarchic life for the Chronicler lay in the restoration of the Yahwistic temple and cult. The emphasis on David and the Davidic dynasty in Chronicles is primarily related to the Chronicler's concern with the temple and cult. David and Solomon are the most significant members of the dynasty in the Chronicler's account, the focus of approximately half of 1 and 2 Chronicles between them (David = 1 Chron. 10–29; Solomon = 2 Chron. 1–9). In the Chronicler's narration of these two figures the preparation for building the temple, the building of the temple, and the dedication of the temple are the central themes. Even in regard to the remaining members of the Davidic line the Chronicler's judgment of their reigns is often related to their fidelity in cultic matters. The relationship of the Yahwistic temple and its cult with the founder of the dynasty (and his son) functions to legitimate them. The Chronicler's primary concern is not David and the Davidic line but the legitimacy that they can lend to the building of the (second) temple, both the climax and conclusion of his narrative.

There are only a few vague references to the continuation of the Davidic line in the sixth-century prophetic literature. Jeremiah 23.5-6 preserves language quite similar to Zechariah 1–8. The unit promises a time to come when a righteous 'branch' will rule over Judah and Israel. The precise referent of this promise is difficult to establish. The apparent play on the name Zedekiah (cf. יהוה צדקנו) in naming the future ruler may indicate that this oracle originated in the final years of the Judahite kingdom.[21] The promises are not extravagant but reflect belief in the preservation of the Davidic line.

The depiction of the future situation regarding the Davidic descendants is much more developed in Jer. 33.14-26. Lang points to this text in conjunction with Ezekiel and Haggai as evidence for early expectation of the restoration of the Davidic throne.[22] This text, however, is

21. Holladay, *Jeremiah*, II, pp. 616-17.
22. Bernhard Lang, *Monotheism and the Prophetic Minority: An Essay in*

rather unreliable evidence for the early Persian period. Holladay notes that several features of the text suggest a late Persian period date. The author of this text has reused earlier portions of Jeremiah and incorporated later administrative developments—note the uses of 'Levite' and the joint administration of civil authority and priest.[23]

The future hope of Deutero-Isaiah, on the other hand, did not lie in the restoration of the Davidic monarchy. In fact, such an idea is never mentioned in Isaiah 40–55. Rather, Deutero-Isaiah saw the Persian empire, and Cyrus II, in particular, as the tool of Yahweh for the future of the people (Isa. 44.28; 45.1-14). 'Deutero-Isaiah was not pro-nationalist or pro-Davidic; he was pro-Persian, with the argument that the fortunes of the Babylonian Jews, if not all Jews, would be best under Persian rule.'[24]

Finally, there is no evidence that Ezekiel expected a restoration of the monarchic state. The governing figure in Ezekiel's visions has been compared with a local mayor with little real authority.[25] References to the return of a Davidic ruler are quite low key in Ezekiel. The description of future rule by David is highlighted by the use of נָשִׂיא as the designation of the governmental office (Ezek. 34.3-24; 37.24-25).

Haggai, Zechariah and Messianic Furor

One aspect of the proposed rebellion under Zerubbabel that should be examined further is the relation of the prophecies of Haggai and Zechariah (1–8) to expectations of the restoration of the Davidic monarchy. These texts provide the only substantial evidence for such theories.

The oracles of Haggai are almost solely concerned with the situation surrounding the rebuilding of the temple. The two texts that have been identified as evidence of messianic excitement are 2.1-9 and 2.20-23. Although commonly used as evidence for expectation among the Yehudite community that a new messianic age would dawn with Zerubbabel as king, the central focus of Hag. 2.1-9 is actually the temple. Zerubbabel and Joshua are singled out by name, but the oracle of Haggai is

---

Biblical History and Sociology (The Social World of Biblical Antiquity, 1; Sheffield: Almond Press, 1983), p. 133.

23. Compare 33.15-16 with 23.5-6; and 33.19-22, 23-26 with 31.35-37. Jer. 33 is clearly an expansive interpretation of these earlier texts. Cf. Holladay, *Jeremiah*, II, pp. 228-31.

24. Berquist, *Judaism in Persia's Shadow*, p. 31.

25. Lang, *Monotheism*, p. 133.

directed at the whole community. There is nothing in this text to suggest messianic expectations, at least in the form of the restoration of a native monarchy, in the Yehudite community of the period. All of the expectations in this oracle center around the splendor and honor to be given to the new temple as a result of the intervention of Yahweh. The alteration of the situation of Yehud described in Haggai 2 has nothing to do with military victories or a new royal administration. The prophet envisions a time when wealth will flow into the soon to be rebuilt temple and make its glory greater than that of the previous temple.

Berquist suggests that the expected shaking of the earth and financial prosperity of the temple result from the close passage of the imperial army and the financial rewards resulting from the provisioning of the army by the Yehudites.[26] Whether or not the prophet consciously made this connection, the expectation of a dramatically new social situation with the completed temple and prosperity as key features may have been an indirect result of the presence of the imperial army. Perhaps this text represents a claim on a portion of the wealth to be generated from the passage of the imperial forces. Or, alternatively, the expectation of an influx of wealth could be related to the expectation of imperial funding to aid the reconstruction of the temple.[27] Whatever the relationship between the needs of the empire and the prosperity of Yehud, the prophet directly connects the coming prosperity and splendor of the temple with the activity of Yahweh. In fact, this theological perception is the key. As in Deutero-Isaiah, the blessing of the people by Yahweh does not depend on the restoration of the Davidic house but could be accomplished even under a foreign ruler.

Meyers and Meyers suggest that the language about the glory of the new temple in comparison with that of the former did have political implications. The connection of the former temple with the Judahite monarchy was an important source of its prestige. The Yehudites reconstructing the temple recognized that the absence of the monarchy could undermine the importance of the temple. This new temple would not be

---

26. Berquist, *Judaism in Persia's Shadow*, p. 66.

27. However, Petersen indicates that the term for wealth (חמדת; 2.7) is often used as part of a construct chain designating 'precious vessels'. This may suggest that Haggai expected vessels for the temple to result from the activity of Yahweh (Petersen, *Haggai and Zechariah 1–8*, pp. 67-68). See also Hans Walter Wolff, *Haggai* (Continental Commentaries; Minneapolis: Augsburg, 1988), p. 81.

connected with a royal palace or function as the central sanctuary of the cult of a state deity. The loss of this political function of the temple could have been a source of the delay in its reconstruction. Haggai's oracle serves as a reassurance that the glory of the new temple will not suffer as a result of the loss of connection with the monarchy but, by the intervention of Yahweh, will be universally recognized as the place of Yahweh's abode.[28] The significance of the temple was no longer dependent upon the existence of the monarchy. The relationship between Yahweh and the people could be mediated solely through the sanctuary.

Both the Deuteronomistic History and Chronicles seem to support this view that the legitimacy and prestige of the temple was not dependent upon the continuing existence of the Davidic dynasty. The account of the institution of the monarchy in the Deuteronomistic History is framed by a narrative (1 Sam. 8) and a speech by Samuel (1 Sam. 12) that both describe the request for a king as contrary to the will of Yahweh. In this way, the origins of monarchic rule are presented as an unnecessary and dangerous innovation that was only tolerated by Yahweh. For the Deuteronomistic History the monarchy is not the central feature of Judahite life which legitimated everything else. Rather, the monarchy was a step in the wrong direction that eventually had disastrous consequences for the nation. The monarchy receives primary blame for the sins of the nation which led to the catastrophe of 586 BCE according to the Deuteronomists' version of the national history.

The Chronicler, on the other hand, never raises questions about the legitimacy of the Davidic monarchy. In fact the origin and early years of the Judahite monarchy are almost completely sanitized of all potentially negative material by the Chronicler. The significance of this lies in the fact that the Chronicler legitimates the temple and the temple cult on the basis of its construction and organization by David and Solomon. In fact, the organization of temple and cult by David and the building of the temple and initiation of the cult by Solomon are the central events in the Chronicler's narration of their reigns. After fulfilling the function of establishing the sanctuary, the institution of the monarchy and the individual monarchs are the chief culprits in the sins and eventual downfall of the nation. The only exceptions are those monarchs who are associated with appropriate reforms (in the view of the Chronicler) of the

---

28. Carol L. Meyers and Eric M. Meyers, *Haggai and Zechariah 1–8* (AB, 25B; New York: Doubleday, 1987), pp. 70-76.

temple cult. For the Chronicler the temple is the vehicle by which Yehud is connected with the national history. While the legitimacy of the construction of the first temple and its organization is tied to David, the king chosen by Yahweh, the monarchy, as an institution, is less important for the Chronicler than the temple and cult. As a consequence, the construction of a Yahwistic temple and the institution of appropriate cultic activity is vital to the theology of the Chronicler but the restoration of the monarchy and the continuation of the Davidic line have become unnecessary.

There may be a reference to the restoration of the Davidic line in Hag. 2.20-23 but such a reading is not the only alternative. The three key terms in the text are 'my servant', 'signet' and 'choose' (v. 23). Meyers and Meyers suggest these terms imply connections with monarchic rule.[29] This is particularly true of the term 'my servant' (עבדי), which is used in several texts as a designation of David, though only once in reference to any other member of the Davidic dynasty. The primary implication of these terms is that Zechariah had a strategic role as an instrument in the work of Yahweh, a work which is primarily focused on the restoration of the temple. The use of this language may give that work royal overtones, but there is nothing in this text that is necessarily suggestive of the unrealistic political expectations suggested by some reconstructions of this period.[30]

The same can also be said of the so-called messianic texts of Zechariah 1–8. The coordination of the terms 'my servant' (עבדי) and 'branch' (צמח) in 3.8 suggests the arrival of a Davidide but it does not seem to reflect fervor for a return of the monarchy. The central implications of the arrival of this figure are the removal of the guilt of the land (v. 9), peace and prosperity (v. 10). The other text commonly associated with messianic expectations is Zech. 6.9-15. This text appears to have originally envisioned a dyarchy of Zerubbabel and Joshua.[31] The

29. Meyers and Meyers, *Haggai and Zechariah 1–8*, pp. 68-70.

30. There is a danger in reading too much into these terms on the basis of our expectations regarding early Persian period expectations. For example the term signet is only used of a Davidide once (Jer. 22.24). There it is not used as an identifier of Coniah as a Davidide, but solely as an image to describe the way in which Yahweh will dispose of Coniah. Cf. Wolff, who leaves the question of messianic expectations open but notes the predominance of Zerubbabel as temple builder (*Haggai*, p. 107).

31. Berquist argues that this text never included Zerubbabel but always only referred to Joshua but this reading seems highly unlikely (*Judaism in Persia's*

manufacture of crowns also implies a shared authority.[32] The reference to the 'branch' who will rebuild the temple (an action attributed to Zerubbabel in 4.8-10) and receive authority, ruling with the priest at his side, certainly is indicative of a dyarchy composed of both political and priestly representatives. The use of הוד indicates the honor of the position but does not exclusively refer to royal honor. The use of משל rather than מלך is also significant. Certainly מלך would be a less ambiguous term if this text was a reflection of early Persian period expectations of the restoration of the Davidic monarchy. The central factor in the description of this figure is that he will be the one to rebuild the temple. The scenario envisioned by this text is not a return to monarchic rule by a Davidide but a joint civil and religious authority in which the primary action of the 'secular' ruler is to oversee the construction of the temple. As in other texts from this period, the central focus of expectations is the restoration of the temple not the restoration of the monarchy.

In Zech. 4.14 the priestly and political leaders are described as 'sons of oil' (בני היצהר). Although this phrase has recently been translated 'the anointed ones' (NRSV), the implication of the text has more to do with the fertility of the land that will result from the joint rule of these civil and religious leaders rather than expectations of a restoration of the monarchy.[33] The absence of משח in this text highlights its absence in the entire corpus of post-monarchic biblical literature. משח is never used in reference to a governing figure in this period.[34] The absence of the root משח in all the literature from this period does not fit a scenario in which there were strong expectations of a restoration of the monarchy. In fact, the use of language associated with the monarchy and messianic expectations in the Persian period seems to have been carefully circumscribed.

Shadow, p. 73). Lester L. Grabbe argues for a dyarchy as the basic form of government in Yehud during the Persian period. He suggests that governors and high priests ruled jointly, although the two positions may have been collapsed into a single individual on occasion (*Judaism from Cyrus to Hadrian* [2 vols.; Minneapolis: Fortress Press, 1992], I, pp. 74-75).

32. Plural in the MT but singular in the versions. The versions appear to reflect attempts to smooth out the difficulties of the text.

33. See Petersen, *Haggai and Zechariah 1–8*, pp. 230-22; Meyers and Meyers, *Haggai and Zechariah 1–8*, pp. 258-59.

34. On two possible exceptions, see below, 'Achaemenid Adaptation of Local Kingship Traditions'.

Significantly, in relation to the possibilities regarding Zerubbabel, the temple and the consequences of domination by a foreign empire, both Haggai and Zechariah temper their anticipation by placing the outcome in the hands of Yahweh. In Haggai it is Yahweh who will shake the earth bringing about both the influx of wealth to the temple (2.1-9) and the appointment of Zerubbabel as signet of Yahweh (2.20-23). Similarly, in Zechariah the anticipated events are specifically said to be the work of Yahweh and not the result of human might or power (4.6). The expectations regarding the rule of Zerubbabel and the restoration of the temple were clearly bound to a theology that removed the outcomes from the realm of human activity and placed them solely within the domain of Yahweh's activity.

Although there are linguistic connections with the Davidic monarchy in some of these texts, none of them can be described as reflecting wild messianic expectations surrounding the figure of Zerubbabel or anyone else. They do, however, reflect an ideology consonant with a local administration headed by a Davidic descendent in tandem with a priestly figure. There is no evidence that the Yehudites sought to reestablish an independent state ruled by a Davidic descendent during the instability surrounding the revolt of Bardiya and the accession of Darius (or at any other time during Achaemenid rule). In the whole corpus of surviving texts from the Persian period the evidence for expectations that the Davidic monarchy would be restored is, at best, very limited and ambiguous. Commenting on the careful use of language in Zech. 6.12 Meyers and Meyers state: 'The intent in either case would be to deal with the delicate situation of a priest with some royal prerogatives, to deflate the emotional potential of the scene, and to impress again upon everyone the limited potential of the role of Zerubbabel in the restoration.'[35] The overall impression is one of caution and perhaps even an intentional suppression of messianic expectations rather than messianic fervor and seething nationalism.[36]

---

35. Meyers and Meyers, *Haggai and Zechariah 1–8*, p. 355.

36. Weinberg (*The Citizen–Temple Community*, pp. 130-31) suggests that there were different plans for renewal of national life in the Mesopotamian and Judahite communities during the period of neo-Babylonian dominance. Those who remained in the land hoped for the restoration of the old order, including return of the exiles and restoration of the Davidic kingdom, while those in Mesopotamia hoped for a radically altered situation with distinct cultic and secular spheres and a head of state with much more limited powers (he views Ezek. 40–48 as the restoration plan of

As indicated above, there is no evidence for a revolt inspired by the desire to restore the Davidic monarchy under Zerubbabel. In addition, there are significant reasons to doubt the likelihood of such an occurrence. The timing, in conjunction with the rebuilding of the temple beginning in late 520 BCE, is after Darius had consolidated his hold on the empire. It strains credibility to suggest that the Yehudites had remained loyal to the empire throughout such a period of major instability and then rebelled when the continuation of imperial control had been assured. Also, the presence of the main forces of the Persian army in Palestine on the way to Egypt would not have been conducive to a revolt.[37] The timing of a revolt to coincide with the arrival of a military force outnumbering the local population is, at best, a highly unlikely scenario.

It is possible that Judah/Yehud continued to be ruled locally by members of the Davidic line from Gedaliah onward. The use of members of the local ruling family to govern conquered territories was a common practice of imperial administrations in the ancient world. The use of members of the Davidic line would have provided the means by which the imperial powers could effect both centralized control and local stability. This would explain the appointment of Zerubbabel, a Davidide according to 1 Chron. 3.17-24, as the imperial representative in Yehud on behalf of the Persians.[38] The exploitation of local royal ideology on a limited scale would have the dual effect of stabilizing Persian rule over the colony and reducing interest in the restoration of the Davidic monarchy. Although under a higher, centralized authority, a Davidide continued to rule the area.

---

the exilic community). The preceding analysis indicates that the scenario that Weinberg attributes to the Mesopotamian community was, in fact, the dominant perspective in the early Persian period.

37. See above, 'Supposed Yehudite Rebellions'; see also Berquist, *Judaism in Persia's Shadow*, p. 62; Grabbe, *Judaism*, I, p. 79; Lemche, *Ancient Israel*, pp. 190-91.

38. However, it must be noted that the connection of Zerubbabel with the Davidic line is uncertain. While the Chronicler's genealogy has Zerubbabel as a Davidide, this is not confirmed in other texts from the period (Ezra–Nehemiah, Haggai or Zechariah). Further, the geneaology in Chronicles has Pedaiah as the father of Zerubbabel, while Ezra (3.2, 8; 5.2) and Nehemiah (12.1) indicate that Shealtiel was the father of Zerubbabel. The evidence is too ambiguous to make a certain determination.

According to Eisenstadt's analysis of imperial mechanisms of control, the connection of an Achaemenid appointee with the Davidic house would have been a powerful means of legitimating that appointee in the eyes of the subject population.[39] The alternative was to appoint a charismatic figure lacking direct connection with the ruling family who embodied the society's sacred values. This option was more dangerous, however, because such a figure would be more likely to present a political challenge to the imperial center. The neo-Babylonian appointment of Gedaliah, a member of the traditional hereditary ruling family, demonstrates the preference of imperial powers for the implementation of this option.[40]

The inherent value to the empire of the use of a loyal member of the traditional ruling house may suggest that they not only would have permitted identifications of Zerubbabel with some traditions of the Davidic line but they may even have encouraged such connections. Such an identification of a Persian appointee with the traditional ideology of the ruling house of Yehud would have created a much more congenial atmosphere for the imposition of imperial demands. The use of terms such as 'Branch' and 'signet' of Yahweh for the Persian governor would merge the ideology and expectations of the society with the imperial goals and administrative structure. In fact, such an adaptation of local kingship traditions was a common factor in Achaemenid imperial policies in their conquered territories.

Achaemenid Adaptation of Local Kingship Traditions
The adaptation of local kingship traditions was an important mechanism utilized by the Achaemenids for the incorporation of conquered population groups into the empire. By participating in the traditional rites and adopting the traditional titles of the local kings, the Achaemenids were able to encourage the acceptance of their rule as a continuation of the native traditions rather than the imposition of a foreign administration.

After conquering Media, Cyrus adopted the royal titles of the Median kings and even lived in the royal palace in Ecbatana for a time. Although he accepted the Median royal titles, Media was, in fact, ruled by a Persian governor.[41] The situation was similar following the

39. Eisenstadt, *Political Systems*, p. 19.
40. Ben Zvi, 'Inclusion', pp. 105, 126.
41. Dandamaev, *Political History*, p. 19.

conquest of Babylon. The transition to the rule of Cyrus occurred with very little disruption of the day-to-day activities of the populace. The economic texts from the period immediately before and after indicate stable prices and the normal continuation of economic activity. Two key factors in this smooth transition were the preference for Cyrus by the priesthood of Marduk and the Persian adaptation of the local kingship traditions. Cyrus was made king of Babylon according to the longstanding traditions of the city and accepted the traditional royal titles. As Dandamaev indicates:

> Of greater significance, perhaps, was the fact that Cyrus' rule in Babylon was not regarded as foreign domination, as he had received his right to rule from the hands of Marduk, and because he carried out the sacred old rites. Cyrus adopted the official title of 'king of Babylon, king of the lands' (only in a small number of texts the simpler title of 'king of the lands' was used). This title was also carried by his successors up to the time of Xerxes.[42]

Similarly, the appointment of Cambyses as king of Babylon in 538 BCE was legitimated by his participation in the New Year festival. 'Thus he became king of Babylon by receiving his authority from the hands of the supreme god Marduk in his temple of Esagila.'[43]

The situation in Egypt was similar. The Achaemenids attempted to legitimate their rule by the adaptation of the Egyptian kingship rituals. Local documents were produced using the traditional Egyptian dating formulae and the Egyptian royal titles were used for the Achaemenids.[44] The Achaemenids also fulfilled the traditional royal roles in the cults of the Egyptian deities.[45]

The Achaemenid worship of local gods and their adaptation of local kingship traditions may reflect a genuine concern to please the deities of the lands they ruled, or they may simply have been actions performed

---

42. Dandamaev, *Political History*, p. 55. 'Moreover, the power of Cyrus in Babylon was not regarded as foreign rule, since he had received the kingdom from the hands of the god Marduk, having performed the ancient sacred ceremonies. Cyrus took the title "king of Babylon, king of the countries", which was preserved by his successors up to the beginning of the reign of Xerxes' (Dandamaev and Lukonin, *Culture and Social Institutions*, p. 90).

43. Dandamaev, *Political History*, p. 56.

44. Such as 'king of Egypt, king of lands' and 'descendant of Ra, Horus, Osiris'.

45. Dandamaev, *Political History*, p. 76.

solely for the purpose of consolidating their rule. Most likely, these Achaemenid practices indicate both a genuine reverence for the deities involved and an understanding of their propagandistic value. In any case, these activities functioned as mechanisms to generate acceptance of Achaemenid rule and create dependence on the imperial center. The pervasiveness of this policy suggests that the Persian kings may also have considered themselves the legitimate successors of the Davidic monarchs. The role of the Achaemenid kings in the restoration of the religious life of Yehud and, in particular, Cyrus ordering the rebuilding of the Jerusalem temple by the authority of the God of Heaven, suggests that a similar identification of the Persian emperor with the local kingship traditions and deity may have occurred.[46] The connection is further enhanced by Deutero-Isaiah's depiction of Cyrus as the 'shepherd' of Yahweh who carries out the purposes of Yahweh (44.28) and the 'anointed' of Yahweh (45.1). Isaiah 45.1 is the only use of the root מָשַׁח ('to anoint') in reference to a monarchic ruler in the period following the end of the Judahite monarchy. Perhaps this identification of the Persian emperor with the מָשִׁיחַ ('the anointed one; messiah') of Yahweh was more than a matter of temporary enthusiasm. The evidence from other lands incorporated into the Persian empire suggests that this connection of the Achaemenid kings with the kingship traditions of monarchic Judah may have been encouraged by the imperial center.

Yehudite Loyalty and Hosea

The loyalty of the province of Yehud to the Persian imperial center is quite striking. As was indicated above, a significant role was played by the community's religious traditions in the acceptance of Achaemenid

---

46. Peter Ackroyd, 'The Written Evidence for Palestine', in Heleen Sancisi-Weerdenburg and Amélie Kuhrt (eds.), *Achaemenid History. IV. Centre and Periphery* (Proceedings of the Gröningen 1986 Achaemenid History Workshop; Leiden: Nederlands Instituut voor het Nabije Oosten, 1990), pp. 207-20. Cf. Ben Zvi, 'Inclusion', p. 133 n. 100: 'Moreover, while the Yehudite priests in the temple stand for the monarchic priests, it is the Achaemenid king who stands for David as the founder of the temple (cf. Ezra 6.14). Therefore, it is not surprising that since David is described as responsible for the establishment of the cult, the Persian king is described as responsible for the proper cult in Jerusalem (cf. Ezra 1.1-11; 6.1-12). True, from a theological perspective akin to the thought of the time, one may claim that the actual founder is Yhwh, but Yhwh chooses to stir up the spirit of the Persian king.'

rule. The area that remains to be addressed is the way in which the prophecies of Hosea could have been read in this context. Although it is impossible to establish the reading of Hosea in this period beyond all doubt, on the whole there is significant overlap between the contents of the book of Hosea and early Persian period questions regarding messianic expectations and foreign rule as they have been sketched in the preceding sections of this chapter. The book of Hosea would generally fit well into the prevailing discourse of the early Persian period regarding both the place of the Davidic line in Achaemenid Yehud and the propriety of foreign rule over the community.

Hosea and Davidic Restoration

There is only a single explicit reference to the Davidic monarchy in Hosea (3.5). Hosea 3 depicts the reconciliation of Yahweh and Israel in the form of a prophetic sign-act report. The prophet purchased a woman, who was an adulteress, from the slave market at the command of Yahweh (v. 1). The first phase of this relationship is described as a time of sexual abstinence for both parties (v. 3). The significance of this prophetic action is that it parallels the experiences of Israel and Yahweh during the exile (v. 4). Both God and Israel find themselves in a situation that disrupts the intimacy of their relationship resulting from the removal of key governmental and cultic contacts. The text suggests that later, however, intimacy will be restored by seeking Yahweh and a Davidic ruler (v. 5).

The significance and interpretation of this text in the early Persian period is difficult to establish with any degree of certainty. Hosea 3.5 could have been used by Yehudite nationalists in the early Persian period as justification for rebellion against the empire and the re-establishment of the Davidic monarchy. There may even have been some who used it in precisely this way. There is, however, no evidence for such nationalistic fervor in this period nor for the use of texts such as Hos. 3.5 to promote national independence. As was argued in the preceding sections, there is little evidence to support the existence of widespread expectations of a restoration of the Davidic monarchy and the establishment of a new monarchic state in the early Persian period. The texts from this period are generally restrained in their use of royal terminology and in their references to David and the Davidic line. The texts in Ezekiel (Ezek. 34.3-24; 37.24-25) that refer to the restoration of a Davidide could have been interpreted as a restoration of the monarchy, in relation to an eschatological hope, or as having been fulfilled by a Davidic governor over the Persian province of Yehud. The same is true of Hos. 3.5. The apparent lack of messianic fervor indicated above and the early Persian period use of messianic termino-logy in relation to Achaemenid rule (Deutero-Isaiah) make it unlikely that Hos. 3.5 was used by the provinicial authorities to encourage hopes for the restoration of an independent, Davidic monarchy. As is often the case with material that is antagonistic to the prevailing outlook, Hos. 3.5 may have been ignored.

Hosean texts that criticize the ancestors for making kings of their own choosing and that indicate the negative consequences of making kings without the guidance of Yahweh would have adapted well to the dominant discourse regarding kingship and the Davidic line in the early Persian period. For example, the accusation that the Israelites estab-lished their royal courts, kings and princes, without concern for the will or knowledge of Yahweh (8.4) underscores the notion that the ultimate criterion in the evaluation of the legitimacy of a ruler is whether the ruler has been selected by Yahweh.[47] This text suggests that one of the significant failings of the ancestors was demonstrated by their frequent coups and constant palace intrigues. They frequently changed king and council and, most importantly, did so without consulting the will of Yahweh (cf. Hos. 7.7).[48] This critique of the appointment of rulers not endorsed by Yahweh is central to the treatment of the Israelite monarchy in the book of Hosea. These texts provide a warning to later readers concerning revolts against a ruler endorsed by Yahweh. The use of a theological discourse, which appeals to the choice of Yahweh and is rooted in the national traditions of hereditary rule, to support the legi-timacy of the local Yehudite ruler provided an environment in which these texts could function as a means of suppressing opposition. Indeed, the Deutero-Isaianic depiction of Achaemenid rule as the choice of Yahweh combined with these texts condemning the ancestors for their rebellion against Yahweh's chosen rulers would also function to sup-press opposition to Persian rule within the province.

In this environment the connection of both the institution and dis-solution of the monarchy with the anger and wrath of Yahweh (Hos. 13.10-11) could also have functioned as a strong caution to Persian period readers about establishing governing institutions not supported

47. Wolff, *Hosea*, p. 139.
48. Davies, *Hosea*, p. 199.

by Yahweh. The suggestion of Andersen and Freedman that this state-ment related to a specific contemporary king in the eighth-century Israelite context may be correct.[49] A later reader, however, looking back from a post-monarchic perspective, would be more likely to see these verses in relation to the beginning and ending of the Israelite monarchy as an institution. This is particularly true of readers familiar with the perspective of the Deuteronomistic History on the origins of the mon-archy (cf. 1 Sam. 8.6).[50] This reading finds further support in the fact that the majority of recent commentaries on Hosea interpret this text from precisely this perspective. For example, Mays places Hosea within the same stream of tradition as the anti-monarchical source of the DtrH.[51] He indicates that these words reflect a rejection of the monarchy as a whole and not just the current monarch. Similarly, Wolff notes: 'In this verse it becomes quite plain that the roots of Hosea's criticisms of kingship go deeper than the present grievances. Almost like the Baal cult (cf. v. 4 after vv. 1-3), kingship from the outset was in opposition to Yahweh's lordship.'[52] Thus parts of Hosea could have been read (and still are read) as a rejection of the monarchy because it was an assertion of the will of the people in opposition to the will of Yahweh. In the early Persian period discourse, such a reading of this text would be amenable to the goals of both the imperial center and the local representatives of imperial rule.

The references to Gibeah (Hos. 9.9; 10.9) and Gilgal (9.15) might also have been read as veiled rejections of the monarchic enterprise. Wolff has suggested reading the references to Gibeah in relation to the rape and murder of the Levite's concubine (Judg. 19).[53] Mays also opts primarily for the connection of Gibeah in this text with the account of the Levite's concubine, but he also suggests the possibility of an allusion to the Israelite monarchy because of the connection of Saul and

49. Francis I. Andersen and David Noel Freedman, *Hosea* (AB, 24; New York: Doubleday, 1980), p. 636.

50. Given both the very limited number of highly literate individuals and the close proximity in time between the production of the final redaction of the DtrH and the early Persian period, some in the Yehudite elite may not only have been interpreters of the DtrH but may also have been involved in its production.

51. Mays, *Hosea*, pp. 177-78.

52. Wolff, *Hosea*, p. 227; cf. Davies, *Hosea*, p. 293.

53. Wolff, *Hosea*, pp. 158, 184; Andersen and Freedman, *Hosea*, pp. 534-35, 564-65; Mays, *Hosea*, pp. 131, 143.

Gibeah.[54] While the linking of this text with the account of the rape and murder of the Levite's concubine may be correct in some interpretive contexts, the association of Gibeah, Saul and the origins of the Israelite monarchy (1 Sam. 10.26; 11.4) opens the possibility of the Persian period reader seeing anti-monarchic rhetoric in these references. The literary context of the reference to Gibeah in Hos. 10.9 strengthens the possibility of such a reading. Both just prior to (10.7) and just after (10.15) this text there are unambiguous threats directed at the monarchy. The threats against the king in this context would encourage the reader to make the connection between Gibeah and the monarchy.[55] The reference is too vague to offer absolute certainty with regard to its reading in the early Persian period.

The reference to Gilgal in Hos. 9.15, 'All their evil is/began at Gilgal', could be interpreted as a negative recollection of the origins of the monarchy there (1 Sam. 11.14-15).[56] As with the references to Gibeah, this connection is somewhat ambiguous and other interpretations are possible. Other references to Gilgal in the book of Hosea have to do with cultic impurities (4.15; 12.11).[57] However, the inclusion of a judgment on governing officials within this verse (9.15b; שׂר designates governing individuals, often indicating royal officials) increases the likelihood of a connection with the monarchy in an early Persian reading.[58] In the end, the text is too vague for absolute certainty.

These texts concerning the monarchy and acceptance of Yahweh's choice of ruler from the book of Hosea provide a good fit with the discourse of the early Persian period regarding local administration and the continuation of the Davidic line. They would easily conform to the ideal, both local and imperial, of a Davidic descendent ruling over Yehud as part of a Persian provincial administration. The texts caution against rejection of a ruler sanctioned by divine selection and selection of a ruler on the basis of human will. These warnings could easily have been read as support for a ruler appointed by the Achaemenids (credited with being the instrument of Yahweh in restoring the 'nation' and temple) who represented the hope of a Davidic descendant ruling in

---

54. Mays, *Hosea*, pp. 131, 143.

55. Mays notes the possibility of such a connection (*Hosea*, p. 143).

56. Wolff, *Hosea*, p. 167.

57. Andersen and Freedman, *Hosea*, p. 545.

58. Both Davies and Mays hold the two, cultic and monarchic, together (Davies, *Hosea*, p. 230; Mays, *Hosea*, p. 136).

Jerusalem. Within the social context of early Persian period Yehud these texts could have been interpreted by the ruling elite as sanction for the rule of an imperial governor with Davidic lineage within the imperial structure with a divinely sanctioned Achaemenid emperor at its head.

Hosea and Foreign Domination

A central question with regard to the reading of Hosea within the Persian period is whether it could be read as supporting submission to foreign imperial rulers. Or, to put it another way, could the Yahwists ruling Yehud have connected faithfulness to the Persian emperor with faithfulness to Yahweh? Such a connection would have the important effect of rooting loyalty to the imperial center in the religious traditions of the local populace. Alternatively, a reading of this text that fostered opposition to relations with foreign powers would have the potential of seriously damaging the relationship between the province and the imperial center.

The uncompromisingly negative stand in regard to relations with foreign powers in the book of Hosea could certainly have presented a danger to the stability of Persian administration over the province of Yehud. In Hosea, all alliances with foreign nations are rejected as acts of unfaithfulness to Israel's relationship with Yahweh. 'For Hosea, as for the other 'literary' prophets of the Bible, a treaty with a foreign power was the same as apostasy from Yahweh because it meant that a foreign god became the titularly sovereign over the country…'[59] In Hosea, Ephraim/Israel and Judah are consistently condemned for their dependent relationships with the great powers. The futility of these relations is depicted by a variety of images. In seeking the aid of Assyria they are said to be like a diseased or wounded person turning to someone incapable of treating the problem (5.13). Seeking relations with the major powers, Egypt and Assyria, is indicative of lack of direction, making the nation like a senseless dove flying back and forth without a clear course (7.11) or a wandering, wild ass (8.9). The wheeling and dealing in international circles from a position of need and desperation is likened by the prophet to a prostitute bargaining for clients. The result of this ill-conceived and faithless policy was the burden of foreign rulers imposing their will on the nation (8.9-10). The futility of

59. Ahlström, *History*, p. 666 n. 3.

seeking relations with foreign powers is related to the multiplication of falsehood and violence and is described as pursuit of the wind (12.2). Finally, in the words of repentance and confession that end the role of the people within the book, the futility of foreign alliances is recognized and such relationships are abandoned as an integral part of the process of reconciliation with Yahweh (14.4).

Yet in contrast to the unremitting rejection of seeking relationships with foreign powers in the book of Hosea, the Persian period is notable for the unfailing loyalty of the province of Yehud to the Achaemenid empire. As discussed above, there is no evidence to suggest that the Yehudites ever attempted to rebel against their Persian overlords and establish a Yahwistic theocracy. How could the reading of a text that so clearly rejects the ancestors' reliance on alliances with foreign powers as faithlessness to Yahweh be harmonized with the Yehudite elites' obvious policy of full cooperation with their Achaemenid rulers? One alternative is that these sections of the text were regarded by the Yehudites as words that were only applicable to their ancestors, the original eighth-century audience of the book of Hosea. Although this scenario is possible, it is inconsistent with the important place known to have been given to the earlier prophetic traditions in Persian period Yehud. As is indicated by the references to the earlier prophets in Zechariah 1–8, these earlier traditions were being read by the early Persian period community both as historical texts about their ancestors and as texts that continued to have significance for the community's life with Yahweh in the contemporary setting (Zech. 1.1-6; 7–8).

A second alternative is that these texts from the book of Hosea were simply ignored by the early Persian period readers, as was suggested in regard to Hos. 3.5. This is indeed always a possibility when there is dissonance between the apparent implications of a text and the prevailing ideology. However, such a treatment of these texts would be more difficult given both the importance that was attached to the words of the earlier prophets and the significance of this theme in the book of Hosea.

A third alternative is that there was a change in the perception of foreign rulers after the fall of Jerusalem and the end of the monarchy that made it possible for the early Persian period readers to differentiate their situation from that of their ancestors. One indication of such a change is found in Jeremiah 42. In this text some of the remaining inhabitants of the land approach Jeremiah for a word from Yahweh regarding their future after the assassination of Gedaliah. The response of Yahweh requires them to remain in the land with the promise that Yahweh will use the king of Babylon to preserve them and restore them to their ancestral lands (42.11-12). This new perception of foreign rulers is extended in the following chapter when Yahweh promises Babylonian rule over Egypt and describes Nebuchadrezzar as 'my servant' (43.10; cf. 25.9).[60] These texts represent a significant change in the perception of foreign rulers and their relationship to the will of Yahweh. They are no longer exclusively regarded as the servants of other deities and, therefore, inappropriate rulers of Yahweh's people.[61]

An even more dramatic alteration in the understanding of foreign rulers is indicated in Deutero-Isaiah. According to Deutero-Isaiah the Achaemenids were not strictly regarded as a foreign power by the Yehudites. The description of Cyrus as the anointed of Yahweh (Isa. 45.1) and as a shepherd of Yahweh's people (Isa. 44.28) indicates that, at least, some segments of the Judahite community in Babylon regarded Cyrus entirely differently than had ever before been the case with a non-Judahite ruler. Particularly the use of the term משיח ('the anointed one; messiah') in relation to Cyrus implies that he was regarded as one specifically chosen by Yahweh as a ruler of Yahweh's people. The significance of this identification can hardly be overstated. As indicated above, this term does not occur in the post-monarchic period biblical literature as a designation for an ethnic Yehudite ruler. It only occurs in reference to Cyrus, a 'foreign' ruler. Thus, the only clear example of messianic expectation in the post-monarchic period is related not to a Davidic descendant, but to the rule of a foreign monarch, Cyrus. This text represents a substantial reconfiguration of the perception of both foreign rule and the domain of Yahweh's choice of a legitimate ruler for Yahweh's people.

These texts also alter one of the substantial objections to relations with foreign powers in earlier eras. Previously the acceptance of foreign rule had also meant the acceptance of foreign gods. To be dominated by a foreign power also suggested the domination of Yahweh by Asshur or Marduk. In the case of Cyrus, the imposition of Persian rule was

---

60. This transition may be foreshadowed in Isa. 10.5 where Assyria is described as the tool by which Yahweh will act.

61. This understanding of foreign rulers is also found in apocalyptic traditions. Note that Nebuchadrezzar is the king 'to whom the God of heaven has given the kingdom, the power, the might, and the glory' (Dan. 2.37) 'and whom he has established as ruler over them all' (Dan. 2.38).

interpreted as the result of the explicit choice of Yahweh.[62] The unambiguous identification of Persian rulers with the kingship traditions of their colonies created an environment in which this was possible for the first time. While it was possible to interpret the activities of foreign rulers as accomplishing the purposes of Yahweh in earlier periods, the imperial participation in the identification between the emperor and the local deities made a much stronger connection viable. The identification of the Achaemenid king and Persian sovereignty with the choice of Yahweh created an environment in which it was not only possible but likely that faithfulness to the rule of the Achaemenid king would be equated with faithfulness to Yahweh. The Achaemenid ruler was chosen by and had the responsibility of accomplishing the purposes of Yahweh.

The evidence from these neo-Babylonian period texts indicates that the negative perception of foreign rulers that is evident in the book of Hosea was no longer the predominant ideology in later periods. An analogy between the objections to reliance on foreign powers in the book of Hosea and the early Persian period social order in Yehud, which was dominated by a foreign ruler, could have provided the means to undermine the social stability of the province, but in this new ideological environment the potential for such an analogy could be averted as a result of the reconfiguration of foreign rulers as the chosen servants of Yahweh in texts such as Jeremiah and Deutero-Isaiah.

At the same time, these texts could still function in this new environment as a warning against inappropriate dealings with powers that were not chosen and legitimated by Yahweh. The fact that the relationship of some foreign rulers to Yahweh and Yahweh's people had been dramatically altered does not mean that this was true of all foreign rulers. In this way these texts could function to support rather than undermine the existing order.

Hosea and Yehudite Relations with Egypt
In one particular area, the early Persian context would have shaped the reading of the book of Hosea to warn against close relations with a foreign power. The constant difficulties experienced by the imperial administration in their efforts to incorporate Egypt within the

---

62. Similarly, Persian rule had also been interpreted as the choice of Marduk in Babylonia according to the Cyrus Cylinder (*ANET*, pp. 315-16). Compare the Verse Account of Nabonidus (*ANET*, pp. 312-15).

Achaemenid empire made the Palestinian provinces, including Yehud, important to imperial goals. At the same time, the proximity to Egypt, which increased their value to the empire, was also a latent source of danger. Their location on the periphery of the empire and near a powerful center of repeated opposition to Persian rule made them potential Egyptian allies in rebellion against the Achaemenids. This duality of Yehud's position in relation to Egypt, as both a valuable source to aid the imperial goals and a potential Egyptian ally, would have dramatically shaped the reading of Yehudite traditions regarding Egypt.

The 13 references to Egypt in the book of Hosea fall into three distinct, but related, categories. First, there are several texts that depict the salvation of Yahweh as an exodus from Egypt. These include both texts that refer to the original, paradigmatic event, and those that depict a later act of salvation within the shape provided by this powerful motif (Hos. 2.15; 11.1, 11; 12.9, 13; 13.4). Significantly, for the early Persian period context, Egypt is portrayed in these texts as the place Israel leaves when they are delivered by Yahweh. There is a clear and consistent connection between departure from Egypt and Yahweh's saving activity.

Second, there are two texts that tie the ancestors' unfaithfulness to Yahweh to inappropriate relations with Egypt (Hos. 7.11; 12.2). In Hos. 7.11, the ancestors, in their alliances with Egypt and Assyria, are depicted as a senseless bird flitting to and fro, only to be captured in a net and disciplined (v. 12). In Hos. 12.2, the ancestors' alliances with Egypt and Assyria are paralleled with pursuit of the wind and the multiplication of violence. These texts clearly portray dependence on Egypt as foolish and contrary to the will of Yahweh.

Third, the portrayal of Yahweh's punishment of the ancestors is often presented in the book of Hosea as a return to Egypt (7.16; 8.13; 9.3, 6; 11.5). In the first set of texts, salvation is presented as departure from Egypt. In these texts, punishment is equated with being sent to Egypt.

The depiction of Egypt within the book of Hosea would have provided a strong sanction for fidelity to the imperial center and a clear basis for opposition to any alliance with Egypt against the Achaemenids. The book of Hosea clearly and consistently depicts Egypt negatively. It is the place from which Israelites must be saved by Yahweh. Relations with Egypt were one of the causes of Yahweh's disapproval and punishment of the ancestors. Finally, Egypt is the place Yahweh sends those whose actions are contrary to the will of Yahweh.

Interpreted by the literate elites, who governed the province for the Persian imperial administration, these texts would have provided substantial theological support for the maintenance of the imperial status quo. Combined with the representation of Persian rule as the result of Yahweh's choice, these texts would have been a valuable tool for the imperial administration in preventing Yehud establishing an alliance with Egypt.

Chapter 4

YEHUDITE RELIGION

A proposed reading of prophetic traditions within the cultural context of the Persian province of Yehud must give prime consideration to religion both in the province and in the wider, imperial context. This chapter will examine: (1) Achaemenid attitudes toward the religions in the territories under their rule; and (2) the religious environment of Yehud with particular attention to the historical developments of Yahwism. The investigation of these aspects of the history of religion in this period will provide vital contextual information for the analysis of the reading of Hosea during the early Persian period.

The Achaemenids and Local Religion

The Achaemenids have acquired a reputation for respecting the local deities and cults of the areas that they conquered. There is clearly a degree of truth to this reputation but the extent of their deference to the various deities within their empire should not be overstated. As with the practice of permitting the return of previously displaced populations, the Achaemenid restoration of and participation in local cults was undoubtedly motivated by a large measure of self-interest. The depiction of the Persian kings as restorers of the traditional local cult and/or worshipers of the local deity functioned as an important mechanism of imperial control over the subject population; this would be particularly true in instances where the Achaemenid ruler is depicted as chosen to rule by the local deity. The Cyrus Cylinder provides a cardinal example of the representation of Achaemenid rulers in relation to local religious institutions. This text depicts Cyrus as an enthusiastic restorer of temples and temple cults under his control. The text is particularly concerned to demonstrate that Cyrus, in contrast to Nabonidus, restored the appropriate, traditional cultic practices of Babylonia. According to the cylinder, he returned deities to their traditional locations and re-established the centrality of the cult of Marduk in the area. These activities are intrinsically related in the text to Marduk's choice of Cyrus as a just ruler for Marduk's worshipers.[1] Clearly the relationship between Cyrus and Marduk was considered to be mutually advantageous by the imperial administration and the Marduk priesthood. The empire benefited from the legitimation of Persian rule of Babylonia inherent in Marduk's choice of Cyrus. Similarly the priesthood of Marduk, which had apparently been marginalized by the administration of Nabonidus, found in Cyrus the opportunity to return to the center of Babylonian life. The mutually beneficial aspects of this relationship are further confirmed by the 'Verse Account of Nabonidus'. Although the text is heavily damaged, it clearly depicts Nabonidus in an extremely negative light while praising Cyrus as the restorer of all that is good and true.[2] These texts functioned as imperial propaganda legitimating the reign of Cyrus and encouraging the local population to accept Persian rule.[3] In this regard, they stand within the Mesopotamian tradition of building inscriptions. These texts must be used cautiously for historical reconstructions of the events of this period. The propagandistic nature of these texts, written after the Persian conquest, prevent an uncritical assumption of the historicity of all details.[4] They do, however, provide a valuable insight into the way in which the Achaemenids wished to be perceived by their subject populations.

The situation in Egypt appears to have been similar to that in Babylonia. Herodotus depicts Cambyses as a madman who had no respect for local religious sentiments and killed the Apis bull in a fit of rage (3.1-38, see esp. 3.27-29). As noted by Olmstead, however, the truth appears to have been quite different from the story Herodotus tells.

---

1. *ANET*, pp. 315-16: 'He scanned and looked (through) all the countries, searching for a righteous ruler willing to lead him (i.e. Marduk) (in the annual procession). (Then) he pronounced the name of Cyrus (*Ku-ra-as*), king of Anshan, declared him (lit. pronounced [his] name) to be(come) the ruler of all the world'.

2. *ANET*, pp. 312-15.

3. Also see the discussion in Chapter 3: 'Achaemenid Adaptation of Local Kingship Traditions'.

4. 'Almost all texts, however, which praise Cyrus, have the character of propagandistic writings and demand a very critical approach, as they were composed by Babylonian priests at a time subsequent to the fall of their country to the Persians, at the command, either of their new king, or of some of his following' (Dandamaev, *Political History*, p. 53).

When the Apis bull died during Cambyses's campaign in Ethiopia he followed traditional practice in the burial. He had the cover of the sarcophagus inscribed with the appropriate royal formula indicating his relationship to the deities of Egypt according to the typical practice of Egyptian pharaohs. Further, on a stele which accompanied the burial, Cambyses is depicted kneeling before the sacred bull in native Egyptian dress.[5] The positive relationship of Cambyses with some Egyptian cults is also confirmed by the inscription of Udjahorresnet, who records Cambyses's restoration of the cult of Neith and the continuation of sacrifices to the great gods in Sais.[6] As with his father in Babylonia, Cambyses respected the local religious traditions, participated in the local cult, and legitimated his reign by means of the local religious ceremonies and titles traditionally related to kingship.

The inscription of Udjahorresnet also indicates that similar conditions continued into the reign of Darius. At some point after restoring the cult in Sais, Udjahorresnet went to Susa, apparently to work as an adviser to the Persian court.[7] He was subsequently sent back to Egypt in the early years of the reign of Darius to restore the Houses of Life. Although the precise function of the Houses of Life is uncertain, their connection with healing, the gods, temples, offerings and religious festivals is clear from the inscription.[8] Again we have evidence of both substantial imperial support for the religious life of subject peoples and the desire of the Persian emperors to be known among the populace as patrons of their local religious institutions. Since this restoration activity preceded a visit by Darius to Egypt, it seems likely that a major factor behind these actions was their value in securing further integration of the recently rebellious province within the imperial structure. These policies should not, however, be viewed as an abuse of the local religious sentiments solely for the benefit of imperial control (though this was clearly an advantage). The Achaemenids apparently worshiped the

---

5. Olmstead, *History*, pp. 89-90. 'We have Egyptian sources which do not corroborate the long and critical account of Herodotus (III, 1-38), rather it seems clear that Cambyses was accepted as a new pharaoh of the twenty-seventh dynasty, and he respected local traditions and honored the Egyptian religion. Like his father in Babylon, so Cambyses in Memphis kept the previous administration intact, only bringing Achaemenid garrisons into the land' (Frye, *History*, p. 97).

6. Lines 19-25. See the translation and discussion in Blenkinsopp, 'The Mission, p. 410.

7. Blenkinsopp, 'The Mission', p. 411.

8. Lines 51-52. Blenkinsopp, 'The Mission', p. 412.

deities of the various lands they conquered believing that it was appropriate to show respect to the deities who controlled these lands.[9]

Xerxes has often been depicted as instigating the destruction of the image of Marduk and Esagila. The primary evidence for this supposition is the reference by Herodotus to his removal of a gold statue from one sanctuary in the temple in Babylon (Herodotus, *History* 1.183). By connecting this reference with the change in royal titulary on Babylonian documents during his reign,[10] it is often suggested by historians that Xerxes retaliated against the Babylonians for their rebellion by melting down the image of Marduk, destroying Esagila, and removing the special status Babylon had previously enjoyed in the empire.[11] If accurate, this scenario might indicate that Xerxes represented a significant turning point in Achaemenid behavior toward the religious institutions of subject populations.

The case for such a major alteration in imperial policy is less than decisive. Even if all of the events indicated above occurred during the reign of Xerxes, they do not individually or collectively require a complete shift in imperial policy regarding the religion and cult of the colonies. The evidence only indicates possible changes with regard to Babylon rather than an empire-wide shift in policy. Also, a destruction of cultic images and temples related to a rebellion would not be an unusual reaction by an ancient Near Eastern imperial administration, nor does it necessarily indicate a permanent change in disposition with regard to the cult site; the cult could subsequently have been restored. Finally, the change in imperial titulary does represent a shift in imperial ideology but it was not a complete rejection of the traditional Babylonian kingship titles; they continued to be used.

In fact, as Kuhrt and Sherwin-White have argued, the evidence cited to support the conclusions regarding Xerxes's destruction of the image

---

9. Dandamaev and Lukonin, *Culture and Social Institutions*, p. 358; Berquist, *Judaism in Persia's Shadow*, p. 25. Contra Olmstead, who suggests that Darius was exclusively monotheistic in his worship of Ahuramazda and that any indication to the contrary can be explained as concession to the polytheistic worship of the subject populations (*History*, p. 195). The suggestion of Dandamaev and Lukonin, however, that the worship of foreign deities by the Persian emperors resulted from the lack of a conception of false faith and the lack of racial hatred in the ancient Near East cannot be correct (*Culture and Social Institutions*, p. 359).

10. Adding 'king of Persia, king of Media' before the traditional Babylonian titles that had been used previously.

11. See, e.g., Olmstead, *History*, p. 237; Cook, *The Persian Empire*, p. 100.

of Marduk and Esagila may have been misread. They suggest that the statue removed from Esagila by Xerxes (according to Herodotus) was not the image of Marduk but another statue. This alternative interpretation is supported by the presence of the cult image within the sanctuary at the time Herodotus was writing his account (cf. *History* 1.181, 183). They also note that the title 'king of Babylon' was not dropped during the reign of Xerxes. Rather, in recently published texts, the title continued to be used after the reign of Xerxes with the latest attestation in documents from the 24th year of Artaxerxes I (441 BCE). In addition, Kuhrt and Sherwin-White note that Esagila was still functioning normally in the reign of Artaxerxes I.[12] Thus there is little evidence to suggest a significant change in the positive imperial policies toward the religions of conquered areas during or after the reign of Xerxes.

In regard to the impact of imperial practices on the situation in Yehud there is little reason to doubt the general depiction given in the biblical texts. While there may be exaggeration and error in certain details, as indicated above, the return of cultic furnishings[13] and the restoration of the cult of Yahweh in Jerusalem would be in keeping with the known imperial policy regarding the religion of conquered territories. Such actions would not represent special treatment of the Yehudites but would conform to common imperial practice.[14] Such policies would be motivated both by a degree of genuine respect for traditional cults and by the desire to create stability in new imperial holdings, particularly Yehud with its close proximity to Egypt.[15]

---

12. Amélie Kuhrt and Susan Sherwin-White, 'Xerxes' Destruction of Babylonian Temples', in Heleen Sancisi-Weerdenburg and Amélie Kuhrt (eds.), *Achaemenid History. II. The Greek Sources* (Proceedings of the Gröningen 1984 Achaemenid History Workshop; Leiden: Nederlands Instituut voor het Nabije Oosten, 1987), pp. 69-78.

13. Ezra 6.5; Hayes also points to the reference to the departure of the temple vessels from Babylon in Isa. 52.11-12 (Miller and Hayes, *History*, p. 446).

14. Berquist, *Judaism in Persia's Shadow*, p. 25.

15. 'The major element is the religious and political tolerance that was established, and also the attempt of the Persian king to build in Palestine a secure staging point for the planned conquest of Egypt. This last aim could be achieved through the return of the exiles to Judah, and these suggestions led to the publication of the edict of Cyrus II in the year 539/538' (Weinberg, *The Citizen–Temple Community*, pp. 110-11).

Yahwistic Monotheism

Central to an understanding of the influence of Yehudite religion on the reading of Hosea within the context of the early Persian period is an analysis of what was actually 'restored' during this period. As was indicated above, the concept of restoration was often used as rhetorical camouflage for innovation. The presentation of the new as the restoration of something old and improperly neglected fostered an acceptance of these innovations among the populace by legitimating them as part of their traditional heritage. Such propaganda also functioned to legitimate the imperial rule by depicting the emperor as the restorer of lost temples, cults and values. Thus the actual relationship between the cult of Yahweh 'restored' by the imperial representatives who 'returned' from Babylon and the monarchic period cult of Yahweh is central to an adequate understanding of the socio-religious environment. An equation of monarchic and Achaemenid period Yahwistic cults in Jerusalem cannot simply be assumed.

The texts of the Hebrew Bible generally present the religious history of the Israelite people as centered in the monotheistic belief in Yahweh from earliest times. From Abram who was called from the polytheism of Mesopotamia forward, Israelites are depicted as strictly monotheistic Yahwists (with some notable exceptions). Those who failed to worship Yahweh as the only deity during the monarchic period (and before) are depicted in the biblical traditions as syncretists who polluted the traditional faith of the Israelite people. There are indications, however, that this depiction is a retrojection of a later theological situation onto Israel's earlier history. There are hints remaining in the biblical texts which suggest that religious plurality did not result from sycretistic accretions to a pure, monotheistic Yahwism, but rather was the common state of affairs in the monarchic period of Israel and Judah. It was only the reading (and writing) of the later normative Yahwism, Yahwistic monotheism, into the earlier periods, as the supposed pristine state of Israelite religion, that caused the plurality of the earlier periods to appear as syncretism. The evidence of these textual hints of religious plurality has been supplemented in recent years by excavations of the material remains of ancient Palestine, which also indicate that plurality and polytheism were the norm in the religion of the monarchic period of Israel and Judah.

The terminology for discussing the faith and cultic practice of ancient

Israel needs clarification. The variety of uses of the terms 'monotheism', 'polytheism', 'henotheism' and 'monolatry', all commonly used in discussions of ancient Israel's faith and practice, necessitates a clear statement about their usage here. Generally, 'monotheism' is used to describe the belief in only one god and 'polytheism' is used to describe the belief in a plurality of gods, that is, they are primarily descriptors of belief rather than practice, although the implications of each respective belief has an effect on practice.[16] 'Henotheism' and 'monolatry' are both used for the worship of a single deity even though the worshiper may believe in the existence of other gods. This is an intermediate position in which only one god is worshiped but the singular focus of the cultic practice does not negate the multiplicity of the divine realm. There is little, if any, practical difference between the terms 'monolatry' and 'henotheism' as they are currently used in the technical literature.[17] Contrary to these generally accepted uses, Baruch Halpern, following Y. Kaufmann, defines monotheism as the worship of a high god, even though such worship may involve the recognition and veneration of a variety of lower, collateral deities.[18] This attempt at a broader definition of monotheism unnecessarily complicates the discussion of ancient Israelite faith and practice. In the following discussion, 'polytheism' will be used to refer to both the belief in and worship of more than one deity; 'monotheism' will indicate the exclusive belief in and worship of a single deity; and 'monolatry' will be used to describe the intermediate position of worshiping a single deity but recognizing the existence of other gods.[19]

16. See, e.g., the discussion of David L. Petersen, 'Israel and Monotheism: The Unfinished Agenda', in Gene M. Tucker, David L. Petersen and Robert R. Wilson (eds.), *Canon, Theology, and Old Testament Interpretation: Essays in Honor of Brevard S. Childs* (Philadelphia: Fortress Press, 1988), pp. 92-107 (97-98).

17. Petersen, 'Israel and Monotheism', p. 98.

18. Baruch Halpern, '"Brisker Pipes than Poetry": The Development of Israelite Monotheism', in Jacob Neusner, Baruch A. Levine and Ernest S. Frerichs (eds.), *Judaic Perspectives on Ancient Israel* (Philadelphia: Fortress Press, 1987), pp. 77-115. See also Yehezkel Kaufmann, *The Religion of Israel: From its Beginnings to the Babylonian Exile* (New York: Schocken Books, 1960).

19. Mark S. Smith, *The Early History of God: Yahweh and the Other Deities in Ancient Israel* (San Francisco: Harper, 1987), p. xix.

Yahwistic Cult of the Monarchic Period

Although the later compositions and editorial additions in the biblical texts present a monolithic Israelite religion from the time of Moses onward, there are texts preserved within the biblical corpus that provide evidence of a much more diverse religious environment in early Israel. The memories of the monarchic period cult of Yahweh preserved in these earlier texts of the Hebrew Bible often portray Yahweh at the head of a pantheon or divine council. In 1 Kings 22 Yahweh is seated on his throne presiding over the divine council surrounded by all the heavenly host (צבא השמים; v. 19). A similar depiction is found in the prose introduction to Job where the sons of God (בני האלהים), including the Accuser (השטן), present themselves on the appropriate day before Yahweh (Job 1.6; 2.1). In Isaiah 6 the prophet reports a vision of the divine throne room in which Yahweh of Hosts (יהוה צבאות; Isa. 6.5) is depicted in a style typical of chief gods in the ancient Near East. Yahweh is depicted in these texts in the manner typical of the chief deity of an ancient Near Eastern pantheon of divine beings.

Behind these depictions of Yahweh at the head of a divine council lies a time when Yahweh presided over a pantheon of deities. In a brief account in the Song of Moses (Deut. 32.8-9), עליון, as chief deity, apportions the various ethnic groups to particular deities as the primary responsibility of each deity. In the text עליון chooses Israel as his portion, although it is difficult to be certain that the identification of Yahweh and עליון is original. In the MT the theologically difficult בני אלהים has been altered to the more acceptable בני ישראל. Not only does the theological difficulty of בני אלהים make it the more likely reading, but this reading is also attested in both the LXX and a fragment of Deuteronomy 32 from Qumran.[20] Similarly, the call in Deut. 32.43 for other deities to worship Yahweh has been eradicated from the MT but is preserved in the LXX and Qumran texts.[21] Finally, a similar call for praise from the בני אלים has survived in the originally Baalistic hymn adapted to the praise of Yahweh (Ps. 29.1). All of these texts

20. See Gerhard von Rad, *Deuteronomy* (OTL; London: SCM Press, 1966), pp. 196-97; Jeffrey H. Tigay, *Deuteronomy* (Jewish Publication Society Torah Commentary; Philadelphia: Jewish Publication Society of America, 1996), pp. 513-15; P.W. Skehan, 'Qumran and the Present State of Old Testament Text Studies: The Masoretic Text', *JBL* 78 (1959), pp. 21-25 (21).

21. Tigay, *Deuteronomy*, pp. 516-18.

attest to an earlier form of Yahwistic faith which has been subsumed, but not entirely eradicated, by the theological orthodoxy of the later compilers of the biblical traditions.

Yahweh is also depicted as head of the pantheon in Psalm 89. In this text Yahweh is the most powerful and awesome of all the divine beings (vv. 6-8 [Eng. 5-7]). As head of the divine assembly, Yahweh is responsible for the creation which is rendered in common ancient Near Eastern mythological form as a battle with chaos personified as a sea monster (vv. 10-11 [Eng. 9-10]). The preservation of these elements in a royal psalm suggests that this depiction of Yahweh was an integral aspect of the theology of the Judahite monarchy. The centrality of pantheon to the theology of the monarchic period is also suggested by the presentation of the ruling monarch as a member of the divine council, one of the אלהים in Ps. 45.7-8 [Eng. 6-7]. The belief that the ruling king was a member of the divine council may also be indicated by the adoption formula (אמר אלי בני אתה אני היום ילדתיך; 'He said to me, "You are my son, today I have begotten you"') in Ps. 2.7, a psalm for the coronation of a new king. Similarly, the coronation hymn preserved in Isa. 9.1-6 uses titles of the king which are most appropriate to a figure of divine or semi-divine stature: פלא יועץ אל גבור אביעד שר־שלום ('wondrous counsellor, mighty god, prince of peace', v. 5). These texts provide evidence of a religio-political hierarchy in monarchic Judah in which Yahweh ruled as chief deity of the pantheon and the king, as son of Yahweh and member of the divine council, ruled on earth as his regent.[22]

A small fragment of this ancient mythology has also been preserved in the well-known, brief narrative introduction to J's account of the flood that recounts sexual unions between divine beings (בני האלהים) and human females (Gen. 6.1-4). This etiology of the ancient heroes provides an additional glimpse into pre-monotheistic Israelite theology. As in other ancient Near Eastern cultures, the boundary between the human and divine realms was not firmly fixed but could be traversed, sometimes to the detriment of those on the mortal side.[23]

---

22. The preservation of these elements in royal psalms may suggest that they suffered less from editing in later periods because the monarchy had come to an end.

23. Claus Westermann, *Genesis 1–11: A Commentary* (Continental Commentaries; Minneapolis: Augsburg–Fortress, 1994), pp. 379-81. Westermann notes that similar tales occur in the mythology of Greece, Ugarit, Phoenicia and the Hurrians.

While the worship of a multiplicity of gods may be portrayed consistently as syncretism from the normative, Yahweh-alone perspective of the later compilers and editors of these traditions (particularly the Deuteronomists), polytheistic belief and cultic practices are also consistently depicted as ubiquitous elements of the officially sanctioned religion of both Israel and Judah during the monarchic period (e.g. 2 Kgs 23.5).[24] This connection between the monarchy and cultic practices that involved the veneration of other deities alongside Yahweh cannot simply be brushed aside as Deuteronomistic, anti-monarchic polemic. The various reforms recounted in the Deuteronomistic History indicate that kings who removed non-Yahwistic elements from the Judahite cult were few. In fact, these accounts of reform provide evidence regarding many of the elements of both the official and popular cults of ancient Judah. Although this evidence is preserved in an account which has been shaped according to the later *tendenz* of the Deuteronomistic editors, that is, as syncretism on the part of the monarchic Judahite population and an aberration from the later norm, a pure, monotheistic Yahwism, it clearly demonstrates the opposite. The worship of a multiplicity of deities *was* the norm in the monarchic period rather than an aberration.[25]

---

24. Note also the evidence of the Nimrud prism of Sargon II, which counts the 'god_s' of Samaria as spoil (lines 32-33). See C.J. Gadd, 'Inscribed Prisms of Sargon II from Nimrud', *Iraq* 16 (1954), pp. 173-201; B. Becking, *The Fall of Samaria: An Historical and Archaeological Investigation* (Studies in the History of the Ancient Near East, 2; Leiden: E.J. Brill, 1992), pp. 28-29; Herbert Niehr, 'The Rise of Yhwh in Judahite and Israelite Religion: Methodological and Religio-historical Aspects', in D.V. Edelman (ed.), *The Triumph of Elohim: From Yahwisms to Judaisms* (Grand Rapids: Eerdmans, 1996), pp. 45-72 (57-58). As Ahlström summarizes: 'The gods are a clear indication that in the kingdom of Israel no monotheistic idea had yet become the official line of thinking concerning the religion' (*History*, p. 670).

25. Saul M. Olyan makes the interesting observation that opposition to Asherah in anti-Baalistic writings in the Hebrew Bible is limited to the Deuteronomistic History and texts reflecting deuteronomistic editing. He suggests that in some circles Asherah was a legitimate part of the cult of Yahweh (*Asherah and the Cult of Yahweh in Israel* [SBLMS, 34; Atlanta: Scholars Press, 1988], pp. 3-5). Day attributes the connection of Yahweh and Asherah to syncretistic circles, but he gives no evidence for this apart from the prohibition in Deut. 16.21. This judgment seems overly influenced by the bias of the deuteronomistic historians (John Day, 'Asherah in the Hebrew Bible and Northwest Semitic Literature', *JBL* 105 [1986], pp. 385-408 [399-400]).

The accounts of the reforms of Hezekiah and Josiah (and the counter-reformation of Manasseh) present the wide variety of non-Yahwistic religious practices that were current in monarchic Judah. In fact, the actions presented as a reform to restore an older, purer form of the cult are more likely to have been cultic innovations.[26] These late Judahite innovations included both the centralization of the cult in the Jerusalem temple and the focusing of that cult on Yahweh to the exclusion of other members of the Judahite pantheon. The 'reform' removed the cultic furnishings, images and personnel related to Baal, Asherah, Molech, Shemesh, Yareah, and the heavenly host, both in the towns and high places of Judah and in the temple in Jerusalem.[27] Josiah's reform also included the end of cultic prostitution and the removal of the horses and chariots dedicated to Shemesh.[28] In other words, even according to the biased presentation of the Deuteronomists, the Israelite and Judahite monarchic states from Solomon to the fall of Jerusalem were predominantly polytheistic and basically similar in cultic practice to the neighboring Iron Age cultures.[29]

26. As indicated elsewhere, 'reform' is often the language used to legitimate and encourage the acceptance of innovative practices.

27. See both the limited and general account of Hezekiah's reform (2 Kgs 18.4) which also included the destruction of the bronze image of a serpent used in healing rituals, and the broad-ranging (and probably exaggerated) reform of Josiah (2 Kgs 23.4-20).

28. The horses and chariots dedicated to the sun may have been dedicated to Yahweh who is, in places, depicted as a solar deity (e.g. Ps. 84.12 [v. 11 Eng.]; Ps. 89). Hab. 3.8 mentions horses and chariots of Yahweh (cf. Ps. 68.18). Regarding solar elements for Yahweh, see J.G. Taylor, *Yahweh and the Sun: Biblical and Archaeological Evidence for Sun Worship in Ancient Israel* (JSOTSup, 111; Sheffield: JSOT Press, 1993).

29. For a detailed examination of the many connections between Canaanite practices and the Israelite and Judahite cultic practices preserved in the Hebrew Bible, see G.W. Ahlström, *Aspects of Syncretism in Israelite Religion* (Horae Soederblomianae, 5; Lund: C.W.K. Gleerup, 1963). Although Ahlström argued that these connections were evidence of substantial syncretism, the pervasiveness of these elements suggests that they were actually integral to ancient Israelite religion. Note even Ahlström's summary: 'The cultus, in common with the culture, was "canaanized": not merely tolerated but accepted as a being necessity in the Canaanite milieu. To set oneself up in opposition to this must have been regarded by the majority as tantamount to an attack on the *normal* religious life' (*Aspects of Syncretism*, p. 88; italics mine). Cf. Halpern, '"Brisker Pipes than Poetry"', pp. 82-83.

In addition to the evidence of religious pluralism already noted, there is also the account of Saul's successful use of a necromancer to summon the long deceased Samuel, who is described as an אלהים arising from the ground (1 Sam. 28), and the narrative of King Mesha's sacrifice of his son during a battle with Israelite forces that achieved the desired effect and resulted in Moab's victory over Israel (2 Kgs 3.27). Both of these texts indicate far more heterodox beliefs in ancient Israel and Judah than the final editors of the Hebrew Bible would like to suggest. The cumulative evidence of these biblical texts alone conveys an image of monarchic Israel and Judah that is far removed from the later monotheistic norm. These societies cannot even be described as henotheistic. The evidence suggests that polytheistic faith and cultic practices were integral to monarchic period society. While the demand of the decalogue that the Israelites worship only Yahweh could be consistent with henotheism, its introduction into monarchic period society would have been revolutionary. The decalogue reflects a substantial alteration to the traditional beliefs and practices of Israelite religion.

On the whole, the cultic practices of Israel and Judah presented in these texts mesh well with our knowledge of other west-Semitic states of the period. On the basis of the textual fragments of pre-monotheistic belief that have survived the editing process of the Hebrew Bible and the many (negative) portrayals of the polytheistic cultic practices that were common in the monarchic period, L. Handy finds evidence in the Hebrew Bible for the existence of a four-tiered pantheon in the religion of monarchic Judah that is strikingly similar to that of other west-Semitic cultures.[30] This pantheon was populated by the high god and his consort at the primary level, various important but secondary deities at the next level, many different deities associated with specific crafts, agricultural activities, and so on, at the tertiary level, and a host of messenger deities at the final level. The various deities and cult practices associated with each of these realms of the pantheon would have impacted Israelite and Judahite society in different ways and at different social levels.

---

30. Lowell Handy, 'The Appearance of Pantheon in Judah', in D.V. Edelman (ed.), *The Triumph of Elohim: From Yahwisms to Judaisms* (Grand Rapids: Eerdmans, 1996), pp. 27-43. For a fuller treatment of the structure of pantheon in West Semitic religions, see Lowell Handy, *Among the Host of Heaven: The Syro-Palestinian Pantheon as Bureaucracy* (Winona Lake, IN: Eisenbrauns, 1994).

Distinguishing between official and popular religion can be a useful heuristic device for analyzing the national or royal cult practiced in the capital separately from the typical religious practices that occurred in the homes and local shrines of the land. There is a danger, however, that such a distinction may become a dichotomy which suggests that there was a wide chasm between the 'popular' cult of the common people who worshiped one set of gods and the 'official' cult of the elite who worshiped only the national god and viewed all other practices as heterodox.[31] In fact, the gods of the pantheon would have been worshiped by most members of the society at times and places appropriate both to the situation of the worshiper and the deity being venerated. The worship of the national deity would occur mainly, though not exclusively, at the national shrine in the capital, while cultic activities associated with lesser deities, cults of the dead, mediums, and so on, would have been far less centralized. This does not mean that the common people in their villages would not have considered themselves worshipers of the national god. Rather, the aspects of the pantheon that most regularly impinged on their everyday existence were the lower-level deities associated with agriculture, crafts, health and fertility. In addition, the cult of the consort of the highest god would have been more widely dispersed throughout the land as the primary representative of fertility. The ubiquity of the fertility cult is indicated by the large number of female deity figurines that have been recovered from household contexts.

The archaeological evidence compliments the pluralistic religious picture drawn from the biblical texts. In summarizing the evidence for religious life in Palestine during the Iron II–III period, G. Barkay notes that the central feature is the discovery of thousands of clay female figurines in domestic contexts. The excavators now commonly associate these female figurines with Asherah and the fertility cult.[32] The ubiquity

---

31. See the discussion of Elizabeth Bloch-Smith, *Judahite Burial Practices and Beliefs about the Dead* (JSOTSup, 123; Sheffield: JSOT Press, 1992), pp. 150-51.

32. Michael David Coogan, 'Canaanite Origins and Lineage: Reflections on the Religion of Ancient Israel', in P.D. Miller, Jr, P.D. Hanson and S.D. McBride (eds.), *Ancient Israelite Religion: Essays in Honor of Frank Moore Cross* (Philadelphia: Fortress Press, 1987), pp. 115-24 (119). Coogan suggests that the female figurines found throughout the Levant are representations of the consorts of the respective national deities. Thus, in Israel, these figurines would represent the consort of Yahweh.

of these goddess figurines indicates a thriving Asherah cult throughout Palestine during the monarchic period. In addition, many animal figurines have been found, particularly horses. Some of these horse figures have a disk between their ears, probably indicating an association with solar worship and the 'chariots of the sun' (2 Kgs 23.11-12). Finally, Barkay notes that several small incense altars have been found in domestic or domestic-industrial contexts.[33] These altars may have functioned in the cult associated with the Asherah figurines and some may also have been used in the worship of other deities associated with crafts or healing. All of this evidence supports the suggestion that religion in late Iron Age Judah was multifaceted and polytheistic.

The inscribed pithoi found at Kuntillet Ajrud and the tomb inscription from Khirbet el-Qom have provided additional evidence to substantiate the centrality of Asherah in the religious life of monarchic Israel and Judah.[34] Inscriptions from both locations offer blessing in the name of Yahweh and his Asherah. Here the supplicant recognizes the protection and blessing afforded by Yahweh and his Asherah. Discussion of these inscriptions has often focused on whether 'Asherah' refers to the goddess or the cult symbol.[35] The conclusions reached in this discussion are secondary to the special significance of these inscriptions for reconstructing Israelite religion in the Iron Age. The goddess Asherah and the asherah cult symbol would have been identified in the minds of the participants in the cult. Whether the primary referent of the Kuntillet Ajrud and Khirbet el-Qom inscriptions was the goddess or the cult symbol of the goddess, both indicate that worship of the goddess Asherah was an important aspect of Israelite and Judahite religion in the monarchic period.[36]

Some have argued that the figures that appear on one of the pithoi from Kuntillet Ajrud are unrelated to the inscription which offers

33. Barkay, 'Iron Age II–III', pp. 361-62.

34. For a translation and discussion of the inscription see Judith M. Hadley, 'The Khirbet el-Qom Inscription', *VT* 37 (1987), pp. 50-62.

35. See, e.g., Olyan, *Asherah and the Cult of Yahweh*; Susan Ackerman, *Under Every Green Tree: Popular Religion in Sixth-Century Judah* (HSM, 46; Atlanta: Scholars Press, 1992), pp. 62-66; Day, 'Asherah in the Hebrew Bible', pp. 401-404.

36. Susan Ackerman, 'The Queen Mother and the Cult in Ancient Israel', *JBL* 112 (1993), pp. 385-401 (389 n. 20). See also the comment of William G. Dever: 'When a/Asherah is invoked in a prayer of blessing for the dead, is it only a "tree" that is envisioned?' ('"Will the Real Israel Please Stand Up?" Part II: Archaeology and the Religions of Ancient Israel', *BASOR* 298 [1995], pp. 37-58 [41]).

blessing by Yahweh and his Asherah. For example, Hadley suggests that the two standing figures are representations of the Egyptian god Bes and the seated figure with a lyre is a representation of another, unidentified deity.[37] Even if Hadley's argument is correct, the blessings by Yahweh and his Asherah provide important evidence regarding the religious environment of the period. But recognizing the connection between the divine figures represented on the jar and the inscription which intersects the headdress of the largest figure provides important additional information regarding ancient Israelite religion. Schmidt has recently presented a persuasive case for interpreting the image of the two figures linked arm in arm together with the inscription. Whether the inscription and figures were added to the pithos at the same time or separately, he suggests that the final combination of divine depictions and inscription presents a unified field of meaning for the final 'redactor' (and readers) of the combined image.[38] In this reading, the two figures represent Yahweh and Asherah depicted in traditional form as high god and consort.[39] Thus the Kuntillet Ajrud pithos provides not only evidence of the typical west-Semitic high god and consort relationship between Yahweh and Asherah during the monarchic period, but a rare example of an iconographic representation of the divine couple.[40]

At a minimum, these inscriptions provide an indication of the connection between Yahweh and Asherah in the popular cultic practice of ancient Israel and Judah. These inscriptions may also, however, provide insight into the national cult of ancient Judah. Ahlström suggests that the parallels between the fortress at Arad and its associated cult site and Kuntillet Ajrud suggest that the latter was also a Judahite fortress with an integral religious center.[41] This connection of Kuntillet Ajrud with

---

37. Judith M. Hadley, 'Some Drawings and Inscriptions on Two Pithoi from Kuntillet 'Ajrud', *VT* 37 (1987), pp. 180-213. See further bibliography cited by Hadley.

38. Brian B. Schmidt, 'The Aniconic Tradition: On Reading Images and Viewing Texts', in D.V. Edelman (ed.), *The Triumph of Elohim: From Yahweh to Judaisms* (Grand Rapids: Eerdmans, 1996), pp. 75-105 (96-97).

39. Schmidt rejects the identification of the figures with Bes, noting that the second figure is most likely female not male ('The Aniconic Tradition', pp. 96-102).

40. There is also an image of a stylized tree flanked by ibexes feeding from the tree on the same pithos, which is most likely another representation of Asherah. See Bloch-Smith, *Judahite Burial Practices*, p. 99.

41. G.W. Ahlström, *Royal Administration and National Religion in Ancient*

the state administration and the military indicates that these inscriptions provide evidence of the official Jerusalemite cult of monarchic Judah. The association of the worship of Yahweh and Asherah in an official national shrine correlates with the biblical evidence for the worship of Asherah in the Jerusalem temple noted above.[42] The implication of both textual and artifactual evidence is that monarchic Israel and Judah were not primarily monotheistic or even henotheistic societies. Rather, these societies fit the common pattern of west-Semitic Iron Age cultures in their religion and cult practices. As Dever summarizes:

> The consensus among critical biblical scholars today, more than ever, is that the majority of ancient Israelites during the monarchy were poly-theists, or at best monolatrous. True, aniconic Yahwistic monotheism was a product of the Exile and the radical reconstruction that was neces-sitated by that experience, under Deuteronomistic, Priestly and other orthodox schools.[43]

The 'Transition to Normative Monotheism'

Dever's suggestion that aniconic, monotheistic Yahwism is a post-mon-archic phenomenon can be demonstrated both by explicit statements of belief and by evidence of changing practices which reflect such a belief. The transition from polytheism to the normative monotheistic religion reflected in the major biblical traditions of the sixth and later centuries (Deutero-Isaiah, P, the Chronicler's history, and late prophetic texts) appears to have occurred primarily in the sixth and fifth centuries.[44] As evidence of an emerging monotheistic faith in this period, all of the extant biblical texts have clearly been edited to reflect a predominantly monotheistic perspective. The Deuteronomistic History and Deutero-Isaiah, both products of the second half of the sixth century, represent

Palestine (Leiden: E.J. Brill, 1982), pp. 40-43.

42. Coogan, 'Canaanite Origins and Lineage', p. 119. Contra P. Kyle McCarter, Jr, who suggests that the Kuntillet Ajrud inscriptions represent a variant of northern Israelite religion in which Asherah was worshiped as a hypostatic form of Yahweh, i.e. not as the Canaanite deity ('Aspects of the Religion of the Israelite Monarchy: Biblical and Epigraphic Data', in *Ancient Israelite Religion*, pp. 137-55 [137-50]).

43. Dever, ' "Will the Real Israel Please Stand Up?" Part II', p. 49.

44. Handy suggests that by the Persian period the Judahite pantheon had been reduced from four tiers to two, the highest level populated only by Yahweh and the lowest populated by the messenger deities now known as angels ('Appearance of Pantheon', pp. 42-43).

the worship of gods other than Yahweh as apostasy, syncretism and futility.

The introduction of Persian rule, the return of the exiles to Palestine and the rejection of idolatry are all connected in Deutero-Isaiah. There is only one God, Yahweh; this one God has chosen Cyrus to be the anointed, and as Yahweh's chosen, Cyrus will be the means of return- ing the exiled community to Jerusalem. The interconnection of these three elements in the theology of Deutero-Isaiah reveals an early rela- tionship between the theology of return and monotheistic Yahwism.[45] Since Deutero-Isaiah is the major document of the theology of return to the homeland, a document produced by and for the Judahite community in Babylonia, it is likely to be representative of the theological per- spectives of the majority of those who decided to immigrate to Yehud. This evidence indicates that those who returned to the homeland of their ancestors from Babylonia and received Persian support to govern the colony and rebuild the temple of Yahweh were most likely represent- atives of the normative monotheistic Yahwism propounded in Deutero- Isaiah and found in the texts of the Hebrew Bible of the Persian period and later.

In an early attempt to clarify the process of the development of Yah- wistic monotheism, Bernhard Lang suggested the following key elements: (1) the west-Semitic tradition of a chief national god; (2) Yahweh's lack of kinship ties to other west-Semitic deities; (3) the practice of temporary monolatry during times of crisis; and (4) the special Israelite expression of these elements beginning in the eighth century, which permitted temporary monolatry to become a permanent feature.[46] Particularly, he sees Yahweh's lack of ties to other deities as the basis for the separateness of Yahweh that could later become mono- theism.[47] While Lang may be correct concerning Yahweh's origins outside of Palestine,[48] the suggestion that the roots of monotheism lie in Yahweh's status as an outsider, a foreigner, among the gods of Canaan seems highly unlikely. This perception of Yahweh's position as one standing outside the pantheon, lacking kinship relations to other Syro-

---

45. See Berquist, *Judaism in Persia's Shadow*, pp. 32-33.

46. Lang, *Monotheism*, p. 54.

47. Lang, *Monotheism*, pp. 35-36.

48. For example, Niehr argues that Yahweh is a southern weather deity that became the chief god of Jerusalem and Samaria ('The Rise of Yhwh in Judahite and Israelite Religion', pp. 45-46).

Palestinian deities is inconsistent with the available evidence. As was indicated above, both the textual and artifactual evidence relating to monarchic-period Israel and Judah reveal that Yahweh was fully integrated into a typical west-Semitic pantheon in this period. If monotheism is to be traced to the singularity and uniqueness of Yahweh in relation to all of the other deities of Canaan then monotheism must have been a very early development in the life of ancient Israel. If, as the evidence indicates, Yahweh became enmeshed in a variety of relationships with other deities in the pantheon then the roots of monotheism must lie elsewhere.

More recently, D. Edelman has proposed a process of development that takes better account of the roots of Yahwism in the west Semitic world. She proposes that the national pantheon of Israel and Judah during the monarchic period was structured and populated along the lines proposed by Handy.[49] The significant change occurred, according to Edelman, during the occupation by the Assyrians and Babylonians when Yahweh, like the deities of other conquered states, was demoted to the status of a second-tier deity in the imperial system. Subsequently, in the transition to Achaemenid rule, the various state deities came to be identified as local expressions of the high god of the empire, Ahura Mazda. This identification was accomplished by use of the abstract term 'God of heaven', אלהי השמים in Hebrew, or אלהא שמיא in Aramaic, as the designation for the head of the imperial pantheon. She posits the influence of Zoroastrianism in the Achaemenid empire as the source for the convergence of a variety of divine manifestations into a single, male, high god and the demotion of the various specialist and messenger deities to the status of messengers or angels.[50] This subsequently developed into an exclusive monotheism in Jewish circles in the Hellenistic period.[51] Although this outline needs refinement and further research, it provides the most useful proposal regarding the most likely line of development at this point in the history of research.

---

49. Handy, 'Appearance of Pantheon', pp. 27-43.

50. Similarly, Davies suggests that the phenomenon of the cult of a high god has its origins in Mesopotamia and that the development of Yahwistic monotheism (if this is the appropriate term) may have been influenced by immigrants brought from Mesopotamia by the Persians, though he suggests that the immigrants had no relation to the previous inhabitants who had been deported by the Babylonians (*In Search*, pp. 91-92).

51. D.V. Edelman, 'Introduction', in *eadem* (ed.), *The Triumph of Elohim:*

There are, however, some significant deficiencies in Edelman's model for the development of monotheism. First, the depiction of Yahweh as a second-tier deity by the Assyrians and the Babylonians would not necessarily alter the perception of Yahweh by the local, indigenous population of monarchic Judah. It is quite possible that, for the local population, Yahweh continued to be viewed as the chief deity of the pantheon. Second, it is unlikely that Zoroastrianism could function as the primary catalyst in the development of monotheism given the lack of clear evidence for monotheism among the Persians during this period. Various divinities within Persian ruled territories may have been subsumed under or identified with Ahura Mazda, but this need not lead to the development of monotheistic beliefs. Finally, this proposal lacks an explanation for apparent moves toward monotheism or, at least, a Yahweh-alone perspective during the monarchic period. Such a development is particularly evident among some of the prophets of the monarchic period, the early edition(s) of the Deuteronomistic history, and in the reforms of Hezekiah and Josiah.

An alternative suggestion is that the early impulse toward Yahwistic monolatry or monotheism has its origins in competition between Yahwists and Baalists in Israel. The materials in the Deuteronomistic history present Omride sponsorship of the Baal cult in an extremely negative manner. The coup of Jehu is substantially attributed to opposition to the influence of the Baal cult on the northern monarchy. In fact, Mark S. Smith has suggested that both Baal and Yahweh were worshiped in the northern kingdom but there was a move to elevate Baal to the position of patron deity of the Israelite monarchy during the reign of Ahab. Smith ascribes this elevation to the desire to create a basis for theopolitical unity between Israel and Tyre.[52] The Elijah cycle (1 Kgs 17–19) and the coup of Jehu reveal a struggle for supremacy between the worshipers of these two deities in the northern kingdom.[53] The antagonism of Hosea to the Baal cult at a later date indicates that this struggle for supremacy continued down to the fall of Samaria. The vehement opposition of Hosea to the Baalistic cult more likely has its

From Yahwisms to Judaisms (Grand Rapids: Eerdmans, 1996), pp. 15-25 (19-23).

52. Smith, *The Early History of God*, pp. 44-45.

53. The presence of a similar struggle in Judah during this period is indicated by the overthrow of Athaliah (2 Kgs 11). Note particularly the prominence of the destruction of the house of Baal and the making of a covenant between Yahweh and the people in this episode (2 Kgs 11.17-19).

roots in his support for Yahweh as the chief god of the Israelite state against the incursions of Baal rather than in a strictly monotheistic faith. Hosea was not an apologist for Yahwistic monotheism, but a defender of Yahweh's position at the head of the Israelite pantheon.[54] This rejection of the cult of Baal only later developed in the direction of Yahweh exclusivism in Deuteronomistic circles in Judah post-722 BCE, as indicated in the reform movements of Hezekiah and Josiah.[55] The continual hostility between Yahwists and Baalists beginning in the ninth century suggests the significance of this period in the transition from polytheism to monolatry and, finally, monotheism.[56] The substantial overlap in the literary imagery used to describe both Yahweh and Baal and common elements in the iconography of the two deities reflect not only the substantive similarities that made coexistence difficult but also the efforts of the Yahwists finally to eradicate the Baal cult by usurping Baal's character and functions for Yahweh.[57]

The reforms of Hezekiah correspond chronologically to the arrival of the Hoseanic (and other) traditions from the north after 722 BCE. Is it purely coincidental that cult reform and the concept of the exclusivity of the worship of Yahweh originated in the south at this time? The fall of Samaria, attributed by Hosea and others to the infidelity of Israel to its primary relationship with Yahweh, would provide the impetus for

54. Lang argued that the opposition to other gods in Hosea is an extension of the struggle for supremacy between Yahweh and Baal. He suggests that Hosea has developed the opposition to Baal supplanting Yahweh into a fully monolatric position (*Monotheism*, pp. 31-33). The suggestion that Hosea was monolatrous is difficult to substantiate, but the recognition of the centrality of the struggle for supremacy between Yahweh and Baal is a very important element in the development of monolatry and, later, monotheism.

55. Carl D. Evans suggests the origins of Israelite aniconism derive from the innovative religious program of Hezekiah and Josiah. He views this not as a reform in which pagan elements were purged from the cult but a redefinition of Yahwism supported by the Deuteronomistic historians by means of a retrojection of this view into the community's past ('Cult Images, Royal Policies and the Origins of Aniconism', in Steven W. Holladay and Lowell K. Handy [eds.], *The Pitcher is Broken: Memorial Essays for Gösta W. Ahlström* [JSOTSup, 190; Sheffield: Sheffield Academic Press, 1995], pp. 192-212 [esp. 209-12]).

56. 'There is no evidence that prior to the ninth century Baal was considered a major threat to the cult of Yahweh' (Smith, *The Early History of God*, p. 47).

57. Smith provides an excellent summary of the substantial overlap in the literary depictions and iconographic representations of these two deities (*The Early History of God*, pp. 49-55).

Yahwistic exclusivism in Judah. The birth and development of a Yahweh-alone party in Judahite circles could explain the 'discovery' of the long-lost, ancient law book during Josiah's reign. The young age at which Josiah ascended the throne would have provided those promoting the exclusive worship of Yahweh with an opportunity to advance their program by influencing the young king. Particularly, the claim to have discovered a long-lost, ancient text, which sanctioned the Yahweh-alone position, could have been used to influence the young monarch to support their cause.[58]

These events are central to the political history of the period as well. Morton Smith suggested that Josiah's opposition to Pharaoh Necho may be an indication of his stupidity.[59] Smith's reading of the events misses an important element in the political dynamic of the period. If Josiah was a supporter of Yahweh exclusivism and pro-Babylonian (like Jeremiah and the Deuteronomist party) then his opposition to the Egyptian army's attempt to aid the Assyrians was not stupidity but the outworking of consistent religious and political policies. With the death of Josiah the Egyptian pharaoh, Necho, appointed a successor to the Judahite throne (2 Kgs 23.33-35). The appointment of the next Judahite king by the Egyptian pharaoh would explain the subsequent abandonment of the religious 'reforms' of the Yahweh exclusivists and the ascendancy of the supporters of a pro-Egyptian foreign policy at the expense of those favoring a pro-Babylonian foreign policy during the final years of the Judahite monarchy.

Following the fall of Jerusalem and the end of the Judahite monarchy, the Deuteronomists, who had supported Josiah's policies (perhaps even been the instigators of his reforms), explained the disaster of 586 as the obvious outcome of the abandonment of the 'reforms'. In contrast, the expatriate Judahite community in Egypt defended its continuation of non-Yahwistic cultic practices by attributing the disaster to the failure to continue such cults in the time leading up to the

58. If a document had been produced during the reforms of Hezekiah (or perhaps even in the north before the fall of Samaria), such a text could have been used as a basis for persuading the young king to initiate a reform movement. Although the origins of these ideas can be traced to this period the precise origins of the text are impossible to establish with certainty.

59. Morton Smith, *Palestinian Parties and Politics that Shaped the Old Testament* (London: SCM Press, 2nd edn, 1987), pp. 38-39.

destruction of Jerusalem (Jer. 44.15-19).[60] Jeremiah 44 preserves a debate between Jeremiah, as a representative of the innovative Yahweh-alone position, and the Judahites in Egypt who wished to continue their ancestral practices; each group attributed the destruction of Jerusalem to the cultic practices of the other. The typical ancestral practices that Jeremiah's opponents wished to continue are described earlier in the book (Jer. 7.1–8.3). The pluralistic religious environment of the late monarchic period is said to have included the worship of Yahweh, Baal, the Queen of Heaven, the sacrifice of children, and astral worship (the sun, moon and host of heaven).[61] Similarly, the vision of Ezekiel dating from c. 591 BCE (Ezek. 8) highlights (negatively) the diversity of Judahite Yahwism at the end of the monarchic period. The Egyptian Judahite community of the sixth century, as heirs of the religion of the Judahite state, represent a continuation of the heterogeneous situation that had existed prior to 586 BCE. The sixth century was a period of substantial conflict between the Yahweh-alone position and those who wished to continue their polytheistic traditions.

Isaiah 45 is indicative of the relationship of the Yahweh-only theology with the return from Babylonia. This chapter depicts Yahweh as the source of light and darkness, weal and woe (v. 7).[62] As in Jeremiah 44 and the book of Lamentations, the attribution of good and ill, destruction and salvation to Yahweh functions at one level to eliminate possible competitors. No other deity could be responsible for the disaster of 586 BCE nor could any other deity be a source of hope for restoration. There is only one deity who is responsible for both. Throughout Isaiah 45 the prophet stresses that there is only one god, Yahweh, that there are no others, and that the hope of the exiled community lies only in Yahweh's anointed, Cyrus (v. 1). This supremacy of Yahweh to the exclusion of all other deities is reflected in a variety of texts of the Hebrew Bible beginning in the late sixth century. The ubiquity of this interpretation is evident by its occurrence in Deutero-Isaiah, DtrH, Jeremiah and Ezekiel. The predominance in these texts of the supremacy of Yahweh to the exclusion of all other gods is the result

---

60. Cf. Smith, *Palestinian Parties*, p. 39 n. 266.

61. For a valuable discussion of the identity of the Queen of Heaven, see Ackerman, *Under Every Green Tree*, pp. 5-35. Ackerman argues that the evidence indicates a melding of the earlier Ishtar and Astarte traditions in the mid-first millennium figure, the Queen of Heaven.

62. Cf. Deut. 32.39.

of the success of the program of attributing the destruction of Jerusalem and the temple of Yahweh to the failure of the reforms to abolish 'syncretism' in the monarchic period.[63] Or, more correctly, to the dominance of those who accepted this interpretation of Israelite history in both the Babylonian Judahite community and the Persian period province of Yehud.

The sketch of the development of Israelite religion provided above agrees in many essential matters with that provided by Mark Smith.[64] The only substantive disagreements relate to the period in which various developments are likely to have occurred. Smith suggests that the first monolatrous Yahwists appeared in the ninth century. Although this may be correct, the evidence is uncertain. The opposition of Hosea to the Baal cult in the northern kingdom of the eighth century seems a more certain date for the innovation of Yahwistic monolatry. But, as was indicated above, this is not entirely certain either. Hosea may simply have been a defender of the supremacy of Yahweh in the face of the threat from Baal. The roots of Yahwistic monolatry may, in fact, lie in the Judahite reaction to the fall of Samaria and the influx of refugees and traditions (such as the prophecies of Hosea) from the north. Similarly, Smith's suggestion that Yahwistic monotheism is first evident in Deutero-Isaiah and Jeremiah may need some modification. The monotheistic faith of Deutero-Isaiah seems quite certain but whether Jeremiah was monotheistic or monolatrous is less certain. The case for Jeremiah is clouded by issues of editorial activity by monotheistic redactors. The late sixth-century text of Deutero-Isaiah is the earliest indisputable evidence for monotheistic Yahwism.

An inescapable conclusion of this analysis is the essentially Canaanite character of much of ancient Israel's religious life.[65] The evolution of Israel's religion over the centuries led to a gradually increasing

---

63. Lang notes that although Deut. 6.4 is still monolatric (henotheistic?) other Dtr texts demonstrate a move to monotheism, i.e. the denial of the existence of any other deity (Deut. 4.35, 39; 1 Kgs 8.60; 2 Kgs 19.19) (Lang, *Monotheism*, p. 45). This view is also apparent in Deutero-Isaiah (43.10; 45.21-22).

64. Smith, *The Early History of God*, pp. 145-60.

65. See Smith, *The Early History of God*, pp. 1-7; Coogan, 'Canaanite Origins and Lineage', pp. 115-24; William G. Dever, 'The Contribution of Archaeology to the Study of Canaanite and Early Israelite Religion', in P.D. Miller, Jr, P.D. Hanson and S.D. McBride (eds.), *Ancient Israelite Religion: Essays in Honor of Frank Moore Cross* (Philadelphia: Fortress Press, pp. 209-47).

distinction between 'Israelite' religion and 'Canaanite' religion. Yah-wistic monolatry and monotheism are late developments in the life of ancient Israel. The witnesses of the biblical texts primarily provide evidence of these later periods in the developmental process. The earlier evidence that does remain in the Hebrew Bible must be separated from the later theological context in which it now resides and read in relation to the more diverse religious environment indicated by the artifactual evidence if we are to arrive at a more accurate understanding of the pro-gression of belief and practice in ancient Israel and Judah.

The Continuation of Early Yahwism at Elephantine

In contrast to the developments in Achaemenid Yehud, the Yahwists of Elephantine represent a continuation and development of the traditional Yahwistic cult of monarchic Judah and Israel. The garrison claims that its temple to יהו pre-existed Cambyses's arrival in Egypt in 525 BCE (A. 4.7). This claim occurs in a context in which the Yahwists of Elephantine are requesting permission to rebuild their temple after its destruction. This raises the possibility that the claim is made simply as a manipulative ploy to strengthen the request for reconstruction and that it does not accurately reflect the history of the temple. There is, how-ever, additional support for the existence of a military garrison at Ele-phantine from the pre-Achaemenid period. The Letter of Aristeas (§13) states that Psammetichus used Judahite mercenaries in a campaign in Ethiopia. In addition, Herodotus (*Hist.* 2.30) indicates that the Persian garrison at Elephantine was a continuation of Egyptian policy from the time of Psammetichus. This would place Judahite mercenaries in Egypt either in the last half of the seventh century, if Psammetichus I is intended, or early in the sixth century, if Psammetichus II is meant.[66] In either case, this would place Judahites in the region of Elephantine well before Cambyses's invasion of Egypt. None of this provides conclusive proof of the presence of Yahwists at Elephantine prior to the arrival of the Persians; indeed, the statement in Herodotus only indicates the

---

66. For Psammetichus I, see Bezalel Porten, 'The Jews in Egypt', in *Cambridge History of Judaism*, I (Cambridge: Cambridge University Press, pp. 372-400 (378-79); Ahlström, *History*, p. 768. For Psammetichus II, see Cowley, *Aramaic Papyri*, p. xvi; Rainer Albertz, *A History of Israelite Religion in the Old Testament Period* (OTL; 2 vols.; Louisville, KY: Westminster/John Knox Press, 1994), II, p. 599 n. 24.

existence of a garrison at Elephantine prior to the arrival of Cambyses. However, Egyptian use of Judahite mercenaries during this period is not only possible but probable. After the death of Josiah at the hands of Necho II Judah became a vassal of the Egyptians with an Egyptian appointed monarch on the throne (2 Kgs 23.33-35). The provision of mercenary soldiers to the ruling power was one of the usual responsibilities of a vassal monarch. This fact, in combination with the previously mentioned textual evidence, makes the presence of Judahite mercenaries at Elephantine during the sixth century likely.

Such an early arrival of Yahwists at Elephantine suggests that their worship, exhibiting devotion to several different deities, may be a continuation of the cultic traditions of monarchic Judah, exempted from the significant alterations that occurred within the territory of Judah after their departure. They may well have been influenced by the surrounding multicultural and multicultic environment, but it is unlikely that their polytheistic Yahwism resulted from the abandonment of a strict monotheistic Yahwism after their arrival in Egypt. Thus the Elephantine community and Achaemenid Yehud represent divergent streams flowing from the Yahwistic faith of monarchic Judah. The Elephantine community probably represents a continuation of the typical cult of monarchic Judah with its worship of various deities alongside Yahweh. Achaemenid Yehud, on the other hand, represents the continuation of the innovative Yahweh-alone perspective represented in the reforms of Hezekiah and Josiah and the Deuteronomistic History.

Yahwism in Achaemenid Yehud

The biblical texts are primarily the production of the literate Judahites of the neo-Babylonian period and the literate ruling elites of Achaemenid Yehud. The theological perspective of the primary textual products of this group(s) indicates that they considered monotheistic (or, at minimum, monolatrous) Yahwism to be the normative religion of the descendants of monarchic Israel and Judah. The major literary texts surviving from this period—Deutero-Isaiah, Jeremiah, Ezekiel, DtrH and Chronicles—all portray the worship of other deities, in preference to or alongside of Yahweh, as illicit. But was this change from the predominance of a traditional, west-Semitic pantheon to the monolatrous or monotheistic worship of Yahweh a widespread sociological development within all strata of the Yehudite population? Or is the exclusive worship of Yahweh a reflection of the official religion of Yehud practiced and promoted by its elites but not necessarily the religion (or the only religion) of the masses? In other words, do the texts that were produced by the provincial elite during the Persian period represent the perspectives of the majority of Yehudites during the period or only those of the elites?

The material remains of Palestine during the Persian period provide some insight into the cultic practices of the population during the period. It is clear that monotheism is not an entirely consistent feature of Yahwistic worship in the Achaemenid period. Smith refers to two seals of Horus, one the property of Obadiah the son of Sheharhor and the other the property of Sheharhor the son of Zephaniah, and one seal of Shamash, the property of Yehoyishmah daughter of Shawashsarusur, dating from the Persian period.[67] Although Smith uses the presence of Yahwistic theophoric names as evidence for the fidelity of Yehudites to Yahweh in this period, the presence of these seals also indicates that the veneration of other deities continued alongside the veneration of Yahweh among some of the population in the Persian period.

The remains of only two temples dating from the Persian period have been found in Palestine: in Makmish and Lachish. They are representative of the two main styles of temples of this period known from Cyprus and Phoenecia.[68] All of the material remains indicate that these temples were used in the worship of deities other than Yahweh. While these temples provide evidence of the continuation of non-Yahwistic cults in Palestine, they do not furnish any direct information regarding cultic activity within the province of Yehud.

In analyzing the extant cult figurines from the period, Stern indicates that in the early Persian period they reflect eastern styles and continue earlier traditions. The production and use of Canaanite-Palestinian style figurines from earlier periods continued into the Persian period. He particularly notes that Baal, 'Pillar Astarte', and horse-and-rider figurines

---

67. Morton Smith, 'Jewish Religious Life in the Persian Period', in W.D. Davies and L. Finkelstein (eds.), *Cambridge History of Judaism* (4 vols.; Cambridge: Cambridge University Press, 1984), I, pp. 236-37. See also Nahman Avigad, 'Seals of the Exiles', *IEJ* 15 (1965), pp. 222-32 (228-29); and Nahman Avigad, *Bullae and Seals from a Post-Exilic Judean Archive* (Qedem, 4; Jerusalem: Hebrew University, 1976).

68. Stern, 'The Archaeology of Persian Palestine', in David and Finkelstein (eds.), *Cambridge History of Judaism*, I, pp. 88-114 (102-103).

have all been found in Persian period contexts in the Levant.[69] Figurines from the later Persian period, on the other hand, indicate influence from Western sources mixed with the Eastern. Based on mineralogical and petrographical analysis of the figurines from Tel Sippor which indicate 25 per cent locally made, 70 per cent from coastal regions, and 5 per cent from Rhodes, Stern concludes, 'The facts stated confirm the generally-accepted assumption that such figurines are to be ascribed to the Phoenician population; this is not contradicted by the finding of several examples on Cyprus, for there was a large Phoenician element on that island'.[70] However, it does not necessarily follow that these were used solely by Phoenician populations simply because their manufacture can be traced to Phoenicia.[71] The discovery of items connected with the worship of other deities within the borders of Achaemenid Yehud suggests the possibility that some non-Yahwistic worship may have continued among the Yehudite population.

Similarly, Stern attributes the incense altars of the period primarily to the Phoenicians. He notes a general pattern of degeneration in style and quality from the early to late Persian period. The style of these altars he attributes to Mesopotamian sources, since they appear in Palestine from the end of the sixth century but were in use in Mesopotamia as early as the seventh century. As with the figurines, he limits the use of these altars to Phoenician populations, but given the wide dispersion of Phoenician-manufactured items throughout the Persian empire, it seems risky to tie the ethnicity of the consumers to the ethnicity of the producers.[72]

Of primary importance for reconstructing the religion of Achaemenid Yehud is the geographical distribution of these material remains of the cult practices of the period. M. Smith suggests that worship at the high places continued unabated throughout Palestine during the Persian period. This observation is undoubtedly accurate for Palestine as a whole but the lack of detailed analysis of the evidence, according to subregions of Palestine and specific chronological periods, makes the

---

69. Stern, *Material Culture*, pp. 179, 181.

70. Stern, 'The Archaeology of Persian Palestine', p. 105. He refers to N. Avigad, 'Excavations at Makmish, 1958: A Preliminary Report', *IEJ* 10 (1960), pp. 90-96, for support for this conclusion.

71. Nor does this limited sample provide a firm basis for such a sweeping conclusion.

72. Stern, 'The Archaeology of Persian Palestine', pp. 106-107.

observation almost useless for a reconstruction of the religion of Yehud in the period.[73] Stern, on the other hand, argues that the distribution of cultic objects in the material culture of the Levant in the Achaemenid period indicates that figurines and altars of non-Yahwistic popular cults are primarily found outside the population centers of 'Jews and Samaritans'. This observation that non-Yahwistic cult remains are predominantly from geographical areas outside Yehud is significant. It should be noted, however, that this factual report is tied to the opinion that 'the two main groups—the Jews and Samaritans—did not utilize such objects in their rites and whenever they did appear among these peoples, they were in direct opposition to their religious precepts'.[74] Thus, ideological bias cannot be ruled out.

If Stern's analysis of the material remains is accurate—that is, that the majority of non-Yahwistic cult objects in the Persian period occur outside the boundaries of Yehud—this would support the belief that the religion of the Achaemenid period reflects the movement toward some form of Yahwistic monotheism or, at least, monolatry in the population as a whole. The discovery of a few scattered objects within the borders of Yehud would indicate that, although non-Yahwistic cults or poly-Yahwism continued during the Persian period, these were probably exceptional rather than generally representative of the religion of the province. The lack of material evidence for the continuation of the worship of gods other than Yahweh in the Persian period indicates a substantial shift from the religion of the monarchic period. In general, this change in the cultic items recovered from the excavation of the material remains conforms to the above suggested pattern of development. Early Israelite and Judahite religion conformed to the common west-Semitic pattern with Yahweh at the head of a pantheon. This early Yahwistic faith only developed into a monolatrous or monotheistic religion similar to that depicted in the biblical texts in the Persian (or Hellenistic) period.

The recovery of non-Yahwistic cult objects within the borders of Yehud may reveal a degree of resistance to the official monotheistic policies of the central authorities of the province. While such opposition indicates a degree of social conflict in Yehud in the early Persian period, the evidence suggests that the magnitude of religious conflict was not substantial. In fact, the evidence of social conflict in this period

73. Smith, 'Jewish Religious Life', pp. 234-35.
74. Stern, *Material Culture*, p. 158.

is not as substantial as some reconstructions have suggested. For example, conflict between those who returned from Babylon and those who had remained in the land has been suggested by many interpreters. Ezra 4.4, which depicts the opposition of the people of the land to the rebuilding of the temple, has been used as the primary evidence for the supposed social conflict during the early Achaemenid period. On the basis of this text, Smith and others have suggested that the population that had remained in the land was, in some way, religiously unacceptable to the returnees; that is, either they were ethnically impure or they participated in polytheistic or syncretistic cults.[75] The problem with such a use of this text for historical reconstruction is that it fails to recognize the composite nature of Ezra 4. Ezra 4.4-6 functions as an editorial bridge to link an account of opposition to the rebuilding of the walls of Jerusalem in the days of Artaxerxes (I?) to the preceding account of the rejection by Zerubbabel and Joshua of the participation of 'the adversaries of Judah and Benjamin' (v. 1) in the rebuilding of the temple. This text appears to be a fabrication by the compiler of Ezra to link the later tradition regarding the reconstruction of the city walls to the earlier situation surrounding the rebuilding of the temple; the editor has retrojected later hostilities and social divisions into the time of the temple restoration.

In fact, there is no evidence of substantive conflict with regard to the rebuilding of the temple during the early years of the reign of Darius I. The opposition between returnees and remainees in this early period is no more than a (much) later fiction of the compiler of Ezra.[76] Additional evidence of conflict between returnees and remainees is virtually non-existent. For example, Smith has used Zech. 8.10 to suggest conflict between competing interest groups in the early Persian period.[77] However, given the rhetorical function of this text in highlighting (exaggerating?) the differing social conditions before and after the beginning of

75. For example, M. Smith connects the phrase 'people of the land', from Ezra 4.4 and other places in Ezra and Nehemiah, with the depiction of the sycretistic practices of the neo-Babylonian Judahites in Ezek. 11.15-21. By doing so, he arrives at the conclusion that the population of Judah post-582 BCE 'was made up for the most part of adherents to the syncretistic cult of Yahweh'. According to Smith, this syncretistic population is to be contrasted with the returnees designated as the בני הגלה (*Palestinian Parties*, pp. 81, 85).

76. See the discussion in Chapter 2, 'Exile, Return and the Desolate Land'.

77. Smith, *Palestinian Parties*, p. 81.

the rebuilding of the temple, this is very tendentious and unreliable evidence for a reconstruction of the social conditions of the early Achaemenid period. Further, Smith argues on the basis of Hag. 2.4 that the priestly faction acted as an agent of compromise between the Yahweh alone party (led by Zerubbabel) and the syncretistic Yahwists, the people of the land.[78] But all that this text actually implies is that Zerubbabel, Joshua and the people (of the land) all received encouragement from Haggai in their common effort to rebuild the temple. This reference (cf. Zech. 7.5) actually reveals that the use of the phrase 'people of the land' as the referent for a distinct opposition group is a much later phenomenon than the period of Haggai, Zechariah and the reconstruction of the Jerusalem temple. While there was certainly social conflict in early Achaemenid Yehud, there is no reliable evidence to support the suggestions of widespread conflict between returnees and remainees. The material remains suggest that the normative religion of the ruling class was, for the most part, willingly accepted by or successfully imposed upon the majority of the population of the province.

Yahweh, Ahura Mazda and אלהי השמים

The relationship of the religion of Achaemenid Yehud to that of the empire is difficult to establish, but the similarities are suggestive. A similar movement from polytheism to monolatry occurred in Persian religion under the influence of Zoroaster. Zoroaster was a reformer of earlier forms of Mazdaism who proclaimed faith in Ahura Mazda alone and the repudiation of tribal deities. In a process similar to that proposed above regarding the collapse of the levels of the Judahite pantheon, many of the 'lesser' deities were subsumed as attributes of the supreme god.[79] The precise nature of the religious beliefs and practices of the Achaemenids and their relationship to this 'reform' movement of Zoroaster is difficult to determine. That they were worshipers of Ahura Mazda is clear and unambiguous. The inscriptional data provides ample evidence that Ahura Mazda was the chief deity of the Achaemenid empire. Whether the Achaemenids were Zoroastrians or not is more

78. Smith, *Palestinian Parties*, p. 85 n. 60.

79. 'Ahuramazda (Greek Oromasdes), according to the teachings of Zoroaster, was the single almighty and omnipresent god of good, who personified light, life and truth. He existed even before the creation of the world, and was its creator' (Dandamaev and Lukonin, *Culture and Social Institutions*, p. 325).

difficult to determine. M. Boyce argues that Zoroastrianism was the religion of the Achaemenids from a very early time on the basis of Zoroastrian names within the Achaemenid family from the pre-empire period. Boyce also suggests the possibility that Zoroastrian Medes supported Cyrus against Astyages because they saw Cyrus as a champion of their religion.[80] The first point does suggest a connection between the royal family and Zoroastrianism but the evidence for collusion between Cyrus and Median Zoroastrians is insubstantial.

In a more moderate proposal, Dandamaev and Lukonin argue that the Achaemenids, beginning with Darius I, practiced one of the early forms of Zoroastrianism but that the differences prohibit claims of an exact correlation.[81] A similar position is posited by Frye:

> Both the followers of Zoroaster and the Achaemenids concentrated their worship on the great god Ahura Mazda and both did not deny the existence of other deities. Both abhorred 'the lie' and extolled 'the truth', as we find in the Gathas and in the OP inscriptions. This should be sufficient to indicate that both followed the same religious system, although surely with some differences in beliefs if not so much in cult or practices.[82]

Although Zoroastrian influence on the Achaemenids was strong, influences from other sources can also be detected. While the homage given Ahura Mazda in the Achaemenid royal inscriptions reflects the high, creator-god theology of Zoroaster, the Achaemenid kings continued to respect and worship other deities in the conquered lands. Also, Dandamaev and Lukonin note that references to Mithra and Anahita become far more common in the inscriptions of the later Achaemenids than those of the early Achaemenids (as does the younger Avesta compared to the Gathas). They attribute this to the growing influence of Iranian popular religion on the official, imperial religion in later stages of the empire.[83]

Could the Zoroastrian emphasis on a single, creator god that appears to have been so influential in the early period of the Achaemenid rule (at least at the level of emperor, state officials, Magi, etc.) have been a

---

80. Mary Boyce, 'Persian Religion in the Achaemenid Age', in Davies and Finkelstein (eds.), *Cambridge History of Judaism*, I, pp. 279-307 (281-82).
81. Dandamaev and Lukonin, *Culture and Social Institutions*, p. 347.
82. Frye, *History*, p. 121.
83. Dandamaev and Lukonin, *Culture and Social Institutions*, pp. 328-29.

significant influence on the development of similar beliefs among the Yehudites in this period? As noted above, it is unlikely that Zoroastrianism could have or did function as the primary catalyst for the development of monotheism among the posterity of monarchic Israel and Judah, but it could have provided additional impetus to the transition that was already underway.

There are several strong parallels between Achaemenid imperial religion and Yehudite Yahwism in the Persian period. The title אלהי השמים or its Aramaic equivalent, אלהא שמיא, is first used in the Persian period to designate the concept of a supreme deity both in Yehud and the ancient Near East generally.[84] The use of this common title to designate both Ahura Mazda and Yahweh does not necessarily indicate that the two deities were considered to be local manifestations of a single deity, although this is possible. This common designation could, however, provide a foundation for the identification of Yahweh as a local manifestation of Ahura Mazda by imperial officials. Such an identification would be beneficial to the status of the Yehudites in the eyes of the empire. The common designation of these two deities could also reflect the influence of imperial ideology on Yehudite Yahwistic theology during this period.

Bolin argues that the Yehudite identification of Yahweh with the God of heaven was a political expediency, that is, that this identification was an attempt to have Yahweh treated as a regional expression of Ahura Mazda for the political advantage of the local administration.[85] He suggests that the Achaemenid empire shifted from an inclusive monotheism in the early years to an exclusive monotheism during the last two-thirds of the fifth century, and so, the equation of Yahweh with אלהא לשמיא was a pragmatic move to create the appearance of adherence to imperial religious policy.[86] The basis of this reconstruction is primarily the Elephantine papyri regarding the restoration of the temple of יהו (A 4.5, 4.7, 4.8). Bolin maintains that the Elephantine

84. Edelman, 'Introduction', p. 21 n. 17. Contra Thomas Thompson, who argues that it originates in the neo-Babylonian period (*Early History of the Israelite People: From the Written and Archaeological Sources* [Studies in the History of the Ancient Near East, 4; Leiden: E.J. Brill, 1992], p. 417).

85. Thomas M. Bolin, 'The Temple of יהו at Elephantine and Persian Religious Policy', in D.V. Edelman (ed.), *The Triumph of Elohim: From Yahwisms to Judaisms* (Grand Rapids: Eerdmans, 1996), pp. 127-42.

86. Bolin, 'Temple of יהו', pp. 135-42.

Yahwists identified Yahweh as אלהא שמיא solely as a means of induc-
ing imperial support for their reconstruction project. The available data
are too limited to allow for a definitive conclusion regarding the veracity of this suggestion.[87] Bolin points to the supposed exclusive focus
on Ahura Mazda in all Achaemenid inscriptions from Xerxes I to Artaxerxes II as evidence for the move to exclusive monotheism by the
later Achaemenids.[88] However, this proposed shift from an inclusive to
an exclusive monotheism in the Achaemenid empire is unsubstantiated;
indeed, given the veneration of the deities of Babylon, Egypt, and so
on, by the Achaemenids, it is impossible to call them monotheistic at
all.[89] The claim of Xerxes to have extinguished all the cults of the 'Evil
Gods' and the promise of blessing on those who worship Ahura Mazda
could provide support for Bolin's suggestion of a move to exclusive
monotheism, but more likely represents propaganda against the gods of
rebellious peoples.[90] Note that these claims occur in the highly tendentious context immediately following the narration of Xerxes's successful defeat of colonial rebellions.

There would, however, have been political advantage in highlighting
similarities between Yahweh and Ahura Mazda for both the imperial
center and the local elites. The use of the same title for both deities
would have functioned as an important mechanism for integrating the
colony into the empire. By using this title for Yahweh,[91] the Yehudite
elites would encourage local acceptance of Achaemenid rule by highlighting the common aspects of local and imperial theology.[92] At the
same time, this emphasis on similarities would also be beneficial in
relations between the local administration and the imperial center.

In addition to the common designation as אלהא שמיא, the similarities
between Ahura Mazda and Yahweh are also suggested by the iconography of the period. Ahura Mazda was most commonly depicted either

---

87. The significant differences in the theology and cult of the Elephantine and
Jerusalemite Yahwists during this period makes impossible a determination of the
beliefs and practices of one on the basis of evidence about the other.

88. Following Cook, *Persian Empire*, p. 147.

89. Note also the analysis of Dandamaev and Lukonin, *Culture and Social Institutions* (pp. 328-29) that other Iranian deities become more common in later
inscriptions.

90. *ANET*, p. 317.

91. Whether purely for political expediency or not is impossible to say.

92. Both Ahura Mazda and Yahweh are depicted as high, creator deities and
were worshiped without the use of idols.

as a winged sun disk or as a winged figure within a solar disk in Achaemenid reliefs and seals.[93] Yehudite seals from the period also commonly occur with representations of winged solar disks. These have often been attributed to Egyptian influence, which is obviously true at one level, as is also the case with the same imagery in Persia, but the more significant relationship is to the use of this symbol in imperial iconography relating to Ahura Mazda. The common use of this important imperial motif in Yehud indicates the (expected) pervasiveness of imperial ideology and imagery within the province. It may also represent further ties between Yahweh and Ahura Mazda. Taylor's recent study of the biblical and archaeological evidence has demonstrated that both solar worship and the use of solar imagery in the worship of Yahweh were common through several centuries in ancient Palestine.[94] The recognition of Yahweh in solar imagery should be expected. The connection of Yahweh with this imagery during the Persian period has recently been strengthened by Edelman's discussion of an early fourth-century Yehudite coin that depicts Yahweh seated on a throne with a winged wheel. She notes that some interpreters have even suggested identifying the deity on the coin as Ahura Mazda because of the congruence with the winged sun disk imagery known from elsewhere.[95] This iconographic bond between Yahweh and the imperial deity, Ahura Mazda, provides an additional mechanism binding the imperial center and the periphery.[96]

93. 'The portals of the palaces of Persepolis and the chief scenes on the stairways were crowned with a depiction of the solar disk with wings, a symbol widespread in Egypt, but most probably interpreted as a symbol of Ahuramazda' (Dandamaev and Lukonin, *Culture and Social Institutions*, p. 342). 'Many seals have been discovered in Persepolis on which a winged Ahuramazda in a solar disk has been depicted' (Dandamaev and Lukonin, *Culture and Social Institutions*, p. 343).

94. Taylor, *Yahweh and the Sun*. See also Smith, *The Early History of God*, pp. 115-24; and the analysis of Niehr, who highlights many of the connections between Yahweh and solar imagery down to the period of the Elephantine papyri, but, surprisingly, never makes the connection with the widespread use of the imagery in Achaemenid inscriptions ('The Rise of Yhwh in Judahite and Israelite Religion', pp. 45-72).

95. D.V. Edelman, 'Tracking Observance of the Aniconic Tradition through Numismatics', in *eadem* (ed.), *The Triumph of Elohim*, pp. 185-225 (esp. 190-96).

96. In this regard, the identification of Darius I as the son of Aten, the sun disk, suggests the operation of the same mechanism in that setting. See the inscription

Hosea and the Yahwism of Yehud

As indicated above, in the early Persian period the religion of the literate elites of Yehud, reflected in the texts which they both produced and read, was exclusively a monotheistic form of Yahwism. There is some artifactual evidence for the continuation of non-Yahwistic worship within the territorial borders of the province among some segments of the population, but this was not the dominant religious expression in this period. Although some of the multifaceted character of the religion of monarchic Judah continued into the Persian period, the most significant change from the monarchic period is the dramatic decrease in the evidence for such activity.

The depiction of the veneration of deities other than Yahweh as infidelity is a significant motif in Jeremiah, Ezekiel and the Deuteronomistic History (and many other later biblical texts).[97] In many of these texts the worship of other deities is explicitly said to be inappropriate for people in a relationship with Yahweh. These texts provide a critical witness to the interpretive environment of the early Persian period. Beginning perhaps as early as the late seventh century, but certainly by the sixth century, these texts demonstrate a strong polemic against any practices which are outside the bounds of a very narrowly defined Yahwistic monolatry.

Further evidence of the religious discourse of the early Persian period is provided by the polemical statements of Deutero-Isaiah. The depiction of other deities as ineffectual (41.21-24; 46.1-2) and the work of human hands (40.18-20; 44.12-20; 46.6-7) contrasts sharply with the consistent depiction of Yahweh as creator and ruler of everything (40.12-17, 21-23; 42.5-6; 43.16-17; 44.24-28; 48.12-13; 51.9-11; 54.5). Note particularly the absolute denunciation of those who trust in gods other than Yahweh (42.17; 43.12; 44.9-11; 45.16), and the explicit claim that there are no other gods (43.10; 44.6; 45.5, 14, 18, 21-22; 46.9). As was indicated above, these texts provide emphatic evidence for the connection between the immigrants from Mesopotamia and monotheistic Yahwism. The Yehudites who were responsible for the

---

cited in Dandamaev and Lukonin, *Culture and Social Institutions*, p. 355.

97. Deut. 31.16-22; Judg. 2.17; 8.27, 33; Jer. 2.20-37; 3.1-10; 5.7; Ezek. 16; 20.27-31; 23 (Oholah and Oholibah); cf. Exod. 34.11-16; Lev. 17.7; 20.5-6; 2 Chron. 21.11-13; Isa. 1.21; Mic. 1.7.

preservation, production and interpretation of the textual traditions of the nation, including the book of Hosea, were almost certainly monotheistic Yahwists.

It may be that Psalm 82, with its unique polemic against other gods (they are all condemned to die like mortals for their failure to maintain justice), belongs in this religio-historical environment as well. This psalm clearly displays elements of the traditional Syro-Palestinian pantheon; the divine council (עדת־אל) composed of the אלהים (v. 1) and the belief that the various gods are all children of עליון (v. 6). Significantly, God (אלהים),[98] acting from within the council, passes judgment on the ethical misconduct of the other members of the council and sentences them to die like humans (כאדם תמותון; v. 7). Resulting from this judgment on the other deities is a call by the psalmist for God to judge the earth, for all peoples (כל־הגוים) belong to God (v. 8). This psalm appears to represent a transitional perspective from a monolatrous position in which every ethnic group worships its appropriate deity to a monotheistic position in which the psalmist's god has become the only god. The judgment and death of all other deities provides a mythic depiction of the subsuming of the various manifestations of divinity expressed in pantheon under the umbrella of a single, high god. Unfortunately, this psalm is very difficult to date with any certainty, and therefore, although it is indicative of the kind of theological transition that occurred, it cannot be primary evidence for the timing of the transition.

In considering the importance of such evidence for the reading of Hosea in the early Persian period, it is important to recall that the guild of skilled individuals capable of producing, reproducing and reading such texts would have been very small in the neo-Babylonian and early

---

98. Hans-Joachim Kraus may be correct in suggesting that אלהים has here been substituted for an original יהוה as part of an elohistic revision (*Psalms 60–150* [Continental Commentaries; Minneapolis: Augsburg, 1989], p. 154). Whether or not this suggestion is correct, the God of Israel, also known as Yahweh, seems to be clearly implied in v. 1. Cf. Frank Moore Cross, who argues that this is not a description of the council of El (of which Yahweh was a member), but a description of the council of Yahweh, with El functioning as a proper name of Yahweh (*Canaanite Myth and Hebrew Epic: Essays in the History of the Religion of Israel* [Cambridge, MA: Harvard University Press, 1973], pp. 44-45). Cross argues, on the basis of the biblical evidence, that Yahweh originated as an El figure (*Canaanite Myth and Hebrew Epic*, pp. 71-72).

Persian periods.[99] These texts, which were produced and preserved by the literary elites of the Persian province of Yehud, furnish vital evidence of the interpretive environment in which the texts of the book of Hosea were being read in the early Persian period. The combination of this substantial body of literary texts with the socio-religious context of the developing orthodox monotheism of Achaemenid Yehud provides substantial interpretive constructs which would have shaped the reading of the book of Hosea in this period. Two of the key factors shaping the reading the book of Hosea in the socio-religious environment of early Achaemenid Yehud are: (1) monotheistic Yahwism with an inflexible emphasis on the exclusive worship of Yahweh within the ranks of the provincial ruling class; and (2) the pervasive ideology of a single, high, creator god within the broader imperial sphere.[100]

Yahweh as the God of Israel
The centrality and uniqueness of Yahweh to the life and cult of Israel is a key feature of the book of Hosea. Yahweh is often designated 'your God' or 'their God' in relation to the Israelites (Hos. 1.7; 3.5; 4.6, 12; 5.4; 7.10; 8.2—'My God'; 9.1, 8—'his God'; 12.6 [2×]; 14.1—'her God'; 14.2). In particular, Hos. 12.2-6 emphasizes that it is Yahweh who is rightfully the God of Israel, tracing the relationship back to the eponymous ancestor of the nation wrestling with God at Bethel (12.4). Twice (12.9; 13.4) the connection of Yahweh, as Israel's God, and the deliverance from Egypt is recollected: 'I am Yahweh your God since the land of Egypt.' In Hos. 13.4 the significance of this event, its basis as the fundamental substance of the relationship between Yahweh and Israel, is developed further: 'you know no God but me and besides me there is no savior'. This primal event, the birth of the nation, is presented as the basis for their relationship with Yahweh. The relationship with Yahweh is integral to both the identity and existence of Israel.

The connection of Yahweh with Israel's beginning as a nation in the exodus traditions is very significant. These traditions provide a

99. See the discussions in Chapter 1, 'Literacy in the Ancient World'; and 'The Social Function of Reading in Yehud'.

100. The distinction between reconstructing an eighth-century reading of Hosea and a sixth/fifth-century reading is essential in the following analysis. The form of the text and its interpretation in the earlier context are beyond the limits of this study. What follows is an attempt to read the book shaped by the reconstructed socio-historical setting of early Achaemenid Yehud.

substantial basis for arguing that Yahweh is the (only) legitimate deity of Israel. Indeed, the restoration of relationship narrated in Hosea 2 depicts the reconciliation in terms of a return to the wilderness period in which a youthful Israel responds to the seductive words of Yahweh (2.16-17 [Eng. 14-15]). The result of this return to the wilderness is an unending marital relationship characterized by faithfulness (2.21-22 [Eng. 19-20]), sowing back into the land, and the reversal of the broken divine–human relationship: 'I will say to Not-my-people, "You are my people"', and he will say, 'My God' (2.25 [Eng. 23]).

Emphasis on Yahweh as the (only) legitimate deity of Israel is one of the central features of the book of Hosea. This is the clear alternative position of Hosea to the various cultic practices condemned in the book. As was argued earlier, however, the original eighth-century context for many of these oracles was one in which polytheism was the norm and Yahweh was regarded as the chief deity of an Israelite pantheon. These Hosean oracles would not have been interpreted as a rejection of this normative religious environment in this earlier interpretive context. Rather, the specific focus of these oracles is the threat posed by Baal to Yahweh's position of supremacy in the Israelite pantheon. The repeated emphasis on Yahweh as 'your' God and 'their' God and the stress given to the innate nature of the relationship between Yahweh and Israel functions to elucidate the ties binding Israel's existence and identity to their recognition of Yahweh as their chief God. The developing relationship with Baal was regarded as inappropriate, and it was depicted as an act of infidelity to Yahweh. At the same time, the relationship with Yahweh is regarded as inherently appropriate to Israel.

The dramatically altered social situation of late sixth-century Achaemenid Yehud would result in a different interpretation of these oracles. In light of the literary and socio-religious context delineated in the preceding sections, these texts from Hosea would most likely have been interpreted as authoritative sanction for the newly emergent Yahwistic monotheism of the period. These texts most likely represented a pro-Yahwistic, anti-Baalistic perspective in the eighth century, but in the new interpretive environment they are much more likely to have been read as support for a strictly monotheistic faith.

The Motif of Sexual Infidelity
The text of the book of Hosea contains a multitude of examples in which the deteriorating and, finally, defunct relationship(s) between

Yahweh and Israel and Judah is depicted by images of sexual infidelity (1.2-9; 2; 3.1; 4.10b-11a; 5.3-4; 6.6, 10; 9.1). This imagery, describing the breakdown of the relationship between Yahweh and Israel, predominantly relates to acts of cultic indiscretion by the Israelites involving the worship of Baal. The analysis below will indicate that these texts, read within the literary and theological context of Persian period orthodoxy, were predominantly understood as the rejection of all non-Yahwistic worship.

As previously noted, the motif of sexual infidelity is employed in Jeremiah, Ezekiel and the Deuteronomistic History as a description of the participation of many Judahites in the cults of gods other than Yahweh. The use of such imagery in these texts was most likely inspired by the similar imagery in the prophecies of Hosea but, for purposes of exploring how the Hosean texts may have been read in the early Persian period, they are representative of the manner in which these images were used in the religious discourse of the period. These later texts became a part of the interpretive matrix through which these earlier prophecies would have been interpreted.

Hosea's marriage to אשׁת זנונים ('a promiscuous woman', 1.2) has long been a point of contention for interpreters. Wolff argues that this imagery ties Israel's guilt to participation in 'Canaanite' cultic prostitution.[101] In contrast, Rudolph has denied that cultic prostitution in ancient Israel can be substantiated from the biblical and extrabiblical evidence.[102] Whether Hosea castigated his Israelite contemporaries for participation in cultic prostitution or not, the oracles of Hosea 1–3 unquestionably indict them for rejecting Yahweh in favor of Baal. This connection between the imagery of sexual infidelity and the ancestors' worship of Baal becomes most obvious in Hosea 2. In a long and emotionally charged interweaving of accusations and threats, the nation's 'unfaithfulness' is connected to their misunderstanding the source of fertility and, arising out of that misunderstanding, their participation in cultic acts devoted to Baal: 'She did not know that it was I who gave her the grain, the wine, and the oil, and who lavished upon her silver and gold that they used for Baal' (v. 10 [Eng. 8]); 'I will punish her for

---

101. Wolff, *Hosea*, p. 16. In view of the previous discussion of Israelite and Judahite religion in the monarchic period the specific connection with 'Canaanite' cult as something foreign is probably unnecessary.

102. Wilhelm Rudolph, 'Präparierte Jungfrauen? (Zu Hosea 1), *ZAW* 75 (1963), pp. 65-73.

the festival days of the Baals, when she offered incense to them and decked herself with her ring and jewelry, and went after her lovers, and forgot me, says the LORD' (v. 15 [Eng. 13]). There can be no doubt regarding the connection between the worship of Baal and the imagery of sexual unfaithfulness in this text. Further, the restoration of the relationship with Yahweh is depicted as an event which forever banishes the name 'Baal' from the mouth of Israel (v. 18-19 [Eng. 16-17]). Ultimately, however, the specific nature of the cultic practices being condemned is not essential to the reading of these texts within the context of Achaemenid Yehud. Whatever the precise referent of זנונים in the eighth-century context, by the early Persian period the phrase, אשׁת זנונים, with its strong sexual overtones, would be read not only as the substitution of a relationship with Baal for that with Yahweh, but as the rejection of all non-Yahwistic worship. It is the ancestor's lack of sexual fidelity in a relationship in which fidelity would have been expected that dominates the reading of this text in the later period. The infidelity of Gomer to Hosea represents 'the great infidelity of the land from Yahweh' (1.2). The common connection of sexual infidelity with the worship of other deities in the religious discourse of the early Persian period would be decisive for the reading of this text from the book of Hosea. The sexual infidelity of Gomer in her relationship with Hosea would function as an image of the ancestor's inappropriate worship of deities other than Yahweh to the Yehudite monotheists of the early Persian period.

In the first person narrative of Hosea 3 the prophet's love of a woman who has a lover and is an adulteress (מנאפת) is a symbolic action representing the love of Yahweh for a people that has turned to other gods (אלהים אחרים) and loves raisin cakes (3.1).[103] Wolff connects the eating of raisin cakes with participation in the fertility cult and the charge that the people attributed the fertility of the land to Baal.[104] Jeremias, on the other hand, associates the raisin cakes with the cult of Ishtar for

---

103. Wolff notes the contact between this verse and Deuteronomy: the term 'other gods' is common in Deuteronomy but is absent from Amos, Isaiah, and Micah. The 'love of Yahweh' is also found in Deuteronomy but is not in the other eighth-century prophets (Wolff, *Hosea*, p. 60). Likewise, Andersen and Freedman indicate that the verb 'to turn aside' is used to designate apostasy in Deuteronomic vocabulary (e.g. Deut. 29.17; 30.17; 31.18, 20) and that the phrase 'other gods' occurs 15 times in Deuteronomy (*Hosea*, p. 298).

104. Wolff, *Hosea*, p. 61.

whom the Judahites of Jeremiah's day made cakes, an activity which is condemned by Jeremiah: 'to make cakes for the queen of heaven' (Jer. 7.18; cf. 44.19).[105] Whether the Yehudites of the Achaemenid period identified the cakes of this text with the worship of Baal, Asherah, Astarte, Ishtar or a composite figure representing a confluence of the attributes of various ancient Near Eastern goddesses from the Iron Age, the connection with a fertility cult would have been clear for an early Persian period reader.

This text represents the most complete rejection of non-Yahwistic worship in the entire book of Hosea. Although other texts oppose participation in the worship of Baal, reject the use of idols and images in the cult, or simply speak of forsaking Yahweh as infidelity, this text explicitly denounces turning to any other gods as infidelity to Yahweh.[106] Clearly, for a Persian period reader, Hosea 3 would have represented an unambiguous rejection of participation in all non-Yahwistic cultic activities. As a result of its congruence with the emerging orthodox monotheism of the late neo-Babylonian and early Persian periods, this forceful statement in favor of the exclusive worship of Yahweh would also significantly influence the reading of other similar but more ambiguous statements in the book.

There are several texts in the book of Hosea which use similar language and imagery to those discussed in the preceding paragraphs, but which do not make an explicit connection between this imagery and language and the worship of deities other than Yahweh. However, such a connection may well have been made within the framework of the Persian period interpretive conventions. For example, the image of sexual infidelity (זנות) is used in Hos. 4.10b-11a to provide a graphic depiction of the charge that the people had forsaken (עזב) Yahweh, and in Hos. 9.1 the joyful celebrations of the nation are ended because of their infidelity (זנית) 'from your God'.[107] Although the explicit

105. Jorg Jeremias, *Der Prophet Hosea* (Göttingen: Vandenhoeck & Ruprecht, 1983), p. 54. Cf. Ackerman, who argues that the Queen of Heaven is a composite figure combining elements of Ishtar and Astarte (*Under Every Green Tree*, pp. 5-35).

106. The more wide-ranging rejection of all other deities may be indicative of a stage of development in Israelite religion later than the eighth century. It is beyond the scope of this analysis to determine whether this text is representative of the theology of Hosea or a later redactional layer.

107. Interestingly, in this last example their infidelity is paralleled by their love of the fee of a prostitute (אתנן), suggesting the possibility of an actual connection

connection with participation in the cult of other deities is lacking in
these texts, given both the wider literary context of the book in which
such a connection is often made and the Persian period context sketched
above, these accusations of infidelity to Yahweh would likely have been
read by an early Persian period reader as an indictment of non-Yahwistic cultic activities. Such a reading is also suggested by a comparison of Hosea's charge of sexual infidelity away from Yahweh with
Deut. 31.16 and Judg. 2.17. Also note the use of this metaphor in regard
to other illicit religious practices (mediums, child sacrifice, etc.) in the
Holiness Code (Lev. 20.2-6).[108]

Similarly, while never mentioning non-Yahwistic cults, Hos. 5.3-4
presents the separation of Ephraim and Israel from Yahweh as the result
of their deeds which are characterized as sexual infidelity: Ephraim
played the whore, Israel is defiled. In this text 'the spirit of infidelity' is
equated with the fact that 'they do not know Yahweh'. There is, in
Hosea's utilization of ידע ('to know'), an intimacy of relationship
which is related to the use of ידע in other biblical texts to signify sexual
union. דעת אלהים ('knowledge of Yahweh') denotes in Hosea the
primary quality lacking in their relationship with Yahweh, a quality
which is both foundational to and transcends right actions. In 4.1 Yahweh indicts the people for lack of faithfulness, loyalty and knowledge
of God. The absence of these qualities has resulted in the presence of a
variety of social evils. In 6.6 חסד ('loyalty') and דעת אלהים are desired
by Yahweh rather than sacrifice and burnt offerings. Appropriate cultic
worship is not sufficient on its own. The uses of ידע in the book of
Hosea emphasize either the creation of a healthy relationship between
God and the people (2.20) or the absence of such a relationship (6.3;
8.2; 11.3). Returning to Hos. 5.3-4, note the way in which Yahweh's
knowledge of the people and their lack of knowledge of Yahweh stand
in stark contrast to one another and frame the charges of infidelity.
Their lack of knowledge and their infidelity provide a graphic indication of the cleft in the relationship with Yahweh. In the immediate
context, the combination of a technical term for cultic uncleanness
(נטמא; 5.3), the reference to priests (5.1) and the implied reference to
sacrifice in 5.6 (seeking Yahweh with flocks and herds) all suggest
a cultic reading of Ephraim's infidelity.[109] This reading is further

between religious 'infidelity' and sexual practices.
  108. Andersen and Freedman, *Hosea*, pp. 169-70.
  109. Andersen and Freedman, *Hosea*, p. 391.

strengthened by the connection made in 4.6 of the lack of knowledge of the people with the failure of the priests. The priests, as mediators of the relationship between Yahweh and the nation, are given special responsibility for the deplorable condition of the relationship.[110] The people should have known Yahweh but their failure to know is both a cause and a result of their infidelity. The knowledge of Yahweh is incompatible with their infidelity which is exhibited in their inappropriate veneration of Baal.

Hosea 6.10 is less obviously connected with non-Yahwistic cultic acts. The immediate context is principally concerned with ethical or social crimes rather than cultic indiscretions. The pairing of the same terms used in 5.3 to describe the state of the house of Israel, Ephraim's infidelity (זנות) and Israel's defilement (נטמא), however, suggests a connection in this text between ethics and cult.

This connection between ethics and cultic activity is a common theme in literature from the Persian period (e.g. Trito-Isaiah: Isa. 56.1-2, 6-7). In Isa. 57.1-13 (note esp. v. 12) the relationship is the inverse of Hos. 6.10, in Trito-Isaiah the appropriate ethical actions are insufficient if they not accompanied by appropriate cultic actions. Also of special interest is the connection of fasting and ethics in Isaiah 58. Religious actions that are self-serving and combined with oppression of the poor are unacceptable.

Zechariah's response to the question regarding the fasts and laments connected with the exile (Zech. 7.1-7) demonstrates an attitude similar to that of Trito-Isaiah. Significantly, in Zechariah, the judgment on the contemporary practices is based on the authoritative words of the former prophets (v. 7). The use of cultic acts in a manner that is self-serving is compared to the oppression and unethical behavior of the ancestors which led to the desolation of the land (7.8-14). Although some aspects of the religious environment which shaped the interpretation of the earlier prophets had changed, the direct connection between ethics and cult which can be seen in Hosea continues to be found in the discourse of the literature of the early Persian period and is also reflected in their interpretation of these earlier texts.

In the eighth-century socio-religious context, the accusations of sexual infidelity may have been heard primarily or solely as a rejection of Baal as a usurper of the rightful place of Yahweh rather than a rejection

---

110. 'The knowledge of God is the peculiar responsibility of the priest...' (Mays, *Hosea*, p. 63).

of the worship of all deities other than Yahweh. Such a determination is, in part, dependent on decisions regarding the redactional history of Hosea and reconstructions of the social history of eighth-century Israel. In Yehud of the early Persian period, however, given the substantial movement that had occurred toward a normative, monotheistic Yahwism which excluded the worship of all deities other than Yahweh, these texts would have been heard more broadly as judgment on all cultic activity that was not exclusively Yahwistic.[111] For Achaemenid period readers these texts represent the words of a former prophet that confirm their contemporary discourse which perceives all non-Yahwistic worship as infidelity against Yahweh. Indeed, in the case of the connection between ethics and cult, the words of this former prophet correspond to and substantively confirm the Persian period discourse. These words from the book of Hosea also function as a warning that the disasters which befell the ancestors resulted from their infidelity to Yahweh (cf. Zech. 1.2-6). Such a reading of the book of Hosea would provide a powerful tool for the maintenance of the normative Yahwism of the ruling elites which excluded the worship of all deities other than Yahweh.

Non-Yahwistic Cultic Practices

There are several references to a variety of cultic practices that are rejected in the book of Hosea. These practices include: festivals and offerings of incense to the Baals (2.15 [Eng. 13]); either sacrifices (MT) or altars (LXX, Syr, Targ) of which they are to be ashamed (4.19),

111. From the latter part of the Persian period comes the depiction of non-Yahwistic worship as infidelity and marriage to the daughter of a foreign god (Mal. 2.10-16). The depiction of infidelity is introduced by the rhetorical questions: הלוא אב אחד לכלנו הלוא אל אחד בראנו (2.10). These questions clearly assume monotheism as the norm in this period. The early Persian period of our proposed reading of Hosea lies toward the monotheistic end of the trajectory of development from Yahwistic monolatry to the Yahwistic monotheism evident in Malachi. For a fuller discussion of the social setting of this text, see Beth Glazier-McDonald, 'Intermarriage, Divorce, and the *bat-'el nekar*: Insights into Mal 2:10-16', *JBL* 106 (1987), pp. 603-11. Hoglund objects to Glazier-McDonald's reading the text both literally (referring to intermarriage) and symbolically (referring to illicit cultic practices). In relation to the covenantal form of the book of Malachi he prefers to read it symbolically and doubts any connection to the intermarriage prohibitions of Ezra and Nehemiah (Hoglund, *Achaemenid Imperial Administration*, p. 36).

apparently related to the worship of idols (4.17); the multiplication of altars which leads to sin (Hos. 8.11); sacrifices to idols and kissing calves (Hos. 13.2); altars and pillars constructed by Israel and threatened with destruction by Yahweh (Hos. 10.1-2); and gashing[112] themselves for grain and wine (Hos. 7.14). Many of these accusations can be directly related to the worship of Baal which was the primary concern of Hosea. The charge in 2.15 [Eng. 13] is specifically tied to the Baal cult. The references to idols could reflect cult images of Baal, an identification that is made more likely in Hos. 13.2 with the reference to the kissing of calves.[113] The practice of gashing the flesh for the fertility of the land is most likely a reference to the practice of laceration associated with the prophets of Baal (1 Kgs 18.28), but laceration was also associated with rituals for the dead (Jer. 16.6). Although such mortuary rituals were forbidden in Deut. 14.1 and Lev. 19.28, both texts depicting these practices as non-Yahwistic, laceration was apparently practiced in the cult of Yahweh in some periods (Jer. 41.5). A few other texts may present veiled references to participation in the cult of Baal: 'they changed their glory into shame' (Hos. 4.7); Ephraim was determined to go after vanity (Hos. 5.11); and the reference to the national traditions, they consecrated themselves to a thing of shame at Baal-peor (Hos. 9.10). Most, if not all, of these practices would have been interpreted in relation to the cult of Baal in the socio-religious environment of eighth-century Israel. It was not Yahweh-exclusivism which motivated the charges and threats of Hosea but the promotion of the supremacy of Yahweh.

The result of these inappropriate cultic practices is Yahweh's rejection of all of their cultic activities. Yahweh refuses to accept their sacrifices (Hos. 8.13), and their sacrifices have become unacceptable like mourners' bread, that is, food offered for the dead, that leads only to the defilement of those who eat it (Hos. 9.4). Their cult sites are destroyed, thorns and thistles grow on their altars (Hos. 10.8; cf. 12.11), and their oracular priests are consumed by the sword (11.6). The end result of

---

112. Following the LXX. The ךs of דדנ have been confused for ךרנ in the MT.

113. This may be a reference to the calf images used in the Yahwistic worship of Israel but the issue is difficult to determine with certainty. Although they came to be regarded as inappropriate images in the DtrH, the use of bull or calf images in the worship of Yahweh may not always have been regarded as inappropriate. The position of Hosea on such imagery is further complicated by the association of such imagery with Baal and the prophet's strong anti-Baalistic stand.

their deeds is being driven from Yahweh's house (Hos. 9.15).

As has been previously suggested, the altered interpretive environment of early Achaemenid Yehud would result in a somewhat different reading of these texts. The development of an exclusive, monotheistic Yahwism resulted in the rejection of all cultic activities associated with any other deity. The rejection of idols and the multiplication of altars may have been specifically related to Baal worship in an eighth-century understanding of these oracles of Hosea, but they would be interpreted much more broadly by the monotheistic readers in late sixth-century Yehud. The disastrous results that Hosea associated with his contemporaries' participation in the worship of Baal would be attributed to the ancestor's participation in the worship of a variety of deities other than Yahweh by the Persian period reader. The ambiguity of the precise reference of some of the practices being condemned in the book of Hosea only makes them more easily transposed to the concerns of the later interpreters.

There are many strong parallels between these inappropriate cultic activities in the book of Hosea and catalogues of cultic crimes in Trito-Isaiah. In Isa. 57.3-13 the various cultic improprieties include lustful acts under trees (v. 5), sacrifices at high places involving beds (v. 7) and the worship of idols (v. 13). Those who participate in such activities are described as offspring of an adulterer and she who plays the whore (v. 3). In Isa. 65.1-16 the rejected practices of some of the population include mortuary rituals (v. 4) and worship at hilltop shrines (v. 7). Of special significance is the connection of these practices which lead to Yahweh's judgment on them with similar practices by their ancestors (v. 7). The striking similarity in the language of Trito-Isaiah and Hosea with regard to the rejection of these practices provides vital evidence of the interpretive environment in which the book of Hosea was being read. Not only do these texts from Trito-Isaiah indicate that texts with similar themes and language from the book of Hosea might also have been read in relation to these practices in the early Persian period, but the specific connection of the contemporary practices and their outcome with those of the ancestors (Isa. 65.7) suggests the possibility that the author of Trito-Isaiah was reading the texts of the former prophets in just this way.

Concluding Comments

The transformation of the socio-religious environment from the eighth-century context to that of the late sixth century resulted in a different interpretation of the oracles of Hosea. With the shift from a Yahwistic pantheon to Yahwistic monotheism, the oracles of Hosea could now be read in relation to activities which may well have been of no concern to Hosea or his eighth-century readers. The evidence of Trito-Isaiah and First Zechariah indicates that some early Persian period readers were using the words of the earlier prophets as warnings about the relationship of themselves and their contemporaries with Yahweh. The predominance of threats and warnings relating to cultic improprieties and the worship of deities other than Yahweh in Hosea becomes extremely significant in this environment. The overwhelming impression created by all of these texts for the Persian period reader is that cultic improprieties and, specifically, non-Yahwistic cultic acts were a primary, if not *the* primary, cause of the disaster that came upon their ancestors. Trito-Isaiah explicitly connects cultic impurity as cause and disaster as effect, and warns that the same outcome is possible for the descendants if they continue the same practices as their ancestors (65.7). Whether the contemporary Persian period practices were actually the same as those of their eighth-century ancestors may be debatable from our perspective, but in the interpretive context of sixth-century Yehud they were equated. Such a reading of Hosea within the social context of Achaemenid Yehud would have functioned as a powerful rhetorical tool for the maintenance of the normative Yahwism represented by Deutero-Isaiah, DtrH and other post-monarchic biblical traditions. By the early Persian period, the Yehudite elite rejected as illicit the worship of any deity but Yahweh. Their position as authoritative interpreters of the earlier traditions, the gate-keepers to the divine, provided them with the platform to establish their perspective on Yahwism as the dominant perspective within the province. The earlier prophetic traditions, like those preserved in the book of Hosea, would have provided vital, authoritative textual support for this strategy.

Chapter 5

REORIENTING THE DIVINE–HUMAN RELATIONSHIP:
READING HOSEA IN THE EARLY ACHAEMENID PERIOD

The relationship between Yahweh and the people of Israel and Judah is the primary concern of the book of Hosea. The various charges against Israel are often presented as concrete examples of infidelity to their relationship with Yahweh. This infidelity primarily relates to religious apostasy involving Baal, but also includes alliances with foreign powers, reliance on military power, and ethical improprieties.[1]

As has been indicated in the preceding chapters, the experience of reading (or hearing) these oracles would be substantially different in the Persian period than would have been the case in the eighth century. The text would be constituted with a considerably different texture when read within the new socio-historical context of early Achaemenid Yehud. The following analysis highlights certain aspects of that texture.

*Reading within the Lines: The Function of the Superscription
and Postscript to the Book of Hosea*

The superscriptions of the prophetic books of the Hebrew Bible appear as titles or headings that have a unique, but ill-defined, relationship to the remainder of the text. The function of the superscriptions of the prophetic books is a question that has often been neglected in critical biblical commentaries. What do they do? Or, perhaps a more precise question in a reader-oriented theoretical environment, 'What happens when they are read?' As was argued in Chapter 1, this is both a question of literary effect and of historical context. In the case of the book of Hosea, the superscription is complemented by a postscript (14.9 [Eng. 10]). Similar questions regarding its function need to be addressed. The physical location of these verses at the beginning and ending of the text

---

1. See Chapters 2–4.

means that they provide the textual boundaries for any reading of the entire book or any reading of parts of the book that is cognizant of the whole. The prophetic texts could be read within any socio-historical context after they were written but the superscriptions (and postscript in the case of Hosea) provide not only a literary but also a historical framework within which to read them. If, as is commonly believed, the texts of many of the prophetic books did not reach their final form until the neo-Babylonian or early Persian periods, what would have happened when these superscriptions were read in that specific socio-historical setting?

The Superscription: Establishing the Story World
The superscription of Hosea opens the book with the affirmation that the text which follows is 'the word of Yahweh' (דבר יהוה). The phrase, דבר יהוה אשר היה אל ('the word of Yahweh that came to') followed by the name of the recipient of the divine revelation, is a characteristic way of identifying a word that had its origin in Yahweh. The same heading is used in Joel 1.1, Mic. 1.1 and Zech. 1.1.[2] This phrase, or minor variations of it, is also used extensively in Jeremiah, Ezekiel and the Deuteronomistic History to introduce the content of a revelation of Yahweh to an individual, or at the head of individual prophetic oracles.[3] Of prime importance is the theological function of such an introductory formula. This heading makes a particular claim about the words that follow, investing them with authority for the Yahwistic reader.[4]

The use of this phrase at the head of a collection of prophetic oracles and narratives, as a means of identifying the whole compilation as דבר יהוה, was probably one of the earliest stages in the transition from oral traditions to the production and preservation of written texts regarded as authoritative scripture. As was previously indicated,[5] the end of the monarchic state, the deportation of many Judahite elites to Babylonia,

2.   Wolff suggests that the common headings of these works (less Joel) may indicate a circle of exilic editors that completed a collection of pre-exilic prophetic sayings (*Hosea*, p. 4). The predominance of the phrase דבר יהוה אשר היה אל in literature from the sixth century (DtrH, Jeremiah and Ezekiel) makes this a likely reconstruction.

3.   1 Sam. 15.10; 2 Sam. 7.4; 1 Kgs 6.11; 13.20; 16.1, 7; 17.2, 8; 18.31; 19.9; 21.17, 28; Jer. 1.2, 4, 11, 13; 2.1; 13.3; etc.; Ezek. 1.3; 3.16; 6.1; etc.

4.   Tucker, 'Prophetic Superscriptions', p. 68; see also Mays, *Hosea*, p. 20.

5.   See Chapter 1, 'Reading Prophetic Texts in Yehud'.

and the subsequent adaptations to life under Persian rule, contributed to a new perception of prophecy. Schniedewind's work indicates that the phrase, דבר יהוה, which had been used in reference to prophetic oracles in the monarchic period, came to be used as a designation for divinely authorized texts in the Persian period.[6] Thus, authoritative texts, including collections of earlier prophetic oracles, assumed the role filled by classical prophecy in the monarchic period. While it would be anachronistic to see this phrase as confirmation of the existence of a canon of scripture in the neo-Babylonian or early Persian period, it does have the effect of raising the reader's expectations regarding the importance of the word (דבר יהוה) which follows, and also functions to create an aura of sacredness about the text. As דבר יהוה, this document, and other sacred books like the book of the Torah (cf. Neh. 8), would be held in higher esteem than documents of purely human origin, such as contracts, provincial administrative documents, and so on, and would be treated with a great deal of reverence.

The authority conveyed by the designation of a text as דבר יהוה is of primary significance to the social setting in the early Persian period. The provincial elites in Yehud, as restorers of the temple of Yahweh and official interpreters of these divinely authorized texts, would derive a substantial benefit from their position in relation to these texts. The establishment of their rule and the imposition of their administrative vision on the provincial population would be heavily dependent on their role as the interpretive gate-keepers to the דבר יהוה that had come to be principally identified with these texts.

The text designated as דבר יהוה, however, is not just any word or a completely decontextualized word. It is a *particular* word of Yahweh; one that came to a particular individual in a particular historical situation.[7] Although these particularizing elements (word which came *to Hosea, in the days of* specific kings of Judah and Israel) are subordinated grammatically to the primary affirmation of divine origin and authorization, their significance must not be neglected. The subordinate clauses, which modify this דבר יהוה, function to root the text in a specific historical setting in the reading community's own past. The first identifies the prophetic agent through whom this particular דבר יהוה came. As was noted above, this was a typical way of introducing

6. Schniedewind, *The Word of God in Transition*, pp. 130-38.
7. See Gene M. Tucker, 'Hosea', in James L. Mays (ed.), *Harper's Bible Commentary* (San Francisco: Harper & Row, 1988), pp. 707-15 (710).

written accounts of prophetic revelation. The identification of the prophet is a consistent element in this formula, perhaps serving to validate the following text in the eyes of the reading community by locating the text's origin in a prophet whose Yahwistic authority was recognized by the community.

The two בימי ('in the days of') clauses also function to provide historical grounding for the text that follows.[8] But the way in which this historical grounding functions needs to be explored further. In the circles of historical-critical scholarship these clauses have generally resulted in the text of Hosea (or at least those parts judged to be genuinely Hosean in origin) being read within the context of a critically reconstructed history of Israel and Judah (and the ancient Near East generally) during the eighth century BCE. While this reading of the text of Hosea within a critically reconstructed history has provided valuable insights regarding both the book of Hosea and eighth-century Israelite and Judahite history and religion, it is certainly a form of reading the book which is unique to modern, critical biblical scholarship. Certainly no one would argue that the final redactor of the book intended that the reader disassemble the final form into its constituent Hoseanic and redactional pieces, critically reconstruct the history of the various periods in which these constituent pieces were produced, and then read the various pieces within the chronologically appropriate, critically reconstructed historical frameworks. Rather, the entire text as it now stands would have been read within the historical framework suggested by the superscription in the ancient world.

What would have been known about the history of the period indicated by this royal date formula in the ancient world some 200 or more years later? Even in our own age with vast amounts of historical research and some requirement of historical study in our standard

---

8.　Jeremias makes this point: 'So betont die Überschrift mit nüchternen Daten, daß Gottes Wort zu bestimmter Zeit an bestimmte Personen ergeht, weil es geschichtliches Wort ist' (*Der Prophet Hosea*, p. 23). Note also the comment of Hans Wildberger regarding the superscription of the book of Isaiah: 'Providing information about the date betrays, of course, an awareness that the understanding of a prophetic message cannot simply ignore details of the time and place in which this occurs. If the reader wants to press on to understand what is written, he or she would have to make an application which is specifically based on what happened "then and there"' (*Isaiah 1–12* [Continental Commentaries; Minneapolis: Fortress Press, 1991], p. 7).

Notice the similar formula in the introduction of Ruth (1.1): בימי שפט השפטים.

educational programs, most modern readers have only a very limited
and unsophisticated knowledge of events 200 or 300 years in our own
past. The history of Israel and Judah known to Yehudite readers of the
final form of Hosea (and prophetic literature in general) would not have
been the history of the modern, critical scholar, but the popular traditions about the nation's past preserved in the stories that circulated in
the court, home and cult.[9] Some of these historical traditions have been
distilled into the narratives of the Deuteronomistic History and Chronicles. Others have been preserved in the prophetic books. Many others,
undoubtedly, passed out of existence long ago. These historical traditions, far more concerned with the theological significance of Israel's
history than with historical veracity, would have been the 'historical'
frame of reference for ancient readers of the words: בימי עזיה יותם אחז
יחזקיה מלכי יהודה ובימי ירבעם ('in the days of Uzziah, Jotham, Ahaz
and Hezekiah, kings of Judah, and in the days of Jereboam').[10]

This is significant for reading Hosea because the superscription then
functions to set the following text within a particular story world with a
very specific narrative and theological shape, not within a general
historical period with little or no specific content, nor within a precise,
scholarly reconstruction of the events of the period. What has functioned as the historical context for understanding the text which follows
this formula, from the final editor(s) and first readers of the text to
recent times, is not 'what really happened' (representing a modern,
positivistic distinction between historical narrative with its interpretive
perspective and the actual, uninterpreted events), but the theologically
charged account of the reigns of these specific kings of Israel and Judah
that circulated in the political and religious traditions of neo-Babylonian Judah and Achaemenid Yehud.[11] The Deuteronomistic History

---

9.   This would have been true not only for readers in the period immediately
following the completion of the text in its final form but also for all readers until the
advent of critical histories of Israel and Judah in the nineteenth century. Indeed, this
remains true for many readers even since the advent of critical histories.

10.   They continue to function in this way. The starting point of every historical
reconstruction of the setting of the words of the eighth-century prophets continues
to be the Deuteronomistic History. Very little about the period can be known otherwise. As Miller has recently argued, although it is possible to write a history of
ancient Israel and Judah without making use of the information contained in the
Hebrew Bible, the resulting volume would be very small and would bear little
resemblance to recent treatments ('History of Israel', pp. 93-102).

11.   Danna Nolan Fewell has made a similar suggestion regarding the function

and the Chronicles provide substantial insight into the theologically constructed history that most likely would have been known to Persian period readers of Hosea.[12] Both of these collections of Israel's historical traditions are concerned with the events of the past, real people and places, but they are more concerned with the theological significance of these historical events than with history for its own sake. The Chronicler's substantial alterations to the events as recounted in the Deuteronomistic History are indicative of the primary value given to the theological interpretation of history, sometimes at the expense of the facts of what actually happened.

Just such a theologico-historical exegetical interest in the monarchic period prophetic traditions is evident in First Zechariah. The book demonstrates a concern in the early Persian period for the relevance of the authoritative words of the 'former prophets' to life in Achaemenid Yehud. The opening oracle of Zechariah calls on the Yehudites, unlike their ancestors, to be faithful to Yahweh. The words of the former prophets spoken to the ancestors are summarized, 'Thus says the LORD of hosts, Return from your evil ways and from your evil deeds'. But, Zechariah notes, the ancestors did not listen to the warnings of the former prophets (Zech. 1.4). The community is reminded that even though both the ancestors and the former prophets are now dead, the words of Yahweh spoken by the former prophets overtook their ancestors. Significantly, both the prophets and their audience are no longer present, but the words of the former prophets remain and continue to be of value to life in Yehud.

The significance of Zechariah's historically grounded exegesis of the former prophets is indicated by the response of the community reported in the concluding summary of the oracle: 'So they repented and said, "The LORD of hosts has dealt with us according to our ways and deeds, just as he planned to do"' (Zech. 1.6). Thus the interpretation of the monarchic period prophetic traditions within the theological and sociohistorical context of early Achaemenid Yehud functioned as the foundation for understanding the contemporary community's relationship

of Dan. 1.1 (*Circle of Sovereignty: A Story of Stories in Daniel 1–6* [JSOTSup, 72; Bible and Literature Series, 20; Sheffield: Almond Press, 1988], p. 34).

12. This does not mean that the Persian period readers of Hosea would have read the text with a copy of the Deuteronomistic History or Chronicles open beside them for reference purposes but that these texts preserve (at least) two versions of the historical traditions that would have been known to these readers.

with Yahweh. Specifically, these traditions functioned as the basis for confession of communal sins so that the broken relationship of the past could be reoriented in the renewed setting of Persian period Yehud. This use of the prophetic traditions in First Zechariah provides an important indication of the way in which the book of Hosea would be heard in this context. The book of Hosea recounts the sin and guilt of the ancestors and then concludes with a graphic description of punishment followed by confession of sin and renewal of the divine–human relationship. This movement in the book well fits the interpretive environment indicated in Zechariah.

By means of the superscription and its royal dating formula, the text of the book of Hosea is set within a framework that provides not simply a historical setting but also a theologico-historical setting for reading the דבר יהוה אשר היה אל הושע ('the word of Yahweh that came to Hosea').[13] The word of Yahweh, then, is heard within both the life setting of the Persian period readers and the story world of Israel's historical traditions as they were remembered and shaped by the reading community. Thus, this is the word of Yahweh not only for eighth-century Israel and Judah but also the contemporary world of the reader, interpreted through the lens of the narrated world of the community's history.[14]

---

13. This is a very different function from the Akkadian and Greek colophons which appear at the end of their respective documents and provide information about scribal production. These colophons provided the assurance that the copied text was accurate but they do not set the text within a particular interpretive horizon. On this issue with regard to the Psalms, see Bruce K. Waltke, 'Superscripts, Postscripts, or Both', *JBL* 110 (1991), pp. 583-96.

14. Commenting on the tension between the original, historical setting of the prophetic oracles and their continuing reuse, Robert Alter suggests: 'Such speech is directed to the concrete situation of a historical audience, but the form of speech exhibits the historical indeterminacy of the language of poetry, which helps explain why these discourses have touched the lives of millions of readers far removed in time, space, and political predicament from the small groups of ancient Hebrews against whom Hosea, Isaiah, Jeremiah, and their confreres originally inveighed' (*The Art of Biblical Poetry* [New York: Basic Books, 1985], p. 141). Similarly, commenting on the effect of the historical elements in the superscription, Francis Landy: 'The distance in time and space, the location in a now vanished *alter ego*, makes of the narrative and prophecy a parable, an image of oneself as other, perceived timelessly and objectively' (*Hosea* [Readings; Sheffield: Sheffield Academic Press, 1995], p. 21. The effect of providing the reader 'an image of oneself as other' seems accurate, but the timelessness and objectivity of this image are problematic.

The Postscript: Re-evaluating the Reading Experience

The world of the reader is the primary and explicit focus of the book's postscript (14.10 [Eng. 9]). While the superscription functions to set the reading of the prophecies of the book of Hosea within the story world of Israel's historical traditions, the postscript shifts the significance of understanding the text of the book to the contemporary situation of the reader. The opening claim of divine origin (דבר יהוה) invests the text with a high level of authority for the Persian period reader but the postscript more explicitly extends the relevance of this word to the reader's current situation. The postscript reminds the reader that the importance of this דבר יהוה is not limited to the community's past, but that it is also pertinent to the community's present. By placing the variation in outcome between walking or stumbling in 'these things' on the perceptiveness of the reader, the postscript warns that there are consequences that result from one's relationship to the words of the book. This is not a text of purely antiquarian interest but one that contains the word of Yahweh for the present.[15]

מי חכם ויבן אלה נבון וידעם
כי־ישרים דרכי יהוה וצדקים ילכו בם
ופשעים יכשלו בם

> Whoever is wise will understand these things;
> whoever is perceptive will know them.
> For the ways of Yahweh are upright and the
> righteous will walk in them,
> but the rebellious will stumble in them (14.10).

The reader is freed to see an image of self through the lens of the text, but this image is subject to shaping by the reader's context, interpretive conventions, and historical knowledge.

15. 'The words of v. 10 [Eng. 9] serve as a reminder to readers of all generations that Hosea's message continues as a message for them. The words are not simply directed to his contemporaries, thus being of no more than arcane interest to us. Rather, the "ways of Yahweh" are a guide to the righteous, and a source of understanding to the intelligent of all successive periods' (Stuart, *Hosea–Jonah* [WBC; Waco, TX: Word Books, 1987], p. 220). 'It is the last addition to the written form of the book and was added in the exilic or post-exilic period. Some reader of the period schooled in the reflections of Wisdom, and painfully aware that Hosea's prophecy had truly disclosed Yahweh's will, commends the book to the wise and perceptive of all generations' (Mays, *Hosea*, p. 190).

It has often been noted that the language of this verse is drawn from the standard vocabulary of wisdom texts of the Hebrew Bible.[16] This is clearly correct as a general observation, but to view this verse simply as a wisdom supplement tacked onto the end of the text would be overly simplistic and would miss important nuances. This final, reflective verse also uses vocabulary from the preceding oracles to reflect several important aspects of the book.[17] The wisdom (חכם) and perception (בין) demanded by the postscript have been noticeably absent in the prophet's depiction of the ancestors:

ועם לא־יבין ילבט

a people without perception will be trampled (4.14);

הוא־בן לא חכם

he is an unwise son (13.13).

Stumbling (כשל), which results from a lack of wisdom and insight, characterizes priests and prophets (4.5), Ephraim and Judah (5.5), and summarizes their situation in the call for confession:

כי כשלת בעונך

for you have stumbled as a result of your sin (14.2 [Eng. 1]).

'Accordingly, what is clearly contrived in xiv 10 (9) is nonetheless carefully and sensitively contrived; its thought is essentially continuous with the material which it seeks to elucidate.'[18]

Beyond the immediate Hoseanic context, this verse is also reflective of the collecting and reinterpreting of earlier traditions that occurred during the neo-Babylonian and Persian periods. This process of editing earlier traditions was particularly concerned with the need to make sense of the new situation in which the community found itself; that is,

16. Davies, *Hosea*, pp. 309-10. Mays, *Hosea*, p. 190. Brevard S. Childs, *Introduction to the Old Testament as Scripture* (Philadelphia: Fortress Press, 1979), p. 382.

17. C.L. Seow, 'Hosea 14:10 and the Foolish People Motif', *CBQ* 44 (1982), pp. 212-24. Seow highlights many similarities in perspective between the postscript and the remainder of the book.

18. A.A. Macintosh, 'Hosea and the Wisdom Tradition: Dependence and Independence', in John Day, Robert P. Gordon and H.G.M. Williamson (eds.), *Wisdom in Ancient Israel: Essays in Honour of J.A. Emerton* (Cambridge: Cambridge University Press, 1995), pp. 124-32 (124).

it was not motivated by an arcane interest in the past but, as this text states, by the belief that these traditions continued to be of value in their contemporary setting. The use of wisdom vocabulary and style in the postscript indicates a common social and theological matrix not only with the classic wisdom texts of the Hebrew Bible but also with the Deuteronomistic texts.[19] The presence of this vocabulary, which is often associated with wisdom circles, indicates the wisdom or, perhaps better, scribal influences that permeate the post-monarchic editorial layers and texts of the Hebrew Bible. Given the relatively small population of Yehud in the Persian period, and the highly limited access to literacy at a level capable of producing and reading these texts, it appears unwise to suggest the existence of a variety of disparate schools or circles. In fact, given the similarities in style and vocabulary in the later biblical texts, a common social milieu among the educated elites of Achaemenid Yehud is most likely for the production of the final forms of many of the texts of the Hebrew Bible.

This postscript indicates that for the wise and discerning reader, the preceding prophetic oracles will provide instruction on living in relationship with Yahweh. The first line of the verse (מי חכם וי ב ן אלה נבון) opens with a pair of coordinated questions, 'who is wise... who is perceptive'.[20] Each of these questions is followed by a jussive with ו indicating a contingent relationship between the question and the verbal action;[21] 'whoever is wise will understand these things' and 'whoever is perceptive will know them'. The realization of the significance of the book is contingent upon the wisdom and understanding of the reader. There is a mirror opposite of this text in Deut. 32.29: 'If they were wise [חכמו], they would understand this; they would discern [יבין] what the end would be.' This verse occurs in a context in which the nation is castigated for its infidelity to Yahweh, including the worship of other deities, and participation in 'strange' cultic practices. Deut. 32.29 suggests that *if* they had been wise they would have perceived the connection between faithfulness to Yahweh and the maintenance of

19. For a detailed discussion of the relationship between Deuteronomistic literature and Wisdom literature see Moshe Weinfeld, *Deuteronomy and the Deuteronomic School* (Oxford: Clarendon Press, 1972), pp. 244-319. See also Wolff, *Hosea*, p. 239; Stuart, *Hosea–Jonah*, p. 219; Mays, *Hosea*, p. 190.

20. The מי being understood at the beginning of the second question.

21. See GKC, §109, i.

their peace and prosperity.[22] Similarly, Deut. 4.6 connects obedience to
Yahweh's statutes with the judgment of others that the Israelites are
wise (חכם) and perceptive (בין). These texts indicate the theological
context in which this warning in Hos. 14.10 would have been interpreted. According to the postscript, the significance of the preceding
text is only available to the wise and perceptive reader; wisdom and
understanding are inherently related to fidelity to Yahweh in this
perspective.[23] This warning corresponds to the earlier observation that
'a people without understanding [בין] comes to ruin' (Hos. 4.14; cf.
Prov. 10.8).

According to the postscript, the ability to understand the message of
the preceding text is vital because the righteous walk (הלך) in the ways
of Yahweh but the rebellious stumble (כשל) in them. The phrase, דרכי
יהוה ('ways of Yahweh'), particularly in conjunction with הלך, is
found almost exclusively in Deuteronomistic texts (Deut. 8.6; 10.12;
11.22; 19.9; 26.17; 28.9; 30.16; Josh. 22.5; Judg. 2.22; 1 Kgs 2.3; 3.14;
8.58; 11.33; 11.38). In addition, the phrase occurs once each in Deutero-
Isaiah ('in whose ways they would not walk', Isa. 42.24) and First
Zechariah ('if you will walk in my ways', Zech. 3.7). Within this (con)-
textual environment, an early Persian period reader would most likely
have correlated 'walking in the way(s) of Yahweh' with fidelity to the
demands of Yahweh, particularly as they are expressed in the Deuteronomistic theology.

Other texts in the Hebrew Bible counsel a similar reflection on the
past. Psalm 107, for example, recounts the (historic) saving acts of Yahweh on behalf of the community, and then the wise (חכם, v. 43) are
admonished to 'give heed to these things, and consider [hithpolel of
בין] the steadfast love of Yahweh'. There is something in the recitation
of the past experiences of the community's relationship with Yahweh
that is understood to be instructive for the reader's present relationship
with Yahweh. A analogous perspective is presented in Jeremiah 9.
Immediately following the oracle about the destruction of Jerusalem
and Judah for a variety of sins, there is a prose section (9.11-15 [Eng.
12-16]) which focuses on the moral of these events: who is wise enough

---

22. This text also contains an appeal to consider the present in relation to the
past: 'consider [בין] the ages past' (32.7).

23. Note also the similarity to the judgment of Yahweh depicted as beginning
with the removal of the ability to perceive (בין) and understand (ידע) in Isa. 6.9-10.

to discern (מי־הזאיש החכם ויבן). This text calls for reflection on the cause of the nation's destruction: their forsaking the law of Yahweh.

All of these texts value reflection on the past and the possibility that such reflection offers insight and perspective on the present situation. Experienceing the past vicariously through the medium of the written text gives direction to life in the present. In the case of the book of Hosea this instruction places the reader in the dual role of listening to the oracles from the perspective of the ancestors (as preserved in Israel's historical traditions), and listening to the oracles from the reader's own contemporary perspective. The reader is placed in a privileged position because now the outcome of these words spoken to the ancestors is known. But, by wise and perceptive reflection on these things, the reader's own situation can be illuminated.

For the Persian period reader the postscript of Hosea demands a decision regarding the significance of the book as a whole.[24] Instruction about life with Yahweh in the present is to be derived from reflection on the word of Yahweh spoken to the ancestors about their life with Yahweh. Such instruction is only available to the reader who is wise and perceptive. Thus the reader is left with a choice. The reader can either be one of the wise, discerning individuals who walk in the ways of Yahweh as a result of their reading of the book or one of the rebellious who stumble in the ways of Yahweh.

The superscription and the postscript of the book of Hosea function much like the frame of a painting, determining how one experiences the scene depicted within the frame. Just as the color and shape of a frame can provide emphasis to certain colors and shapes within the painting and de-emphasize others, so these verses provide a frame that dramatically shapes the reading of the text which lies between them. This shaping functions effectively for both a sequential reading of the whole and for readings of portions of the text by those who are cognizant of the whole. Even the experience of reading a few verses from the middle of the book is affected for the reader who is aware of the contextualizing framework provided by the superscription and postscript. All readings of the book, past and present, would be significantly different without the context provided by these verses.

24. Cf. Wolff, *Hosea*, p. 240.

The Shape of Reading Hosea in Early Achaemenid Yehud

The following sketch of a Persian period reading of Hosea will more fully develop one coherent structure that can emerge from a reading of the whole book and will indicate the rich possibilities offered by a reader-oriented analysis that is cognizant of the socio-historical setting in which the reading occurred. As indicated above, the superscript and postscript of the book of Hosea create specific expectations for a Persian period reader. The superscription signals that the text that follows will present the words of Yahweh concerning a past generation which, from the reader's privileged vantage point, was judged unfaithful and punished with exile.[25] The book of Hosea is primarily concerned with what constitutes faithfulness to the relationship with Yahweh and this perspective dominates the depiction of the monarchic period ancestors. Various aspects of the life of the ancestors are subsumed under the image of infidelity in the book. This perception of the past forms an important part of the interpretive framework for reading Hosea in the early Persian period.

The Depiction of Judah in Hosea

An examination of the portrayal of Judah in the book of Hosea highlights the value of a reading of the book which is cognizant of the shape of the whole. A great deal has been written concerning the status of Judah in the text of Hosea. The interest has primarily focused on whether these references are original to the preaching of Hosea or whether they are the result of redactional activity in Judean circles. In a reader-oriented analysis, the questions shift away from concerns about the origin of these references to the reader's encounter with them within the literary context of the book as a whole and the socio-historical context of the period in which they are read. Since the superscription establishes the story world of the book within the eighth century BCE, the reader's expectations regarding the referents of the terms 'Israel' and 'Judah' are shaped by the knowledge that they referred to two kingdoms, inhabiting specific geographical areas at that time. This is highlighted immediately by the separate listing of the kings of Judah and the king of Israel who ruled during the period covered by the

---

25. On the significance of exile to the Persian period community see the discussion in Chapter 2, 'Exile, Return, and the Desolate Land'.

contents of the book (Hos. 1.1). This initial separation of the two establishes an environment in which the reader is able to distinguish Israel
and its relationship with Yahweh from Judah and its relationship with
Yahweh. This is immediately reinforced by a strong distinction between
the two in the opening verses of the book. The clearly separate identity
of the two kingdoms at the beginning of the book provides the basis for
a gradual merging of the two during the reading process. From the
perspective of the Achaemenid reader, the understanding of Judah and
its relationship to Yahweh changes within the book from one which is
initially positive to one in which it is almost entirely identified with the
negative judgment on Israel.

The first reference to Judah (1.7) is one of unrestrained compassion
by God toward Judah. In contrast to the surrounding context of accusations and threats against Israel, Judah is distinguished in this text by
Yahweh's concern. Yahweh pledges to have compassion on Judah
(רחם), which clearly distinguishes it from the total breakdown in the
relationship between Yahweh and Israel, depicted as לא רחמה ('not
pitied') in 1.6. Yahweh not only promises Judah compassion but also
salvation. This salvation is based not on military preparations and
actions but solely on Yahweh their God. Although a Persian period
reader might experience a degree of dissonance reading these words in
a historical and social context in which the memories of defeat and
deportation were still vivid, the story world of the text, created by
reading the superscription, permits this to be attributed by the reader to
a time before Judah came under the judgment of Yahweh. Thus, the
reader's initial encounter with these two central 'characters' in the book
is one in which Judah is depicted in a very positive manner.

There is a certain lack of clarity to the characterization of Judah in
the first salvation oracle of the book (2.2 [Eng. 1.11]). Without the
knowledge of the destruction of Jerusalem and the exile to Babylon, a
reader could interpret this reference to the gathering together of Israel
and Judah as a return of Israel to the positive status enjoyed by Judah.
Within the context of the historical knowledge of a Yehudite reader,
however, the depiction is ambiguous. Clearly, Israel is the primary
focus of the salvation oracle. In relation to the immediately preceding
context, it is the Israelites who are once again called 'Children of the
living God' (2.1 [Eng. 1.10]). But this primary focus on Israel, which
involves a gathering of both Israelites and Judahites under a single
head, would have been shaped in the early Persian period by the

recognition that both Israelites and Judahites needed to return to the land. The experience of reading this text in a period after the destruction of Jerusalem and the exile of a significant number of the local populace would create some tension for the Yehudite reader. Within the space of a few verses, Judah is promised protection and salvation and then included in an oracle of salvation that presumes preceding punishment. Although Judah has not been singled out for criticism in the book, the Yehudite reader has knowledge of the events that came later in the nation's history and hears a faint hint of those later events in this oracle of salvation.

Upon reaching 4.15 the reader's perception of the depiction of Judah is further complicated when the Judahites are the subject of a warning: 'Do not let Judah become guilty.' The contrast with the infidelity of Israel is reminiscent of ch. 1 but the warning of possible guilt is a significant shift from the promise of salvation in 1.7. The ambiguity that would have been created for the Yehudite reader by the inclusion of Judah in the oracle of salvation (2.1-2) would be strengthened by this warning of possible guilt. The possibility that the Judahites may share the fate of the Israelites would be reinforced by the community's theologico-historical traditions regarding the guilt and eventual punishment of both Israel and Judah.

The ambiguity regarding Judah is entirely erased and replaced with a negative judgment beginning in ch. 5. In Hos. 5.5 Judah begins to merge with Ephraim and Israel, 'Judah also stumbles with them'. No longer are the Judahites distinguished from the Israelites by their positive relationship with Yahweh. The preceding references to Judah, which created a sense of ambiguity, are perceived as indications of the shifting place of Judah in the movement of the book. By Hosea 5, the Judahites are not the subject of warnings about possible guilt but rather are equally guilty of crimes against Yahweh. The princes of Judah are the subject of serious accusations, and become a target for God's wrath (5.10). Finally, God threatens to be like rottenness (כָּרָקָב; 5.12) and a young lion (5.14) to Judah. In both 5.12 and 5.14 the threat to the Judahites parallels a similar fate for Ephraim. By the end of Hosea 5, the fate of Judah has become identified with that of Israel. Both the Israelites and the Judahites are rejected by Yahweh and under the same threat of punishment.

Thus, when the people are given their first opportunity to speak in 6.1-3, the Judahites have been assimilated with the Israelites; the two share a common fate before Yahweh. A reader familiar with the history of the two separate kingdoms would recognize that, although a geographical distinction still existed, the two separate peoples with separate fates have now become one. Now both speak with a single voice in the text. This impression of common status is confirmed by Yahweh's parallel rhetorical questions in 6.4, 'What shall I do with you, O Ephraim? What shall I do with you, O Judah?' From this point on in the text, 'Judah' becomes little more than another synonym for 'God's sinful people'. Although the historical reality of separate kingdoms remains, Judah and Israel stand together as one people under the judgment of Yahweh.

The reference to Judah in 12.1 has often been interpreted as reflecting a different status for Judah than that of Israel. Note the NRSV translation (12.1 [Eng. 11.12]):

> Ephraim has surrounded me with lies,
> and the house of Israel with deceit;
> but Judah still walks with God,
> and is faithful to the Holy One.

This translation of the MT depends on understanding רוד as a positive description of Judah's 'walking with God' but the usual translation of רוד ('to roam'), would normally indicate a negative activity in relation to one's relationship with Yahweh.[26] The connection of אל with Yahweh, the God of Israel and Judah, is possible but not the only possibility. Further, the translation of קדושׁים by 'Holy One' understands this term as a majestic plural which would be a highly unusual usage. Wolff has suggested that the קדושׁים are those prophets and Levites who were associated with Hosea and, because they were persecuted in Israel, who sought refuge in Judah.[27] The translation of this verse as a positive contrast of Judah against Israel is both unexpected and difficult to justify on the basis of the MT.

Alternatively, Mays suggests that this text would more obviously be translated:

> He still wanders after El [the Canaanite high god]
> and is faithful to the Holy Ones [members of the heavenly court of El].

---

26. Cf. Gen. 27.40; Jer. 2.31. Both of these texts suggest a breaking free from an appropriate authority.

27. Wolff, *Hosea*, p. 210.

On the basis of this translation, he suggests that the text was originally a continuation of the negative depiction of Israel that has been
subsequently altered by the insertion of ויהודה ('and/but Judah') by an
editor.[28] This translation of the text has the advantage of not requiring
recourse to highly unlikely readings of the Hebrew of this verse.
Whether Mays's suggestion that ויהודה is secondary in the text is
correct or not, the negative assessment of Judah is consistent with the
developing portrayal of Judah within the book of Hosea. Only a positive evaluation of the Judahites would be unexpected for a reader familiar with the contents of the book. Thus in the course of the reading
experience, the reader of the book of Hosea moves from viewing Judah
as standing in sharp contrast to the evils of Israel in the opening
chapters, to seeing absolutely no difference between the two ancient
Yahwistic kingdoms.

Topography of a Persian Period Reading of Hosea
The following analysis is an attempt to present an overview of the
experience of reading the book of Hosea from within the reconstructed
Persian period context. As a topographical map depicts the variations in
terrain, this examination will highlight the changing terrain experienced
in reading the book in this context—a topography of Hosea in the early
Persian period. One of the most substantial differences between a late
sixth-century reading of Hosea and readings in earlier socio-historical
settings is that it is actually possible to propose a topography of reading
the book. It is unlikely that the book, as it now stands, existed in earlier
periods. The arrangement of the oracles, the key turning points in the
progression of the events of the book, and the influence of these on
the interpretation of the individual oracles are all new considerations
for the interpretation of the words of Hosea. While some aspects of the
interpretation of specific oracles may be quite similar in both the eighth-
century setting and the late sixth-century setting, the existence of a
book of Hosea and the effect of this format on the interpretation of the
parts is a significant transformation in the reading of these oracles.

---

28. Mays, *Hosea*, p. 160. Andersen and Freedman strongly favor reading this
text as a negative judgment of Judah and a reference to gods other than Yahweh
(*Hosea*, pp. 602-603). Davies appears to consider a reading similar to this the most
likely understanding of the MT but does not clearly opt for a particular interpretation (*Hosea*, pp. 270-71). Cf. James M. Ward, *Hosea: A Theological Commentary* (New York: Harper & Row, 1966), pp. 208-209.

One of the difficulties in establishing a topography of the book of Hosea in the Persian period is identifying the key transitional points in the text for a reader of that period. It is possible, however, that the important points of transition could be similar for a variety of readers through time. Past studies of Hosea have often noted breaks or shifts in the text between chs. 3 and 4, and to a lesser degree, between chs. 11 and 12. Although the major demarcation of the text between chs. 3 and 4 has often overstated the cleft,[29] these analyses are reflective of a common experience shared by a variety of readers. These observations can be supplemented by the additional observation that ch. 14, both as a result of its position at the conclusion of the book and in light of its content, functions as a (the?) primary break or turning point in the experience of reading the book. Finally, the dramatic depiction of failed reconciliation (6.1-3) rises above the surrounding context of harsh accusations, and functions as a significant turning point in the reading process.

All of these suggested turning points share in common their function as the climax to a movement from judgment to (promise of) reconciliation. It was suggested earlier that this movement is a common feature of the structure of prophetic texts deriving from this period. The analysis by Ben Zvi has indicated that there is a common tripartite structure to Isaiah, Jeremiah (LXX), Ezekiel and Zephaniah, involving movement from accusation/threat against Israel and Judah, to oracles against foreign nations, and ending with oracles of salvation. He attributes this common structure to the editing of these texts in the Persian period.[30] Similarly, each section of Hosea ending with one of these key texts follows—with the modification of omitting the oracles against foreign nations—this common pattern of organization evident in other prophetic texts edited during this period. The existence of this common structure, evident in different prophetic texts whose form evolved from editing in the neo-Babylonian or Persian periods, indicates that this structure expressed something of the contemporary understanding of the words of the earlier prophets. The arrangement of the prophetic oracles that moves from judgment to salvation is common to most of the texts which derive from this period. This common arrangement indicates a perception of the words of earlier prophets that focused on

29. At the most extreme even positing 1 and 2 Hosea: Kaufmann, *The Religion of Israel*, pp. 368-77.

30. Ben Zvi, *Zephaniah*, p. 346.

renewal of relationship with Yahweh. The presence of this organizational principle in the collection of Hosea's prophetic oracles derives from the conventions of textual production and reading in which they achieved this form. In other words, the key textual turning points identified by modern interpreters would have been the same for those who first produced and read this text.

The movement from accusation to promise in each of these sections of Hosea provides a different experience of that movement and its consequences which, in a reading of the book that is cognizant of its overall shape, creates a much more intricate and elaborate image of the process of judgment and promised reconciliation than could possibly result from reading any of the individual sections alone.[31] The reading of these sections of text within the overall literary context provided by the book as a whole, creates a much more expansive movement from accusation to promise of salvation, with many subtle nuances.

Hosea 1–3. This movement from accusation/judgment to promise of reconciliation occurs three times within the first major section (Hos. 1–3): 1.2–2.3; 2.4-25; 3.1-5.[32] These three individual units are bound together by their common use of the imagery of family breakdown and reconciliation as the metaphor describing the fluctuations in the relationship between Yahweh and Israel. In turn, this use of domestic imagery differentiates these chapters from the remainder of the book. The diverse uses made of this common basic image give a greater depth to the perspective on the divine–human relationship by highlighting different aspects and repeating the movement from accusation through judgment to reconciliation. In all three units the wife, as the partner guilty of the infidelity which has caused the breach in the relationship, is the central character, but the perspective varies in each. In the first unit Gomer, the unfaithful wife of the prophet, is the embodiment of the

---

31. Although a reading of the individual sections that was cognizant of its location within the whole would be similarly more elaborate.

32. See Tucker, 'Hosea', p. 709: 'The order of the narratives and speeches suggests but does not actually specify a theological as well as chronological sequence. Thematically, the movement is from sin and accusation, to indictment and announcement of judgment, to renewal through purchase and purging, to announcement of salvation. That progression expressed the theology of the final editors of the section; whether Hosea himself saw history unfolding in such an order is unclear.'

unfaithful people of Yahweh. The children, however, are the prime
vehicles for both the announcements of judgment and the promise of
reconciliation. This focus on the children, the next generation, brings
already in Hosea 1 the expectation that both punishment and salvation
are an experience of future Israelites. The second unit is primarily composed of Yahweh's recitation of the sins of the wayward spouse. In this
text the wife's actions are the cause of the breakdown of the relationship, while Yahweh's actions are the source of reconciliation in the
salvation oracle. This unit highlights the human sin which results in the
breach, and the unexpected actions of Yahweh which renew the relationship. The final unit is principally concerned with the motivation for
the promised restoration. The prophet is to love a woman whose deeds
are unlovable, just as Yahweh loves the Israelites who turn to other
gods (3.1). Finally, the perspective on the divine–human relationship is
also deepened by the variety of literary styles used to present the
images: a third-person narration about the prophet, a first-person monologue by Yahweh, and a first-person narrative 'by' the prophet.

The third-person narrative of Hos. 1.2–2.3 presents a report of a sign-
action by the prophet. In these verses the marriage of Hosea to Gomer,
an אשת זנונים ('a promiscuous woman'), and the resulting children,
ילדי זנונים ('children of promiscuity') provide a vivid depiction of the
deterioration of the relationship between Yahweh and Israel. Although
Wolff may be correct in connecting this description of Gomer and the
children to the 'Canaanite' fertility cult,[33] it is uncertain that such a
reading would be likely in the early Persian period. There are no unambiguous references to improper cultic activity in this unit. In fact, the
only explicit crime which gives substance to the accusation of infidelity
in this unit is the reference to the bloodshed related to Jehu's coup
(v. 4). However, the immediate correlation between the description of
Gomer and children by the term זנונים is the land's infidelity, straying
from Yahweh (כי־זנה תזנה הארץ מאחרי יהוה, v. 2). Thus both the land
and its inhabitants are guilty.[34] As was noted in the previous chapter,

---

33. Wolff, *Hosea*, p. 15; cf. Mays, *Hosea*, p. 24.

34. Note the comments of Phyllis Bird: 'Although *zenunim* can be understood to
refer to the woman in both expressions and thus to characterize the children as the
product of her promiscuous activity ("children [born] of promiscuity"), the mimick-
ing construction of the paired terms and the linkage without an intervening verb
suggest that the author intended to claim for the children the same nature as their
mother. The message of the sign-action, enunciated in the following *ki* clause and

although such language is also used to describe reliance on foreign alliances and military power to the exclusion of Yahweh, the primary force of this accusation in the book of Hosea is illicit participation in the Baal cult, or, for the Achaemenid period reader, all non-Yahwistic cultic activities. Although this text may not have been related to a specific form of fertility cult by a Persian period Yehudite, it would certainly have been read as the condemnation of any action which substitutes reliance on anything, human or divine, for total dependence on Yahweh, and specifically in relation to inappropriate cultic acts.

The names of each of the three children of Hosea and Gomer, which threaten the disintegration of the relationship between Israel and Yahweh, present what has become a theologico-historical reality for the Persian period reader. The first name, Jezreel, relates the end of the kingdom of Israel to the bloodshed of the violent coup of Jehu (vv. 4-5). The phrase פקד על in this text is often translated by an active verb suggesting a cause and effect relationship between the coup of Jehu and an act of punishment by Yahweh.[35] Rather, this phrase indicates that the effect of the Jezreel bloodshed will be allowed to overtake the nation.[36]

The second and third names, Not-Pitied and Not-My-People, provide a theological perspective on the end of the kingdom, that is, the end of the kingdom is the result of the end of Yahweh's compassion for the nation and the breaking of the divine–human relationship that had

---

elaborated in ch. 2, is that the land "fornicates"—and so do its inhabitants (children)' ('To Play the Harlot: An Inquiry into an Old Testament Metaphor', in Peggy Day [ed.], *Gender and Difference in Ancient Israel* [Minneapolis: Fortress Press, 1989], pp. 75-94 [80-81]).

35. 'Punish', NRSV; cf. Wolff, *Hosea*, pp. 17-18; Andersen and Freedman, *Hosea*, p. 175.

36. Tucker, 'Sin and "Judgment" in the Prophets', pp. 373-88. 'The sinister significance of Jezreel is now clearer. If the original "blood of Jezreel" included not only Naboth's but also Ahab's, then the text tells us not *why* Jehu's house was punished, but *how* it is to be punished. The pattern is not one of historical cause and effect, but a theological pattern in which the hidden hand of God is briefly glimpsed when something that once happended happens again in a similar way (cf. Gen 27.36 with 29.25 and 48.18; II Sam 12.11 with 16.22)' (Andersen and Freedman, *Hosea*, pp. 186-87). Cf. Thomas Edward McComiskey, 'Prophetic Irony in Hosea 14: A Study of the Collocation פקד על and its Implications for the Fall of Jehu's Dynasty', *JSOT* 58 (1993), pp. 93-101 (93). McComiskey argues for an ironic relationship between the bloodshed of Jehu and the bloodshed which will end the kingdom.

previously existed (vv. 6, 9). The interpretation of this last name expresses the break in relationship most forcefully: כִּי אַתֶּם לֹא עַמִּי וְאָנֹכִי לֹא־אֶהְיֶה לָכֶם ('for you are not my people and I am not "I am" for you', v. 8). These words reverse the traditional covenant formula found in Exod. 3.14 and 6.7.[37] The centrality of this formula for the understanding of the relationship between Yahweh and 'Israel' during the early Persian period is highlighted by the almost exclusive use of this phrase in contexts concerning the restoration of the relationship between Yahweh and the people in Jeremiah, Ezekiel and Zechariah.[38] The reversal of the existing relationship depicted in Hos. 1.8 is reversed again in texts from the neo-Babylonian and early Persian periods. Indeed, the promise of a reversal of this reversal of the relationship is given at the end of the second unit of this section: 'Then I will say to Not-My-People, "You are my people" and he will say, "My God"' (2.25). For early Persian period Yehudites these texts reflect a theological perception of the changing historical fortunes of their nation/community. The relationship that once existed between Israel and Yahweh was broken, and the break in that relationship resulted in disaster and exile. The promise of a restoration of the relationship provides a link across the intervening gap between monarchic Judah and Persian Yehud, between first temple and second temple. This theological interpretation of the preceding century provides the means of rooting their present reality in the national traditions. The new reality is legitimate because it is the re-establishment of the relationship that existed before the disaster which befell the ancestors.

The first unit ends with a description of the promised restoration of the divine–human relationship (2.1-3 [Eng. 1.10–2.1]).[39] These verses stress the promised restoration of relationship in terms of the reversal of the judgments of 1.2-9. Not-My-People becomes My-People and Not-Pitied becomes Pitied once again. This reversal of names indicates a

---

37. Wolff, *Hosea*, p. 21; Mays, *Hosea*, p. 29.

38. Jer. 11.4; 24.7; 30.22; 31.1; 32.38; Ezek. 14.11; 34.24; 36.28; 37.23; Zech. 8.8.

39. Wolff notes that the perfect consecutives function to distinguish 2.1-3 from 1.2-9 (*Hosea*, p. 24); cf. Mays, *Hosea*, p. 30 n. a. Ward suggests that the waw is more naturally understood as an expression of continuity rather than discontinuity (*Hosea*, p. 24). However, this view is entirely dependent on his unlikely redaction-critical rearrangement of the text and is of no consequence to an attempt to understand the text in its present form.

dramatic reversal of fortunes which is partially presented in language strongly reminiscent of the promise to the patriarchs:[40]

והיה מספר בני־ישראל כחול הים

And the number of the Israelites will be like the sand of the sea (2.1).

It is likely that a Yehudite reader would have made the theological connection between the promise of the land to the ancestors and the promised return to the land in Hos. 2.1. Such an interpretation of this text in ancient times is suggested not only by the language of the text but also by the expansive version of this text which includes additional material from the promises to the patriarchs in 4QXII[d].[41]

The depiction of the restoration of relationship in this text correlates with the perception of the exile as *the* punishment of the ancestors, a punishment that had left the land desolate. The promise of renewal clearly anticipates a time in which both the Israelites and Judahites would, under a single head, return to the land (2.2). This text would be read by Yehudites of the early Persian period in relation to the reconstitution of the community of Yahwists around Jerusalem. A similar understanding of the restoration community is found in Ezekiel 37. In fact, the depiction of a combined group of Judahites and Israelites returning to the land, having a single ruler, and removing all the former 'sycretistic' elements in Ezek. 37.15-23 could be read as an expansive interpretation of this promise in Hosea. Compare the closing affirmation of the oracle in Ezekiel with the reversal of Yahweh's rejection of Israel in Hosea:

והיו־לי לעם ואני אהיה להם לאלהים   (Ezek. 37.23);

והיה במקום אשר־יאמר להם לא עמי אתם יאמר להם בני אל חי   (Hos. 2.1).[42]

While Wolff's suggestion—that this is an original Hoseanic oracle envisioning a reunification of Israel and Judah before the fall of Samaria—likely reflects an accurate perception of the interpretation of this text in the eighth-century context, a Persian period reader is much more likely to have read it in relation to the exile and return.[43] Within

40. Cf. Gen. 22.17; 32.13. Cf. Wolff, *Hosea*, p. 26; Mays, *Hosea*, p. 31; Davies, *Hosea*, p. 60.

41. Davies, *Hosea*, p. 60.

42. Cf. also Hos. 2.25b.

43. Wolff, *Hosea*, p. 27.

the theological and socio-historical environment of Yehud, this promise in Hosea would correspond to the common perception of the progression of the community's history from the end of the monarchy to the establishment of the Persian colonial administration, a perspective entirely unavailable to an eighth-century reader.

The second unit (2.4-25 [Eng. 2.2-23]) within this first major section presents both the breach in the relationship and the promise of reconciliation primarily by means of a divine monologue. This section both continues and expands the narrative of 1.2–2.3.

> Section two presupposes section one, at least to the extent of establishing the cast of characters and the critical moment in the family life of the prophet when the implications of the ominous statement in 1:2 have become present reality… Here 2:3 provides a transition from section one to section two since the children are the subject of the climactic statement in 2:3. Almost instantly the picture of renewal is dissolved in a flashback, a return to a less happy occasion involving the children, when their names were as yet unchanged and they were cast in the somber role of accusers of an errant mother in behalf of a distraught father.[44]

Whatever their original referents may have been within the context of an independent, eighth-century prophetic oracle, the familial characters in this unit—mother (2.4, 7), children (2.6; also the assumed addressees of 2.4) and husband (2.4, 9)—have a narrative pre-existence as a result of the literary context of the unit within the book of Hosea. This monologue both presumes the characters and setting of the preceding section and also mirrors the movement from accusation and threat (2.4-15) to promise of salvation (2.16-25). Any reader aware of the overall shape and content of the book of Hosea will only sunder this connection between the characters of 1.2-9 and 2.4-22 by a conscious decision to interpret the unit independently of its literary context.

One of the powerful rhetorical features of this monologue is the ambiguity regarding the identity of the speaker that results from its location immediately following the narrative of Hosea 1. Immediately, from the initial words of the spurned husband and father in v. 4 onward, it is unclear whether the speaker is Yahweh or Hosea. The reference to Baal is the first possible indication that Yahweh, not Hosea, is the speaker (v. 10 [Eng. v. 8]). But even this accusation—that the wife is using the gifts of the husband in the Baal cult—could refer to the relationship of Hosea and Gomer. The lives of Hosea and Gomer and

44. Andersen and Freedman, *Hosea*, p. 211.

Yahweh and Israel have become deeply intertwined.[45] The reader shares the pain, anger and frustration of the infidelity. These highly emotive words give expression to what could well be the experience of the prophet in facing and opposing Gomer's infidelity. Finally, the ambiguity ends with the very last phrase of the monologue: וְאֹתִי שָׁכְחָה נְאֻם יְהוָה ('but me she forgot, says Yahweh', v. 15). The pain, horror and brokenness of these words becomes all the more shocking and powerful once it is realized that they give expression to Yahweh's perception of the relationship with Israel.

The accusations in this second section are far more specific than those of section one. There are unambiguous indications that the dominant transgression that lies behind these accusations and threats is participation in worship of the Baals (vv. 10, 15). The emphasis on the source of the fertility of the land is also suggestive of the Baal cult (vv. 5, 7, 10-11, 14). The relation between participation in non-Yahwistic cult and the judgment of Yahweh on the ancestors could not be missed by a Yehudite reader. In fact, the extreme emotion and violence of the language of this unit, some of the most emotive and violent language in the entire book, would suggest that the participation in non-Yahwistic worship was the most significant crime of the ancestors.[46] As was indicated above, the key to these crimes is that they result in the abandonment of Yahweh in favor of an alternative: 'but me she forgot, says Yahweh' (v. 15).

As in the preceding section, the shift from accusation and threat to promise of salvation is abrupt and surprising.[47] The promise of restoration (2.16-25) opens with language of seduction, 'I will allure her' (מְפַתֶּיהָ) and 'I will speak to her heart' (וְדִבַּרְתִּי עַל־לִבָּהּ). This is followed by the betrothal of Israel to Yahweh (וְאֵרַשְׂתִּיךְ לִי, 3× in

---

45. 'The two stories of Hosea and Gomer, and of Yahweh and Israel, are told as if they are one. Hos. 1–3 is not a simple allegory in which a story told on one level (the human) has a meaning on another level (the divine). Gomer's story is Israel's story, and although Hosea and Yahweh cannot be identified in the same way, the prophet and his God are faced with similar problems' (Andersen and Freedman, *Hosea*, p. 284).

46. Note also the threat to end all religious celebrations (v. 13).

47. 'The typical sequence is indictment + *laken* + penalty, and thus, "therefore" is often the first word in a judgment oracle. Here, however, it begins a salvation oracle. That the ultimate sin of forgetting Yahweh (v 15) should be the reason for a mighty act of salvation (v 16) is startling, and the use of "therefore" to make the connection flouts all logic' (Andersen and Freedman, *Hosea*, p. 269).

vv. 21-22), which climaxes in Israel knowing Yahweh (וידעת את־יהוה,
v. 22b). The restoration is depicted in explicitly sexual terms.[48] This
explicit sexuality in the depiction of the relationship of Yahweh and
Israel stands in sharp contrast to the fertility elements and the cult of
Baal in the preceding accusations. The identification of Yahweh as
אישׁי ('my husband') rather than בעלי ('my Baal [lord])' functions to
distinguish clearly Yahweh from Baal, whose name is removed from
the mouth of Israel. In the new relationship it is Baal, not Yahweh, who
is forgotten.

As with the previous section, the depiction of the promised restoration of relationship relies heavily on the ancestral traditions of Israel,
specifically, the exodus and wilderness traditions (vv. 16-17). The response of Israel to Yahweh's wooing is explicitly connected to their
response at the exodus: וכיום עלתה מארץ־מצרים ('like the day of her
departure from Egypt', v. 17). Although the use of המדבר ('the wilderness') as a positive period in the relationship between Yahweh and
Israel contrasts with the Pentateuchal depictions of the same period, the
wilderness, as a place in which Israel is removed from all the entangle-
ments that distract her from Yahweh, is a powerful image of the re-
establishment of a relationship based on the utter dependence of Israel
on its only God. But the connection with the exile and return is tacitly
indicated not only by the use of the exodus traditions but also by the
depiction of the restoration as a sowing in the land (וזרעתיה לי בארץ,
v. 25). The effectiveness of this image depends on the underlying
assumption that the punishment had involved removal from the land.
All of these images—exodus, wilderness and sowing in the land—
require absence from the land as a prerequisite of their effectiveness as
depictions of Yahweh's deliverance of the people. The Persian period
reader, particularly the ruling elites, many of whom had migrated to
Yehud from Babylonia, would associate such imagery with the 'exile

---

48. Cf. Stuart: 'The textual variants which expand the wording to "know that I
am Yahweh" are unlikely to represent the original. Rather, since Hebrew ידע is the
most common Old Testament euphemism for cohabitation, i.e., the consummation
of the marriage in this case (e.g., Gen. 4.1; Num. 31.18; 1 Kgs 1.4), Yahweh and
the new Israel will this time live together as man and wife' (*Hosea–Jonah*, p. 60).
Unfortunately, he then diminishes the significance of this observation by suggesting
that ידע implies not sex but intimacy in this context. In fact, it is the perception of
the intimacy of human sexual intercourse that provides the power of the metaphor.
Cf. Mays, *Hosea*, p. 52.

and return', the most striking and historically immediate event involving absence from and return to the ancestral homeland.

In the third unit of this section (3.1-5), the accusations and promises are combined in a single, first-person narrative. The initial command of this prophetic sign-action report collapses action, metaphor and significance (v. 1). The accusation of inappropriate behavior and the promise of reconciliation are bound together within this initial command. The people's infidelity against Yahweh is both the factor against which Yahweh reacts, and the foundation for the expression of Yahweh's love for them.

The remainder of the narrative reports Hosea's compliance with the commanded action, and further develops the significance of the sign-act. Hosea's purchase of a woman who is an adulteress, in fulfillment of Yahweh's command to go and love such a woman, highlights the depths to which both Gomer and Israel have sunk. Although this unit may originally have been a variant account of the narrative in Hos. 1.2-9, the reader, cognizant of the literary context and noting the עוֹד of 3.1, will most likely read this latter unit as a later stage in the course of the relationship between Hosea and Gomer.[49] This pre-existing relationship between Hosea and the woman of Hosea 3 heightens the impact of the metaphor. Just as Hosea seeks to restore a relationship broken by Gomer's seeking other lovers, so Yahweh seeks to restore the relationship with a people who have opted for other gods: וְהֵם פֹּנִים אֶל־אֱלֹהִים אֲחֵרִים ('they turn to other gods', v. 1).

This use of this phrase, פֹּנִים אֶל־אֱלֹהִים אֲחֵרִים, makes explicit in this third unit the connection between the metaphor of infidelity and the worship of gods other than Yahweh. As was the case in the previous section, this participation in cultic activities venerating other deities is the source of the conflict between Yahweh and Israel. As was also the case in the previous section, the resolution of this conflict is described in terms that would almost certainly have been read as descriptive of the loss of the monarchic state and temple (v. 4). The absence of the paired items listed in v. 4 removes the political, sacrificial and oracular activities that were central to Israel's life in the monarchic period. The removal of all of these elements deprives them of everything, legitimate and/or illegitimate, that could mediate between them and the divine.[50] This period in which they are deprived of these mediating elements

49. Cf. Mays, *Hosea*, pp. 55-56.
50. Wolff, *Hosea*, p. 62; Mays, *Hosea*, pp. 58-59.

parallels the period of sexual abstinence in the relationship of Hosea
and Gomer in v. 3. Just as Hosea and Gomer were to forgo all sexual
activity whether licit or illicit, לא תזני ולא תהיי לאיש גם־אני אליך
('you will not act as a prostitute and you will not be with a man, nor I
with you', v. 3), all objects and activities which provided the basis for
contact and intimacy between people and deities would be removed to
establish a period of abstinence in the divine–human relationship (v. 4).
For a reader in early Persian Yehud the time between the fall of Jerusalem and the restoration of the Yahwistic temple in Jerusalem would
be the most obvious period to associate with the loss (and then
restoration) of these social and religious elements which mediated the
relationship between Israel and the divine realm.

Hosea 4.1–6.6. The second major section of the book (4.1–6.6) paints a
picture of a failed attempt by the people at reconciliation with Yahweh.
As has already been the case previously, there is an abrupt transition
from an oracle of salvation to words of accusation and threat. While the
focus of 3.1-5 was primarily the process of reconciliation initiated by
Yahweh, Hosea 4 shifts the focus entirely to indictment of the people
for their crimes. The sense of disjunction between 3.5 and 4.1 is
heightened further by the opening imperative of 4.1a, שמעו דבר־יהוה
בני ישׂראל ('Listen to the word of Yahweh, O Israelites'). This phrase
functions as the heading to the new section of the book in a manner
similar to the way in which the superscription functions as the heading
for the entire book.[51]

The consistency of the pattern established in the first section of the
book predisposes the reader to expect this series of accusations to end
with a salvation oracle that promises resolution of the conflict between
Yahweh and the people. This expectation is heightened by the progressive lengthening of the oracles of salvation that occurs through the three
units of the first section; ending with a unit in which the accusation of
infidelity has been collapsed into the promise of a restored relationship
with Yahweh. The reader's expectations are frustrated both by the
lengthy focus on accusations and threats and by the aborted attempt at
reconciliation initiated by the people in 6.1-3. The pattern established

---

51. Wolff suggests that 4.1a is a redactional heading added by the same redactor
as 1.1 (*Hosea*, p. 66). Whether or not this redactional analysis is correct, it is indicative of the function of this verse in creating a significant disjunction between the
preceding and following text.

by the opening section of the book (1–3) is broken in 4.1–6.6, and this has a disorienting effect on the reader.

Hosea 4–5 presents, up to this point in the book, the longest enumeration of the accusations and threats of Yahweh against the people. The opening imperative (4.1a), 'Listen to the word of Yahweh, O Israelites', functions both to reaffirm the identification of these texts as דבר יהוה and to stress the importance of giving heed to these words.[52] The necessity of listening to these words is amplified by the threefold imperative formula of 5.1. These three groups—priests, Israelites (בית ישראל) and royal household (בית מלך)—are all implicated in the accusations of the book, but in this section the priests are the primary focus.

The indictment (ריב) of 4.1-3 encapsulates the ethical offenses of the people, surrounding the enumeration of their offenses with an analysis of both their source and consequences. The ethical transgressions of the nation result from the absence of אמת ('faithfulness'), חסד ('loyalty') and דעת אלהים ('knowledge of God', 4.1), that is, the lack of these qualities is integral to the ethical crimes of the people (4.2). The result (על־כן) of this poisonous stew of absent values and lawless behavior is a disaster that envelops the entire ecosystem; land, humans and creatures of land, air and water are all facing a complete catastrophe (4.3). This brief indictment correlates human infidelity and ethical transgressions with the imminence of an all-encompassing cataclysm within the natural world. Chaos in the ethical sphere leads to the dissolution of the created order and a return to chaos in the physical sphere.[53] This text integrates both a juridical (ריב, v. 1) and a dynamistic perspective of the relationship between actions and their consequences. The chaos that envelopes the land and all its inhabitants results from the sins of the people. At the same time, these disastrous consequences are announced in an indictment of the people's acts by Yahweh.[54]

Beginning with 4.4 and running through the remainder of Hosea 4–5, the priests are the focal point of the oracles. The rejection of knowledge by the priests explains the lack of knowledge among the people which leads to their destruction (4.6). Their personal gain from the sins of the

52. Cf. Wolff, *Hosea*, p. 67.

53. Mays notes the fact that these few verses distill a substantial portion of the message of the book: 'In spite of its brevity the oracle is virtually a paradigm of Hosea's message of judgment' (*Hosea*, p. 61).

54. Tucker, 'Sin and "Judgment" in the Prophets', pp. 386-87.

people had the consequence of making them desirous of sin within the populace (4.8). The result is that the outcome of their ways (both priests and people) will be allowed to come back upon them (ופקדתי עליו דרכיו, 4.9).

This attack upon the priesthood is integrally related to the cultic improrieties of the ancestors. This section clearly connects infidelity of the nation with participation in inappropriate cultic activities:

עמי
בעצו ישאל ומקלו יגיד לו
כי רוח ו זנונים התעה ויזנו מתחת אלהיהם
על־ראשי חחרים יזבחו ועל־הגבעות יקטרו
תחת אלון ולבנה ואלה כי טוב צלה
על־כן תזנינה בנותיכם וכלותיכם תנאפנה
לא־אפקוד על־בנותיכם כי תזנינה ועל־כלותיכם כי
תנאפנה
כי־הם עם־הזנות יפרדו ועם־הקדשות יזבחו
עם לא־יבין ילבט

> My people inquires of their stick and their rod gives oracles to them because a spirit of prostitution has caused them to stray and they prosti- ute themselves from their God. They sacrifice on every mountain top and burn offerings on the hills, under oak, poplar and terebinth because their shade is pleasant. Therefore, your daughters work as prostitutes and your daughters-in-law commit adultery. I will not bring the prostitution of your daughters nor the adultery of your daughters-in-law upon them because the men go to prostitutes and sacrifice with cult prostitutes. A people unable to perceive will be trampled (4.12-14).

They consult wood and receive oracles from a rod, and they sacrifice at a variety of local shrines. They also have involved themselves with idols and multiple altars (4.17, 19). All of this is summarized as ויזנ מתחת אלהיהם (cf. 4.10; 5.3-4). The resulting image would indicate to the Persian period reader that the priesthood was not only a participant in the sins of the ancestors which led to their downfall, but that the priests were instrumental in that sin.

All of these sins are intimately related to the ancestors' lack of know- edge of Yahweh. The lack of knowledge of God is an underlying basis for the crimes that lead to the catastrophic destruction of both land and inhabitants (4.1). Yahweh claims that the people are destroyed because they lack knowledge which the priests have rejected (4.6). The cultic sins of the people are summarized by: 'a people without understanding

comes to ruin' (4.14).[55] Finally, the spirit of infidelity (רוח זנונים)
parallels the fact that they do not know Yahweh (5.4). The connection
between lack of knowledge of Yahweh by the people, the rejection of
knowledge by the priests and the destruction of both is condensed into
their common destiny: 'like people like priest' (4.9). Note the irony that
the people who claim a desire to know Yahweh (6.3) are consistently
depicted as being entirely without knowledge of Yahweh. The rejection
of knowledge by the priests lies at the base of the ancestors' infidelity
to Yahweh. But there is also a critical relationship between the priests'
rejection of knowledge and the Torah or instruction of Yahweh. Hosea
4.6 exhibits a chiastic structure:

> A People destroyed for lack of knowledge
>   B Priests have rejected knowledge
>   C God rejects the priests
>   B₁ Priests have forgotten the Torah of God
> A₁ God will forget the priests' children (the people).

The lack of knowledge which led to the destruction of the ancestors
is a direct result of the willful neglect (ותשכח) of the Torah of Yahweh
by the priests. These texts in the book of Hosea place responsibility for
the sins of the nation and their outcome on the failure of the priests to
provide adequate instruction (Torah of Yahweh) to the people. As the
evience from Ezra, Nehemiah and Chronicles examined earlier indiates,
the priests and Levites were intimately connected with the teaching and
interpretation of the extant textual traditions of the nation in the Persian
period. This responsibility for instruction and interpretation is also
evident in Malachi 2 where the contemporary priesthood is compared
unfavorably with the eponymous ancestor, Levi, and castigated for its
poor and perverted instruction to the community.[56] Failure by the
priests to provide adequate instruction to the community in the monarchic period is singled out in the book of Hosea as a primary cause of
the ensuing disaster. Whatever the meaning of תורת אלהיך ('Torah of
your God') in the northern kingdom of the eighth century, this phrase
would be read in relation to the traditional texts that were achieving a
normative status within the community in the early Persian period.
Instruction in the Yahwistic traditions from the past, the דבר יהוה of

---

55. 'Verse 6aA and v. 14bB constitute a well-formed discontinuous bicolon'
(Andersen and Freedman, *Hosea*, p. 321).
56. See esp. Mal. 2.4-9.

the Torah and prophetic collections became an important aspect of the Yahwism of the second temple. The authority ascribed to the former prophets, the communal interpretation of the exile as punishment for the crimes of the ancestors (particularly cultic improprieties), and the delineation of the priestly role in contributing to that course of events all intersect to enforce a strictly exclusive Yahwism on the priesthood and, in turn, on the entire community of Achaemenid Yehud. These texts in Hosea would have functioned as a strong warning to the priesthood of the early Persian period that much of the responsibility for the faithfulness of their community to Yahweh rested in their hands. The material from Malachi 2 indicates that this perception of the role of the priesthood continued into the later Persian period.

The fact that Judah is equally incorporated into the condemnation and subject to the same judgment as Israel in Hosea 5 (vv. 10, 12, 14) would have suggested to a reader in the early Persian period that the Judahites had reached this condition before the end of the Israelite state. Within the historical limits defined by the group of monarchs listed in Hos. 1.1, it is most likely that such a reader would assume that the situation in monarchic Judah had degraded sufficiently from the beginning of Hosea's preaching so that the Judahites, who had not been under judgment at the beginning (1.7), were equally threatened by Yahweh before the end of the Israelite kingdom in 722 BCE. From this point in the text forward, all of the monarchic period ancestors, Israelite and Judahite, are under the judgment of Yahweh for their infidelity.

A striking change of speaker occurs in the opening lines of Hosea 6. Prior to this point in the book, we have heard from a narrator relating events about the prophet and his family (1.2-9), a first-person narration by the prophet (3.1-5), and predominantly, the voices of Yahweh and Hosea intermingled in such a way that they are virtually impossible to separate. Now, for the first time in the book, the people speak for themselves (6.1-3). In place of the oracle of salvation that would conform to the previously established pattern of the book is a call to return to Yahweh:

לכו ונשובה אל־יהוה
כי הוא טרף וירפאנו יך ויחבשנו
יחינו מימים ביום השלישי יקמנו
ונחיה לפניו
ונדעה
נרדפה לדעת את־יהוה כשחר נכון מוצאו
ויבוא כגשם לנו כמלקוש יורה ארץ

Come, let us return to Yahweh, for he has torn and he will heal us, he struck us and he will bandage us. Within two days he will restore our life, by the third day he will raise us up and we will live in his presence. Let us know, let us pursue the knowledge of Yahweh. His appearance is sure like the dawn. He comes to us like the rain, like the spring rain waters the earth.

This call for repentance and knowledge of Yahweh provides a new and dramatically different perspective on the ancestors. They are no longer simply the mute objects of divine accusation and threat. They have a voice, and the words uttered express contrition and the desire for relationship with Yahweh. The plural cohortative of שׁוּב indicates the desire to restore that which has been lost. The following motive clauses introduced by כִּי ('for') indicate a recognition that Yahweh is both the source of their difficulties and the potential source of healing (v. 1). The emphatic construction created by the combination of the cohortative of יָדַע ('let us know') and the cohortative of רדף ('let us pursue') followed by the object of their pursuit, לָדַעַת אֶת־יהוה ('to know Yahweh', v. 3), amplifies the sense of urgency of vv. 1-2. This attempt at reconciliation is completed by the expression of confidence in Yahweh's action on their behalf.

This strong expression by the ancestors of a desire to revive their relationship with Yahweh contrasts starkly with the image of them that has been created through the process of reading the book up to this point. Those evil people, who deserved what they got,[57] abruptly enter into the dialogue, not with evil words or with words attempting to justify themselves, but with words seeking a restored relationship with Yahweh. This unexpected attempt at restoration by the ancestors introduces narrative tension into the Persian period reader's experience of the text. Suddenly, the reader faces an interpretive dilemma. Up to this point, the reading of the accusations and threats of the book, within the context of the community's theologically shaped memory of the exile as a justified punishment of the monarchic period community, has constantly confirmed the reader's expectations regarding the past. Now, however, the people have spoken words of repentance. Will there now be an oracle of salvation for this historical community? How will that correlate with the reader's expectations?

57. Such a reading in the Persian period is suggested by the interpretation of the words of the 'former prophets' in Zech. 1.1-6 and 7.1-14.

The reader's dilemma is deepened by the response of Yahweh which rejects the possibility of restoration of the relationship (6.4-5). Wolff proposes that Yahweh's response to the penitential words of the people occurs where one would expect a priestly salvation oracle in the cult.[58] This suggestion reinforces the difficulty created for the reader by Yahweh's response to the Israelites' repentance. The arrangement of the oracles of Hosea into the form of a book has created additional tension for the reader. Precisely at the point at which a Persian period reader, a participant in the recently (re)instituted cult of Yahweh (eventually in the new Jerusalem temple), would expect to hear the reassuring words of a salvation oracle, there is a rejection of the human attempt at reconciliation. Both the characteristic cultic response to similar penitential words and the preceding experience of the book, in which promise of salvation has consistently followed accusations and threats, would lead the reader to anticipate a salvation oracle here. The lack of a salvation oracle would frustrate the expectations of the reader, but the presence of words of repentance that are rejected by Yahweh function to create very substantial dissonance.

Contrary to Wolff's extremely negative judgment of this penitential song,[59] the content of this unit is representative of appropriate words of repentance. In the first strophe (6.1-2) there is a call for repentance, an acknowledgment that Yahweh's judgment is the source of their trouble, and an expression of confidence that Yahweh will respond to their repentance. The second strophe (6.3) shortens this formula by moving directly from a call to return to Yahweh, let us seek to know Yahweh, to the statement of confidence. If these words occured in another context, such as a psalm of lament, the sincerity of the penitent would never be questioned by commentators. It is only the theologically unacceptable rejection of appropriate words of repentance which has caused the difficulty for interpreters. This unexpected act of penitence by the people following immediately on Yahweh's stinging condemnation and withdrawal from them creates significant narrative tension for the Persian period reader. This tension is heightened by the direct opposition between Yahweh's previous departure and the ancestor's confidence in his imminent return (cf. 5.15 and 6.3). The immediate divine repudiation of the people conspicuously confounds the reader's

58. Wolff, *Hosea*, p. 119; cf. Mays, *Hosea*, p. 96.
59. 'These words sound like a kind of self-appeasement...' (Wolff, *Hosea*, p. 117).

expectations and creates an environment in which the reader's previous perceptions of both the past situation and Yahweh can be altered.

Andersen and Freedman attempt to resolve the tension by suggesting that Yahweh's response in 6.4-6 is chronologically contemporary with the threats of 5.14-15, and that both precede chronologically the repentance of 6.1-3.[60] While this solution permits the people's words of repentance to stand as an expression of genuine contrition, it fails to take seriously the chronological experience of these words in a sequential reading (or a reading that is cognizant of the sequence of the text as a whole). The difficulty of Yahweh's rejection of apparently genuine repentance by the Israelites is not removed by placing these words after the response. The words of repentance stand out clearly from the entire surrounding context from 4.1 to 10.15. The most plausible reading of 6.4-6 within the literary context of the book is to view it as the rejection of the repentance of the people by Yahweh.[61]

Many commentators who read 6.4-6 as a divine rejection of the people's repentance attempt to explain this rejection by suggesting that it is the result of the insincerity or instability of their devotion to Yahweh.[62] Certainly, a portion of Yahweh's lament in 6.4-6 regards Israel and Judah's lack of constancy in their relationship. But this inconsistency is not given as the immediate cause of Yahweh's rejection of their repentance, but represents the long-term problem in the relationship. Ultimately, the relationship between Yahweh and the people cannot survive because the people's commitment to it continually waivers. There is no indication that the people's inconsistency in their relationship with Yahweh is intentional or an act of concious rebellion. In fact, given the religio-historical environment of the northern kingdom in the eighth century, most in ancient Israel would have seen no difficulty in the simultaneous veneration of Yahweh and other gods. Hosea, on the other hand, was concerned that the veneration of Baal to the growing exclusion of Yahweh was evidence of a lack of fidelity and constancy to their appropriate relationship with Yahweh. Whatever the

60. Andersen and Freedman, *Hosea*, pp. 327-30.

61. Wolff, *Hosea*, p. 119; Mays, *Hosea*, p. 96; Stuart, *Hosea–Jonah*, p. 109. Contra: Davies, *Hosea*, pp. 149-50.

62. 'But Israel's covenantal loyalty is far too unsteady' (Wolff, *Hosea*, p. 119). 'The covenant loyalty of both Israel and Judah was fleeting' (Stuart, *Hosea*, p. 109). 'Without reserve God discloses the frustration caused by the inconstancy of his people' (Mays, *Hosea*, p. 97).

significance of these words in an eighth-century setting, there is no indication in this text that the words of repentance are in any way insincere. In fact, these words of the people expressing their desire to return (שׁוּב) to Yahweh mirror the foreshadowed beginning of reconciliation in 3.5: אַחַר יָשֻׁבוּ בְּנֵי יִשְׂרָאֵל וּבִקְשׁוּ אֶת־יְהוָה אֱלֹהֵיהֶם ('Afterward, the Israelites will turn and seek Yahweh their God'). For the Persian period Yehudite reader, this text presents a situation in which apparently genuine words of repentance are rejected by Yahweh. This narrative linking of human repentance with divine repudiation raises substantive narrative and theological dissonance for the reader.

Yahweh's (negative) response to this attempt by the people to restore the relationship shifts all of the reader's dilemma directly onto God. Suddenly the reader is directly confronted with a God who rejects words of repentance in favor of horrible violence. At least two responses are possible at this juncture: the confusion either destabilizes the reader's confidence in the book or it destabilizes the reader's confidence in knowing Yahweh. The dissonance between the progression of the narrative at this point and the reader's expectations, based both on the theological expectation of Yahweh's positive response to words of repentance and the preceding movement of the book from accusation and threat to promise of salvation, would cause the reader either to question the veracity of the text or the veracity of the reader's existing theological presuppositions. The first response, though possible, is highly unlikely in the early Persian period. Given the regard for the words of the former prophets in this period, it is more likely that this text would cast doubt on the reader's existing assumptions about Yahweh. In Yahweh's refusal to accept the words of repentance, God's freedom is juxtaposed with the people's attempts to re-establish the relationship. This unexpected reaction of Yahweh suggests that human words are unable to elicit a particular (desired or expected) response from God. Even if these words are interpreted as an insincere attempt by the people to coerce a favorable reaction from Yahweh through appropriate cultic activities, the resulting response still highlights the freedom of God in such a circumstance. The reader learns that mortals cannot manipulate Yahweh.

This contradiction of expectations also has the effect of causing the reader to re-evaluate the trajectory of the reading. Previously, a consistent pattern of narrative development had been established, but now that expected pattern has been substantially disrupted. Now the contours of the unfolding reading are uncertain and the eventual outcome unpredictable.

Hosea 6.7–11.11. Immediately following the unanticipated rejection of the Israelites' words of repentance, the third major section (6.7–11.11) represents the longest and most comprehensive account of the accusations and threats against the ancestors in the entire book of Hosea. The reader, now in doubt as to whether God's actions can be predicted, continues on, trudging through threats and accusations chapter after chapter: 6, 7, 8, 9, 10. Roughly the middle third of the book is devoted to this compendium of Israelite crimes and their eventual consequence. The list of charges cover all the areas mentioned previously. They are accused of political intrigue and palace coups. They consume their rulers:

כלם יחמו כתנור ואכלו את שפטיהם
כל־מלכיהם נפלו אין־קרא בהם אלי
(7.7; cf. vv. 3-6);

and they set up kings without the approval of Yahweh:

הם המליכו ולא ממני השירו ולא ידאתי
(8.4).

They are also accused of a variety of cultic improprieties, including: participation in forbidden cultic acts:

על־דגן ותירוש יתגוררו יסורו בי
(7.14; cf. 9.10);

the production and veneration of idols:

כספם וזהבם עשו להם עצבים למען יכרת
זנח עגלך שמרון חרה אפי בם
עד־מתי לא יוכלו נקין
כי מישראל
והוא חרש עשהו ולא אלהים הוא
כי־שבבים יהיה עגל שמרון
(8.4b-6; cf. 10.5-6);

and the erection of altars and the offering of sacrifices which are unacceptable to Yahweh (8.11-13; cf. 10.1-2).

They are also chastised for dependence on foreign alliances instead of Yahweh: flitting back and forth between the great powers of the ancient Near East seeking stability but neglecting Yahweh (7.11-13);

and bargaining with other nations that only results in their being consumed (8.8-10). Finally, they are castigated for reliance on military power rather than Yahweh (8.14; 10.13-14). All of these crimes can be subsumed under the overarching metaphor of infidelity to their relationship with Yahweh:

כי זנית מעל אלהיך
אהבת אתנן על כל־גרנות דגן

> for you have prostituted yourself from your God.
> You have loved the fee of a prostitute upon every threshing floor
> (9.1; cf. 6.7, 10).

This catalogue of offenses of the monarchic period ancestors would function as a warning to the Persian era reader to avoid these crimes which resulted in the disaster that came upon the ancestors. The connection between these transgressions and the deportation of some to Babylonia is repeatedly affirmed for the Persian period (postexilic) reader by the regular depiction of the result of these sins as removal from the land throughout this section (7.16; 8.10, 13; 9.3, 6, 15, 17; 10.6; 11.5).

The impact of Yahweh's rejection of their repentance is significantly increased by this extensive listing of accusations and the multiple threats of expulsion from the land. Apparently the crimes of the ancestors had become so serious that repentance was impossible or, at least, would no longer be accepted. A similar perspective is reflected in Isaiah 6, where the function of the prophet is described as dulling the senses of the people so that they are unable to repent:

השמן לב־העם הזה ואזניו הכבד ועיניו השע
פן־יראה בעיניו ובאזניו ישמע ולבבו יבין ושב ורפא לו
(Isa. 6.10).

The commission of Isaiah is to last until the land is desolate (v. 11) and everyone has been sent away (v. 12). The result will be a vast emptiness in the land (v. 12).

Upon reaching Hosea 11, the reader finally hears some tender and compassionate words coming from the mouth of God. But initially they are words only about God's past tenderness toward Israel (11.1, 3-4), reminiscent of Hos. 9.10a, which served only as the introduction to further accusations and threats. Here the recollection of Yahweh's historical acts of salvation are initially only used to heighten the severity of the accusations by contrasting God's compassion with the people's unfaithfulness (11.2, 5-7). Thus, the primary significance of these reminiscences of Yahweh's past acts of compassion is to justify Yahweh's judgment against this faithless people.

In the twinkling of an eye, however, Yahweh's past tenderness is suddenly resurrected to new life. The unexpected rejection of the people's words of repentance (6.4-5) is now reversed by an equally unexpected gracious refusal to punish, even in spite of the people's sins (11.8-9). As in the earlier rejection of repentance, this startling change of heart by Yahweh is introduced by rhetorical questions. The previous pair of questions gave expression to a sense of exasperation on the part of Yahweh that punishment was the only remaining option.

מה אעשה־לך אפרים מה אעשה־לך יהודה

> What shall I do with you, Ephraim?
> What shall I do with you, Judah? (6.4)

In this text, a series of four questions indicates Yahweh's revulsion at the prospect of completely destroying the nation.

איך אתנך אפרים אמגנך ישראל
איך אתנך כאדמה אשימך צבאים

> How can I surrender you, Ephraim?
> How can I deliver you up, Israel?
> How can I surrender you like Admah?
> How can I make you like Zeboiim? (11.8)

Reading Hosea 11 in particular, and the larger unit in general, creates an impression of divine uncertainty and inner struggle. Yahweh is wrestling with the situation and the available options. In contrast to the apparent certainty with which Yahweh rejected the words of the people in 6.1-3 here Yahweh struggles with uncertainty, apparently without any prompting.

The salvation oracle (11.10-11), abruptly abutting on to a catalog of threats and accusations, restores the previously established pattern of chs. 1–3, but the sense of predictability with regard to the outcome of the divine–human relationship has now been entirely obliterated. At this point in the text, Yahweh's actions seem completely beyond the reader's ability to control or anticipate. The reading experience has destabilized the reader's expectations concerning God, sin, and punishment. Yahweh cannot be controlled by human manipulation through the cult, nor is Yahweh bound to a course of action by human sinfulness.

Hosea 12–14. One crucial effect of the reading experience to this point in the text has been to unsettle the reader's expectations regarding the relationship between human and divine actions. On the one hand, substantial portions of the book have reaffirmed a link between human actions and divine response. Sin brings about accusation, threat and judgment. Repentance, reconciliation and blessing by Yahweh are bound together. On the other hand, certain texts, particularly chs. 6 and 11, have linked human action and divine response in totally unexpected ways. How can the reader make sense of a text in which human repentance leads to divine accusation and judgment (6.1-5), and human sin leads to divine compassion and refusal to punish (11.1-11)? The disorientation created by these unexpected events provides an environment in which the reader is unable to foresee a resolution to the tension that has been created, but the way has also been opened to a new theological orientation.[63] The reader's anxiety is heightened further upon being thrust once again under a tirade of accusations and threats by the God who has just moments earlier refused to play the part of an exasperated parent punishing a chronically disobedient child. The charges against the Israelites in this fourth section include many of the elements familiar from the preceding sections:

the multiplication of deceit and violence

(12.2); כזב ושד ירבה

extortion and trust in the resulting prosperity

ויאמר אפרים אך עשרתי מצאתי און לי
(12.9); כל־יגיעי לא ימצאו־לי עון אשר חטא

dependence on foreign alliances

(12.2); וברית עם־אשור יכרתו ושמן למצרים יובל

and cultic improprieties, including the worship of other deities

(12.1b); ויהודה עד רד עם־אל ועם־קדושים נאמן

אם־גלעד און אכ־שוא היו בגלגל שורים זבחו
(12.12); גם מזבחותם כגלים על תלמי שדי

---

63. Compare the functional analysis of the psalms suggested by Walter Brueggeman. He proposes three categories on the basis of their effect on the reader: orientation, disorientation and reorientation ('Psalms and the Life of Faith: A Suggested Typology of Function,' *JSOT* 17 [1980], pp. 3-32).

כדבר אפרים רתתנשא הוא בישראל
ויאשם בבעל וימת
ועתה יוספו לחטא ויעשו להם מסכה
מכספם כתבונם עצבים מעשה חרשים כלה
להם אמרים זבחי אדם עגלים ישקון (13.1-2).

The accusations and threats of chs. 12–14 are interwoven within a framework of references to the national historical traditions. These chapters make use of traditions regarding Jacob (12.3-6, 13), the wilderness (13.5) and the origins of the monarchy (13.10-11). These traditions are predominantly used to underscore the sin of the people. As such, they function both to justify Yahweh's judgment and to prepare for the necessary reconciliation which occurs at the end of the book. Secondarily, the Jacob and Exodus traditions have the implicit effect of connecting the contemporary reader with the ancestors. Persian period Yehudite readers believed themselves to be the legitimate continuation of all preceding generations of Israelites, finding their origins in the Jacob and Exodus traditions. The story of Jacob is introduced into the text in such a way that Judah and Jacob (Israel) are identified:

וריב ליהוה עמ־יהודה
ולפקד על־יעקב כדרכיו כמעלליו ישיב לו

Yahweh has a contention with Judah
and will visit Jacob's sins upon him (12.3).

The first two lines of the tricolon parallel Judah and Jacob as the (co)recipient(s) of Yahweh's judgment. The final line draws the two characters together into a single existence before Yahweh: 'He will repay him according to his practices.'

In 12.1-2, Ephraim, the house of Israel, and Judah have all equally been the subject of Yahweh's accusations. The tricolon of 12.3 functions to identify these national characters with the eponymous ancestor whose story will be used to emphasize the deep-rooted nature of their struggle with God.[64] The use of Jacob is particularly important in this

64. Cf. Hos. 12.13, the second reference to the Jacob tradition. In this text Jacob and Israel are identified by their occurrence in successive parallel lines.

Although the separate existence of kingdoms called Israel and Judah would have been known to a Persian period reader (cf. the Deuteronomistic History), these terms would both equally apply to the contemporary community as the legitimate continuation of the Yahwistic faith of these ancestral communities. See further,

regard. Wolff suggests that Judah has been introduced into this context secondarily by a later redactor.[65] This may be an accurate assessment of the transmission history of the text. More important for a Persian period reading of this text, however, is the effect this combination of Ephraim, Judah and Jacob has on the reader's perception of the interrelationship of all these characters, and the relationship of these characters to the contemporary Yehudite community. Ephraim and Judah are identified by means of a common eponymous ancestor. As Wolff notes: 'It thus emphasized not the geographical aspect which separated Israel from Judah but the common history of salvation which united them.'[66] Compare also Hos. 5.9-10 and Hos. 10.11 where these three are also paralleled. The pairing of Ephraim and Judah and the highlighting of their common bond by the use of the common eponymous ancestor tradition functions for the Persian period Yehudite reader as a link across both time and space.

The importance of the Jacob traditions for bridging the gap between the monarchic Judahite community and the post-monarchic Judahite and Yehudite communities is demonstrated by the numerous uses of 'Jacob' as a designation of these communities in the late Isaianic literature from the neo-Babylonian and Persian periods. In Deutero-Isaiah Jacob is almost always used in parallel with Israel as names of the community of Yahweh.[67] In Isa. 44.5 the names 'I am Yahweh's', 'Jacob' and 'Israel' are specifically chosen by the members of the restoration community as terms of self-designation. Note also the important interconnection of Israel, Jacob and Judah in Isa. 48.1: the 'house of Jacob' who are called 'Israel' are those who have come forth from 'Judah'. These texts clearly indicate an environment in which the community of the period identified with the national ancestral traditions through the names of this eponymous ancestor.[68] In spite of the divided kingdoms of the monarchic period and the subsequent exile from the land (resulting in a desolate land according to the perspective of contemporary texts), both the ancestors and the Persian period Yehudites

---

Chapter 2, 'Exile, Return, and the Desolate Land', and the analysis of Ben Zvi, 'Inclusion', pp. 95-149.

65. Wolff, *Hosea*, p. 206; Ward, *Hosea*, pp. 208-10.

66. Wolff, *Hosea*, p. 211.

67. 40.27; 41.8, 14, 21; 42.24; 43.1, 22, 28; 44.1, 2, 5, 21, 23; 45.4, 19; 46.3; 48.1, 12, 20; 49.5.

68. Cf. the following texts from Trito-Isaiah: 58.1, 14; 59.20; 65.9.

are Israelites in the eponymous ancestor, Jacob, and in the religio-political designations, Israel and Judah. Within the interpretive environment demonstrated by these neo-Babylonian and Persian period texts, the similar texts from the book of Hosea would most likely have been interpreted by a Persian period reader as indicative of the community's identification with the ancestors through these key figures and names in the national traditions.

The stories of Jacob in the womb and Jacob at Penuel are used in Hos. 12.4-5 to highlight his contentious nature; in the womb he struggled with his brother and deceived him, in his adulthood he struggled with God. Jacob, the eponymous ancestor who supplanted his brother by deceit and who strove (שׂרה) with Yahweh at Penuel, is representative of the nation's contentious relationship with and departure from Yahweh. This theme of Jacob's struggle continues into v. 5, with the acknowledgment that he prevailed in his wrestling with the messenger (מלאך). Just as the relationship between the eponymous ancestor and Yahweh was filled with stuggle and difficulty, so the descendants of Jacob have experienced struggles and difficulties in their relationship with Yahweh. The second line of v. 5 highlights Jacob's pleading with God. His struggles were accompanied by weeping and pleading. This recollection of the traditions about the eponymous ancestor has the effect of creating an identification between the events preserved in the tradition and the life of the community:

בית־אל יצאנו ושם ידבר עמנו

He found us at Bethel and there he spoke to us.

It was not just the ancestor who was found by Yahweh at Bethel, but all of the descendants of this eponymous figure. The recognition that the origins of the community lie in Jacob/Israel, who is primarily identified with Bethel in the traditions, is placed into the mouth of the reader. This has at least two key effects. First, the present community of readers is identified with the eponymous ancestor and, as a result, is provided with a link to the monarchic period ancestral communities. Second, the reader is identified not only with an ancestor who struggled with God but also with an ancestor who recognized his need to weep and plead before Yahweh. This first-person recognition is immediately followed by a (liturgical) creedal formula,

ויהוה אלהי הצבאות יהוה זכרו

Yahweh is the God of Hosts,
Yahweh is his name (12.6).

and a call for repentance:

ואתה באלהיך תשוב
חסד ומשפט שמר וקוה אל־אלהיך תמיד

But you will return to your God,
keep loyalty and justice
and continually wait for your God (12.7).

As was suggested above, the use of the national traditions functions: as a means of constructing the identity of the present community of readers in relation to the ancestors; to highlight the national sins which led to exile; and, finally, to prepare the reader for the formula of reconciliation which forms the climax of the book (14.2-4 [Eng. 1-3]).

The combination of the Jacob and exodus traditions in 12.13-14 provides an example of the way in which the use of national traditions in the book of Hosea can function as the lens through which the community's recent history is interpreted by a Persian period reader. The brief allusion to the tradition of Jacob serving for a wife in Aram (12.13), followed immediately by the reminder that Yahweh brought Israel up from Egypt by a prophet (12.14), functions as a paradigm for interpreting the Yehudite community's recent past. The reference to Jacob serving for a wife in Aram does not stress his unfaithfulness in relation to Yahweh, but his servitude in a foreign land in which he prospered and from which he was delivered, both by the power of Yahweh.[69] The implication of the deliverance of Jacob by Yahweh is emphasized in this context by the juxtaposition of the 'exile' of the eponymous ancestor from the promised land with the deliverance of the nation in the exodus from Egypt. These two brief accounts from the national traditions, particularly as they combine servitude in a foreign land with the memory of the exodus from Egypt, implicitly recall, for the Persian period reader, both the exile of (some of) the monarchic

---

69. Cf. Peter R. Ackroyd, 'Hosea and Jacob', *VT* 13 (1963), pp. 245-59 (246): 'In the context, in v.14, the stress rests upon God's protective activity in regard to Israel. The general indications of the tradition point in the same direction, for both the flight to Aram and the acquiring of a wife represent the establishing of hope for the descendants of Jacob.'

period population and the return to the land which followed the decree of Cyrus.

Nor is such a use of the exodus traditions in relation to the exile to Mesopotamia unique. The exodus motif is often employed in biblical literature from this period to represent the return of the exiles from Mesopotamia as a new, but essentially similar act of salvation by Yahweh. This use of the exodus traditions functions to underscore the similarities between the community's experience of exile and restoration and their traditions of national origin.[70] This experience of finding a reflection of recent circumstances in the origin traditions would create the perception that these recent events were not unique in the history of the relationship between Yahweh and Israel, but rather, that they were a new development of Yahweh's saving activity on behalf of the ancestors. Just as Jacob and the Israelites had survived, prospered and eventually returned to the land in spite of their exile to Aram and Egypt, respectively, the recent generations of Israelites had survived exile in Mesopotamia and returned to the land with the hope of prosperity and blessing.[71]

There are two occurrences of the liturgical formula, 'I am Yahweh your God since the land of Egypt' (12.10; 13.4) in this final section of the book of Hosea. The use of this formula functions, for the Persian period reader, as a means of highlighting the intersection between Yahweh as Israel's God, Israel's existence, and the act of Yahweh which provides the founding event for both. The creation of the nation—that is, its birth in the exodus event—is integrally tied in this liturgical formula to the recognition of Yahweh as Israel's God: 'your God *since* the land of Egypt'. Israel came into existence by an act of Yahweh and that same act represents the point at which Yahweh became Israel's God. The implication throughout is that Israel would not have come into

---

70. See Michael Fishbane, 'The "Exodus" Motif/The Paradigm of Historical Renewal', in *idem*, *Text and Texture: Close Readings of Selected Biblical Texts* (New York: Schocken Books, 1979), pp. 121-40. He provides an excellent discussion of the pervasiveness and importance of this motif in the Hebrew Bible.

71. 'It seems much more probable that Hosea is in reality making an allusion to the marvel of the divine purpose by which through such vicissitudes the patriarch was brought to prosperity and blessing. The Genesis traditions show a hero who is devinely blessed no matter what his opponents try to do to him. Laban's imposition of servitude—like Pharaoh's treatment of Israel in Egypt—looks like defeat of God's purposes. But it is not; it is the occasion for the demonstration of divine blessing, as the story reiterates' (Ackroyd, 'Hosea and Jacob', p. 247).

existence and cannot continue to exist unless Yahweh is their God. The same activity which created Israel inaugurated their relationship with Yahweh and the two cannot be separated. The same perception of the role of the exodus events in establishing the bond between Israel and Yahweh is indicated in Hos. 11.1, 'Since Israel was a child I have loved him, and I have called him my son since Egypt'.

In the second occurrence of this liturgical formula (13.4) the importance of Israel's fidelity to this relationship is emphasized. The special relationship created as a result of Yahweh's act of salvation continues while they are totally dependent upon Yahweh but is lost when they become self-satisfied. As in the salvation oracle of Hosea 2, the wilderness is equated with a time of special intimacy between Yahweh and Israel (אני ידעתיך במדבר, 'I knew you in the wilderness', 13.5). It was only after they entered the land and became satiated and haughty that they abandoned Yahweh (על־כן שכחוני, 'therefore they forgot me', 13.6). Yahweh knew Israel, but in their pride and self-satisfaction Israel forgot Yahweh. The disparity between the intimacy of the wilderness period and Israel's forgetting Yahweh provides the basis for Yahweh's judgment, which is described as a wild animal ripping open its prey (vv. 7-8). The uses of this formula underscore that Israel's existence is established and guaranteed only on the basis of their relationship with Yahweh. Their failure to remain faithful to this relationship results in their destruction. For the Persian period reader, the intertwining of Israel's creation and continued existence with their faithfulness to Yahweh has the effect of establishing proper relationship to Yahweh as a central feature of the community's life.

The last recollection of Israel's past focuses on the request for a king (13.10-11). In their attempt to identify specific kings that were given and taken away in Yahweh's anger, Andersen and Freedman appear to deal with the text in too literal a manner.[72] Rather, the text rejects the monarchy as an institution. This is not a simple matter of rejecting a single king for evil activities. The quotation of the people's request for a king (13.10b) and the account of the angry giving and taking of the king by Yahweh (13.11) is most similar to the perspective represented by 1 Samuel 8 than any other biblical text. In 1 Samuel 8 the origins of the Israelite monarchy are depicted as rebellion against the express will of Yahweh. The people ask for a king to be like the other nations. This

---

72. Andersen and Freedman, *Hosea*, p. 635.

request is specifically said to be a rejection of Yahweh (1 Sam. 8.7), and is equated with serving gods other than Yahweh (1 Sam. 8.8).[73] In addition, the deuteronomistic antagonism to the monarchy, represented in the speech of Samuel in 1 Samuel 12, presents a very similar account of the origins of the monarchy, emphasizing the negative aspects of a human king and the sinfulness of the people in asking for a king. In 1 Samuel 12 the king is the one 'whom you have chosen, for whom you have asked' (v. 13). The response of the people to Samuel's speech is to confess that they 'have added to all our sins the evil of demanding a king for ourselves' (v. 19).

Even if it was not the implication of these words in Hos. 13.10-11 for an eighth-century Israelite reader/hearer, the Persian period reader, who would most likely have been familiar with the perspective represented in 1 Samuel 8 and 12, would have read this text within this existing theological context. This text, read within this particular horizon of reading, suggests that the monarchy itself, not individual kings, was contrary to Yahweh's will for the nation.[74] Such a perspective would have already been suggested to the Persian period reader of Hosea in the earlier reference to the ancestors making kings by their own volition (Hos. 8.4), and possibly also in the connection of the beginning of the ancestor's evil with Gilgal (Hos. 9.15). Given the post-monarchic situation within which this text would have been read and the anti-monarchic perspective of the deuteronomistic literature which formed a substantial part of the literary context, this text would certainly have been read as a negative judgment not just on an individual king, but on the institution of monarchy as a whole.

Each of these historical allusions contrasts the faithfulness of Yahweh with the infidelity of Israel. The interweaving of specific accusations of inappropriate practices within these allusions provides the motive and justification for Yahweh's rejection and punishment of Israel. This complex explanation of Yahweh's judgment on Israel leads to the most repugnant description of punishment in the entire book (13.15–14.1 [Eng. 13.15-16]).

---

73. Cf. the discussion of P. Kyle McCarter, Jr, who considers 1 Sam. 7–8 reciprocal texts that present first the positive argument for a Yahwistic theocracy, and then the negative argument that human kingship is a curse (*1 Samuel* [AB, 8; New York: Doubleday, 1980], pp. 159-62).

74. Davies, *Hosea*, p. 293; Wolff, *Hosea*, p. 227.

Finally, the book ends with the reconciliation of Yahweh and Israel. This reconciliation occurs in a form (call to repentance, confession of guilt and promise of restoration) that would have been expected prior to reading the text, but it is experienced quite differently as a result of the process of reading through the preceding sections of text.

1. Call to repentance:

שׁוּבָה יִשְׂרָאֵל עַד יְהוָה אֱלֹהֶיךָ כִּי כָשַׁלְתָּ בַּעֲוֹנֶךָ
קְחוּעִמָּכֶם דְּבָרִים וְשׁוּבוּ אֶל־יְהוָה אִמְרוּ אֵלָיו

Return, O Israel, to Yahweh your God,
for you stumbled as a result of your wickedness.
Take words with you and return to Yahweh.
Say to him… (14.2-3a).

2. Confession of guilt:

כָּל־תִּשָּׂא עָוֹן
וְקַח־טוֹב וּנְשַׁלְּמָה פָרִים שְׂפָתֵינוּ
אַשּׁוּר לֹא יוֹשִׁיעֵנוּ עַל־סוּס לֹא יִרְכָּב
וְלֹא־נֹאמַר עוֹד אֱלֹהֵינוּ לְמַעֲשֵׂה יָדֵינוּ אֲשֶׁר־בְּךָ יְרֻחַם
יָתוֹם

We are finished, forgive (our) guilt.
Accept the good and we will offer the sacrifices of our lips
as recompense.
Assyria cannot save us, we will not ride on a horse.
We will no longer say 'Our God' to a product of our hands,
since in you alone orphans find compassion (14.3b-4).

3. Promise of reconciliation:

אֶרְפָּא מְשׁוּבָתָם אֹהֲבֵם נְדָבָה
כִּי שָׁב אַפִּי מִמֶּנּוּ
אֶהְיֶה כַטַּל לְיִשְׂרָאֵל יִפְרַח כַּשּׁוֹשַׁנָּה
וְיַךְ שָׁרָשָׁיו כַּלְּבָנוֹן
יֵלְכוּ יֹנְקוֹתָיו
וִיהִי כַזַּיִת הוֹדוֹ וְרֵיחַ לוֹ כַּלְּבָנוֹן

I will heal their apostasy, loving them freely,
for my anger has turned away from them.
I will be like dew to Israel;
he will bloom like the lily,
he will strike his roots like Lebanon.
His shoots will spread out,
his splendor will be like the olive tree
and his fragrance like Lebanon (14.5-7).

The call to repentance seems to place the reader back on familiar ground in regard to understanding the divine–human relationship. This familiar ground becomes even firmer when the people respond with pleas for mercy and promises of better behavior. But how will Yahweh respond? Will this be another opportunity for Yahweh to go off and hide in 'God's place'? As with the call for repentance and the appropriate response of the people, this time Yahweh responds according to prior expectations and promises restoration and healing. However, as a result of the total experience of reading Hosea, the meaning cannot be reduced to a simplistic direct correspondence between sin and punishment on the one hand, and repentance and salvation on the other. The experience of reading the book disorients prior understandings of divine–human relations in favor of the complete, sovereign freedom of God.

This final depiction of reconciliation draws together many of the themes found in the preceding chapters of the book to create a new relationship between Yahweh and Israel. The origin of Israel's relationship with Yahweh is based in Yahweh's love for them (כי נער ישראל ואהבהו, 11.1). Specifically, Israel is the son that Yahweh called out of Egypt in love. In the earlier narrative description of the potential restoration of the divine–human relationship, the prophet was told to love a woman (אהב) who was an adulteress, just as Yahweh loved the Israelites in spite of their worship of other gods (3.1). This emphasis on Yahweh's love for the people is also reminiscent of the rejection of לא רחמה ('not pitied', 1.6-7) and the promise of a new relationship with רחמה ('pitied', 2.3, 25). In this final act of reconciliation, the renewal of the relationship between Yahweh and Israel is based on Yahweh's loving them freely (אהבם נדבה, 14.5). The centrality of Yahweh's love and compassion for the people in the book of Hosea is picked up and incorporated into their reconciliation in ch. 14.

Yahweh's healing of the people is a significant theme in the book which is incorporated into this final chapter. In the failed attempt at reconciliation in Hosea 6, the people seek Yahweh because 'he will heal us' (וירפאנו, 6.1). The belief that Yahweh is the source of healing for Israel is expressed in this typical confession and statement of confidence. In contrast, one of Yahweh's accusations against Israel is that they had failed to recognize that it was he who healed them (ולא ידעו כי רפאתים, 'They did not know that I healed them', 11.3). In ch. 14, the final reconciliation is predicated upon Israel's confession that it is

Yahweh who will heal their apostasy (ארפא משובתם, 14.5).[75] This is another example of the way in which the same themes and terms recur, either for good or ill, in the central turning points in the book (3.1-5; 6.1-3; 11; 14).

The earlier, failed attempt at reconciliation opened with the call to return to Yahweh (לכו ונשובה אל־יהוה, 6.1). In 11.5 the same Hebrew root is used in an interesting contrast in which the refusal of Israel to return to Yahweh results in their return to the land of Egypt. The call to repentance in 14.2-3 both opens and closes with the call to return to Yahweh (שובה ישראל עד יהוה אלהיך, 14.2; ושובו אל יהוה, 14.3).

Finally, the people's recognition and confession that Assyria cannot save them in 14.4 (אשור לא יושיענו) acts as a reversal of an earlier depiction of their punishmement by Yahweh in which they are to serve Assyria as their king (ואשור הוא מלכו, 11.5). Wolff has noted the connections between ch. 14 and earlier texts (particularly ch. 11), but he describes these connections simply as catchwords.[76] This analysis fails to recognize the important function of 14.2-9 in gathering up the most striking accusations and threats of punishment from the remainder of the book and reversing them, in one all-encompassing act of reconciliation between Yahweh and Israel. Many of the hopes for renewed relationship from preceding chapters are realized, and many of the elements which are the causes of broken relationship in preceding chapters are removed. Unlike the failed attempt in 6.1-5 or the one-sided effort of Yahweh in 11.1-11, this text presents both parties as active participants in reconciliation and the restoration of their broken relationship.

The recognition of this function of 14.2-9 in reversing the judgment on the ancestors and the particularly close verbal relationship between Hosea 14 and Hosea 11 provides the basis for understanding the enigmatic phrase: 'since in you alone orphans find compassion' (אשר בך ירחם יתום, 14.4). This seems a very strange motivation for national repentance, especially since it is the only motive given, unless the connection is made with ch. 11. In 11.1-7 Israel is depicted as an orphan that is adopted as Yahweh's son in the event of the exodus.[77] Yahweh is

75. Note that their destruction is said to result from their stubborn holding to their apostasy (משובה, 11.7).

76. Wolff, *Hosea*, p. 234.

77. Hos. 11 clearly depicts the relationship between Yahweh and Israel in terms of an adopted child and parent. Cf. Wolff, *Hosea*, pp. 197-98.

described as teaching Ephraim to walk (11.3), taking them in his arms, and healing them. Yahweh's treatment of Israel is compared to those who lift an infant to their cheeks, and Yahweh is said to be the one who fed infant Israel (11.4). Finally, in accusing them of calling on Baal, Yahweh claims that Baal is incapable of completing their rearing (11.7).[78] In light of this description of the relationship between Yahweh and Israel in 11.1-7 and the other connections between this text and 14.2-9, the motivation for repentance in 14.4 becomes intelligible. In their confession, the people recognize that they are an orphan and that only in Yahweh will orphan Israel find the love and nurture that is necessary for their growth from childhood to adulthood. All of the interrelationships between ch. 14 and the preceding sections of the book, particularly the perception of 14.4 in relation to 11.1-7, demonstrate the value of a reader-oriented approach to the book of Hosea that is cognizant of the structure and shape of the whole. This shaping of the reader's expectations and perception of the content of ch. 14 only occurs in such a reading. It is only in a reading of the book that is attentive to the literary relationship of the oracles within the structure of the book that these interrelationships become intelligible.

The Function of Reading Hosea in Persian Yehud

One significant aspect of the experience of reading this book in the Persian period must have been the congruence between the contents of the book and the communal history.[79] The movement from threat of punishment to promise of restoration after punishment would ring true to the historical memory of the community, a memory which encompassed both exile and return. The centrality of exile and return to the communal psyche, as demonstrated by the ubiquity of this theme in the extant traditions from the period, would coalesce with the reading of Hosea to confirm the reliability of the prophetic word. Thus the reader's expectation that the book contains 'the word of the Lord' is reinforced by this correspondence between the reading of the text and the community's historical memory. One effect of this correspondence would be the validation for the reader of the claim of the superscription that

78. Cf. Isa. 1.2, where Yahweh's raising of the rebellious child, Israel, is also described by the verb רום.

79. Of course, it is important to remember that the congruence would in large measure be due to the fact that the interpretive environment of the period would fundamentally shape the way in which the book was read.

this is דבר יהוה. The opposite would also be true: the correspondence would also function to validate the community's self-understanding by rooting it in the authoritative words of a Yahwistic prophet. The accuracy of Hosea's words regarding judgment would raise the expectation that his words about salvation could also be trusted.

The manner in which the book encompasses accusation, judgment and reconciliation permits the Persian period reader vicariously to experience the community's past relationship with Yahweh as a learning experience. The communal reading of Hosea would have constituted an experience of the complete process of sin, rejection and reconciliation. The communal perception of themselves and their God was dramatically reconfigured to recognize both their post-punishment situation and the sovereign unpredictability of Yahweh. The references to the earlier prophetic traditions in the book of Zechariah indicate that these earlier prophets were being read in just this way in the early Persian period.

The confirmation of the veracity and authority of the words of Hosea is amplified by the privileged position of prophets in the text of the book. In contrast to the presentation of kings, the royal household and officials, and priests, prophets are almost entirely exempt from criticism. Hosea 4.5 is the only text that suggests any criticism of prophets, and it is very limited in scope. In fact, the prophets are depicted as having been inappropriately ignored or regarded as lunatics by the ancestors (9.7-9). This characterization of past generations' dealings with Yahwistic prophets highlights the dangers of similar attitudes for the contemporary reading community. This danger is further emphasized by the portrayal of the prophets as both the means of destruction and deliverance for Israel (6.5; 12.11, 14 [Eng. 10, 13]). Not only is the veracity of the prophetic word established by reading Hosea but also the power or effectiveness of the word for both good and ill.

By emphasizing the role of the prophets both in Israel's destruction and deliverance, the reading of Hosea (and other prophetic texts) in this period would have functioned to impress the importance of these texts upon the ruling class. The effect would have been similar to the transition from valuing prophetic oracles to valuing prophetic texts proposed by Schniedewind.[80] If the prophetic words were understood to have both threatened and produced the events which came upon the

---

80. Schniedewind, *The Word of God in Transition*.

ancestors then the interpretation and dissemination of the prophetic texts would be very important to the political and religious leadership of Persian period Yehud.

A central function of reading Hosea in this setting was the creation and maintenance of a national, religious identity. By casting the history of the people 'Israel' in terms of sin, punishment and restoration, the book of Hosea (and a significant proportion of the prophetic literature) establishes a paradigm within which it is possible to construe continuity between monarchic Israel and Judah and Persian period Yehud. As was suggested previously, the identification of the entire Yehudite population of the late sixth and early fifth centuries with the exiled population from sixth-century Judah provided the basis for establishing continuity with the ancestors. The inhabitants of Persian Yehud could be assumed to be the descendants of the populace of monarchic Judah because they all had returned from exile. This continuity is further reinforced in reading the book of Hosea by the numerous connections with the origin traditions of the nation highlighted above. These traditions not only create identity for the reader as a result of their status as stories of national origin, but they also shape the self-understanding of the Persian period Yehudites because the use of these traditions (exodus, wilderness, and the exile of the patriarch) within the book of Hosea highlights the parallels between the community's recent experience of exile and return and the narration of their origins that encompasses moves from outside to inside the land.

Just as significantly, this connection with the exiled population provided the contemporary Yehudite community with a necessary discontinuity in relation to the ancestors. They were not the generation to whom these threats of punishment were directly related. Rather, they were the generation of repentance and restoration. Their ancestors had failed to heed the words of the prophet and the community had paid the price of exile. Persian period Yehudites could now understand themselves as living in a post-punishment relationship with Yahweh. They could both preceive the threats of the book as warnings and the promises of the book as their potential future. Both by means of continuity and discontinuity with their ancestors of preceding generations, the Persian period Yehudite community defined itself as the legitimate descendant of monarchic 'Israel'.

A central factor in establishing Yehudite society as the legitimate continuation of monarchic Israelite and Judahite society was the re-establishment of appropriate Yahwistic faith and practices. By rebuilding the Yahwistic temple in Jerusalem and (re)establishing the worship of Yahweh, the Yehudite community staked claim to the legacy of their monarchic period ancestors. The reading of Hosea suggested above would have been an important feature of this project. The denunciations of non-Yahwistic worship, which according to the book of Hosea had resulted in exile from the land, and the promise of a new future based on repentance and reconciliation with Yahweh (esp. Hos. 14.2-9) provided the foundation for a Persian period Yahwism, practiced in the new Jerusalem temple, which rejected as illicit the worship of all other deities.

Finally, the reading of Hosea proposed above would have functioned as a central means of establishing and maintaining political and religious control over the population. The productive and interpretive practices of the literary elites both shaped and were shaped by the texts with which they worked. The production and interpretation of sacred texts, including Hosea, was a key factor in the creation and continuation of the social, political and religious life of the Persian province of Yehud. The provincial elites, by virtue of their role as producers and interpreters of divine texts, would have functioned as mediators of the divine to the community. The means both to achieve present and future blessing and to avoid a repetition of the disasters of the past were monopolized by the scribal and priestly intermediaries who controlled access to the texts, their production and their interpretation. These same individuals functioned as the intermediaries between the populace and the central, imperial authorities. This dual intermediary function endowed the literary elites of the province with an unparalleled measure of social control over the population of Persian period Yehud.

Chapter 6

CONCLUSION

The preceding inquiry has presented one possible reading of the book of Hosea within the reconstructed socio-historical environment of early Persian Yehud (c. 539–516 BCE). There are several benefits that result from this type of analysis.

The reader-oriented perspective adopted in this analysis has permitted insight into some of the many potential meanings of the text. The meaning of the book of Hosea, or any other text, is not an immutable object, latent within the words on the page, that can be distilled from the book. The meaning of the book of Hosea is experienced by the reader reading the text. It is a diachronic event that is given its shape by the setting in which it is read, and the interpretive conventions employed in the reading. One significance of this observation is that the meaning of a text changes as the reader, setting and interpretive conventions change. In certain ways, every reading of every text is unique, including this reconstructed reading of the book of Hosea.

Although one implication of this theoretical understanding of the process of reading is the essentially private nature of meaning, it also provides a basis for understanding shared meaning through the communal nature of interpretive conventions and the shaping effect of the social setting of reading. As social beings, we read texts through the interpretive lens provided by the reading practices of our community(ies). When we share both setting and interpretive conventions then we can arrive at shared or overlapping interpretations of a text. There will always be differences in specific details, but that which is shared will be larger than that which is idiosyncratic. It is possible to see this operative by comparing modern reading communities reading the biblical texts. Membership in a particular religious community, particularly fundamentalist communities with interpretive conventions that are enforced with communal sanctions, may result in common, communal readings of the biblical texts, which are unique to that community of readers. Alternatively, membership in another reading community, such as the community of modern critical, biblical scholars, may create common readings within the community that cut across the boundaries of the religious communities represented by the individual scholars. The point is, although there will always be unique elements to any reading at any particular time and by any particular individual, there will also be large areas of commonality between individual readings which occur within a common socio-historical setting and which result from a shared set of interpretive conventions.

By combining a reader-oriented approach to the book of Hosea with historical and sociological analyses of a particular reading community, it becomes possible to reconstruct a reading of the book by that particular community. Such a reading will always be imperfect and provisional, but this is true of all readings that attempt to bridge the gap between unique, idiosyncratic readings of a text and communally shared, intersubjective meanings of a text. The difficulties of doing this with an ancient reading community are not different from understanding the reading(s) of a text of a contemporary reading community, but the cultural and chronological distance does magnify the difficulty. The degree of success always depends on making the best possible use of the available evidence to reconstruct accurately the social forces that shaped the reading practices of any particular community.

The examination of the reception of the book of Hosea (or any of the other eighth-century prophetic books) within the context constituted by the reading conventions of late sixth-century Yehud highlights the continuing, but altered, role played by earlier traditions in the ongoing life of the community of worshipers of Yahweh. These traditions were not restricted in their relevance to the socio-historical setting of their eponymous prophet. In fact, although they are often treated as primary evidence for the period in which the named prophet lived, the prophetic books, as they now exist, are more directly related to the situation in which they were given their final shape. The task of reading the, so-called, eighth-century prophets within the reconstructed interpretive horizons of eighth-century Israel and/or Judah is, in fact, an even more precarious task. In addition to the difficulties involved in the recreation of the situation in which the words were received, it is necessary to reconstruct which words from the existing text were actually received in that earlier context. A reading set within a context after the completion of the final form at least has the advantage of rendering this difficult deconstructing of the existing text unnecessary. For a sixth-century reading of Hosea it is ultimately unimportant whether there was actually an eighth-century prophet called Hosea, or which, if any, of the words of the book might derive from this prophet. The reception of the book of Hosea in this later period is determined by the interpretive context of the sixth century, including their beliefs about their past, rather than the actual events of the past. Reading the prophetic books of the Hebrew Bible within the socio-historical context of the period of their production, or its immediate aftermath, has the advantage of shifting the focus of interpretation to a period in which they were actually being read, in a form which still exists, by the ancient community of readers.

One aspect of the interpretive environment of sixth-century Yehud, which has been highlighted in this study, is the strong influence of the imperial context on the production and reading of texts. Some of the factors that would have shaped the reading of texts in this environment would be common to similar colonial situations. The relation of imperial center and periphery is an aspect of the interpretive environment which will always have a dramatic effect on the shape of readings which occur in a colonial context. There are also, however, unique factors within the relationship between the Persian imperial administration and colonial Yehud which contributed to the shape of readings within that specific socio-historical environment. In the end, it is the interplay of all of these factors, whether common to a certain type of social structure or unique to a specific instance of social organization, which shaped the reading of texts in Persian Yehud. For example, colonies at the periphery of an empire are always caught in webs of relationship that bind them to the imperial center on the one hand, and to social structures which lie beyond the boundaries of the empire on the other. In the late sixth century, the dangers of relations with Egypt would have been highlighted in all of the Persian colonies in Palestine. The threat of colonies on the Palestinian periphery of the empire being induced to support Egyptian rebellion against the imperial center would have been a significant factor in the administration of all of these colonies. In the case of Yehud, the existence of textual traditions depicting Egypt as a source of danger and a place of punishment may have facilitated the general imperial goal in this specific colony, but these traditions alone would not necessarily have been the source of warnings about relations with Egypt in late sixth-century Jerusalem. It is the context of imperial difficulty with Egypt which provides the interpretive environment that results in a particular reading of these traditions.

The dominant role of the colonial administration of Achaemenid Yehud in the production and interpretation of the traditional texts is another important feature of the period stressed in this study. The extremely limited dissemination of literacy at a level capable of producing and interpreting texts as complex as those preserved in the Hebrew Bible had the effect of concentrating the interpretation of these texts in the hands of a small number of educated elites. The provision of writing materials and the training and support of scribes would have been an expensive undertaking in the ancient world. As a result of the expense involved, the financial support of scribal schools and scribal activities would have been the domain of the administrative structures of royal courts. A wealthy individual may have paid for the services of a scribe for a specific task from time to time, but only a governmental administration would have had the need or the resources to support a scribal class. This means that the production and interpretation of the texts of the Hebrew Bible were not only the province of a small number of highly trained individuals, but they were also the province of individuals who were trained and supported by the imperial administration. This does not exclude the possibility of readings which are opposed to imperial policies, but it does make them much less likely. The dependence of the scribal class on the existing structures for their livelihood would encourage them, implicitly and explicitly, to produce texts and interpretations of texts that support the status quo.

The transition to monotheistic Yahwism was an important element of the interpretive environment of this period which shaped the reading of the book of Hosea. Given the polytheistic environment of eighth-century Israel, it is likely that the original Hosean oracles within the book which condemn inappropriate cultic activities were primarily concerned with the struggle between Baal and Yahweh for supremacy of the Israelite pantheon. By the late sixth century, however, monotheistic Yahwism had become the dominant religion in Yehud (at least among those who produced and interpreted the texts that have survived from the period). This very different interpretive environment would have shaped the reading of the book of Hosea. The condemnations of inappropriate cultic activities would have been interpreted more generally as a rejection of all cultic activities that are not appropriate to a strict Yahwistic monotheism. It is the later religious environment, not the earlier context or the intentions of the prophet, which would have dominated the reading of these texts in Achaemenid Yehud.

Finally, I would suggest that reading the book of Hosea within the reconstructed interpretive context of late sixth-century Yehud allows a discernible shape of the book as a whole to emerge. In this environment, the belief that the monarchic period population had been deported, that the land had been left desolate, and that the faithful Yahwistic community had then returned from their exile to restore the community's life was a central interpretive convention. The centrality of this interpretation of the community's past can be seen in the ubiquity of this perspective in the texts that were produced in the Persian period. Interpretively shaped by this understanding of the past, the book of Hosea reveals a movement from threat of punishment, to punishment, to post-punishment reconciliation. Such a reading of the book of Hosea (and other prophetic traditions) in this period permitted the population of Achaemenid Yehud to create a self-understanding which placed them in a post-punishment relationship with Yahweh. They could use the traditions of the past as a warning to avoid the disasters which came upon their ancestors, and, at the same time, to support their construction of a new social and religious structure. Such an interpretation created enough continuity with the past to permit them to view themselves as the legitimate continuation of monarchic period society. This interpretation also provided enough discontinuity with their past to legitimate their new social structures as alterations designed to avoid the disasters of the past. Thus, this interpretation created a self-understanding which viewed their very different society as the appropriate continuation of monarchic Israel and Judah.

BIBLIOGRAPHY

Ackerman, Susan, *Under Every Green Tree: Popular Religion in Sixth-Century Judah* (HSM, 46; Atlanta: Scholars Press, 1992).

—'The Queen Mother and the Cult in Ancient Israel', *JBL* 112 (1993), pp. 385-401.

Ackroyd, Peter, 'Hosea and Jacob', *VT* 13 (1963), pp. 245-59.

—*Exile and Restoration: A Study of Hebrew Thought of the Sixth Century B.C.* (Philadelphia: Westminster Press, 1968).

—'The Jewish Community in Palestine in the Persian Period', in W.D. Davies and Louis Finkelstein (eds.), *The Cambridge History of Judaism* (4 vols.; Cambridge: Cambridge University Press, 1984), I, pp. 130-61.

—'The Written Evidence for Palestine', in Heleen Sancisi-Weerdenburg and Amélie Kuhrt (eds.), *Achaemenid History. IV. Centre and Periphery* (Proceedings of the Gröningen 1986 Achaemenid History Workshop; Leiden: Nederlands Instituut voor het Nabije Oosten, 1990), pp. 207-20.

Ahlström, G.W., *Aspects of Syncretism in Israelite Religion* (Horae Soederblomianae, 5; Lund: C.W.K. Gleerup, 1963).

—*Royal Administration and National Religion in Ancient Palestine* (Leiden: E.J. Brill, 1982).

—*The History of Ancient Palestine* (Minneapolis: Fortress Press, 1993).

Albertz, Rainer, *A History of Israelite Religion in the Old Testament Period* (OTL; 2 vols.; Louisville, KY: Westminster/John Knox Press, 1994).

Albright, W.F., *From the Stone Age to Christianity: Monotheism and the Historical Process* (Garden City, NY: Doubleday, 2nd edn, 1957).

—*The Biblical Period from Abraham to Ezra: An Historical Survey* (New York: Harper & Row, rev. edn, 1960).

Alter, Robert, *The Art of Biblical Narrative* (New York: Basic Books, 1981).

—*The Art of Biblical Poetry* (New York: Basic Books, 1985).

Andersen, Francis I., and David Noel Freedman, *Hosea* (AB, 24; New York: Doubleday, 1980).

Avigad, Nahman, 'Excavations at Makmish, 1958: Preliminary Report', *IEJ* 10 (1960), pp. 90-96.

—'Seals of the Exiles', *IEJ* 15 (1965), pp. 222-32.

—*Bullae and Seals from a Post-Exilic Judean Archive* (Qedem, 4; Jerusalem: Hebrew University, 1976).

Baines, John, 'Literacy in Ancient Egyptian Society', *Man* NS 18 (1983), pp. 572-99.

Barkay, Gabriel, 'The Iron Age II–III', in Amnon Ben-Tor (ed.), *The Archaeology of Ancient Israel* (New Haven: Yale University Press, 1992), pp. 302-73.

Becking, B., *The Fall of Samaria: An Historical and Archaeological Investigation* (Studies in the History of the Ancient Near East, 2; Leiden: E.J. Brill, 1992).

Ben Zvi, Ehud, *A Historical-Critical Study of the Book of Zephaniah* (BZAW, 198; Berlin: W. de Gruyter, 1991).

—'Inclusion in and Exclusion from Israel as Conveyed by the Use of the Term "Israel" in Post-monarchic Biblical Texts', in Steven W. Holloway and Lowell K. Handy (eds.), *The Pitcher is Broken: Memorial Essays for Gösta W. Ahlström* (JSOTSup, 190; Sheffield: Sheffield Academic Press, 1995), pp. 95-149.

—*A Historical-Critical Study of the Book of Obadiah* (BZAW, 242; Berlin: W. de Gruyter, 1996).

—'The Urban Center of Jerusalem and the Development of the Old Testament/Hebrew Bible Literature', unpublished paper delivered at the conference on 'Urbanism in the Ancient Near East', Lethbridge, January 1996.

Berquist, Jon L., 'The Social Setting of Early Postexilic Prophecy' (PhD dissertation, Vanderbilt University, 1989).

—*Judaism in Persia's Shadow: A Social and Historical Approach* (Minneapolis: Fortress Press, 1995).

—'Postcolonialism and Imperial Motives for Canonization', *Semeia* 75 (1996), pp. 15-35.

Bird, Phyllis, 'To Play the Harlot: An Inquiry into an Old Testament Metaphor', in Peggy Day (ed.), *Gender and Difference in Ancient Israel* (Minneapolis: Fortress Press, 1989), pp. 75-94.

Blenkinsopp, Joseph, 'The Mission of Udjahorresnet and Those of Ezra and Nehemiah', *JBL* 106 (1987), pp. 409-21.

—*Ezra–Nehemiah* (OTL; Philadelphia: Westminster Press, 1988).

Bloch-Smith, Elizabeth, *Judahite Burial Practices and Beliefs about the Dead* (JSOTSup, 123; Sheffield: JSOT Press, 1992).

Bolin, Thomas M., 'The Temple of יהו at Elephantine and Persian Religious Policy', in D.V. Edelman (ed.), *The Triumph of Elohim: From Yahwisms to Judaisms* (Grand Rapids: Eerdmans, 1996), pp. 127-42.

Boyce, Mary, *A History of Zoroastrianism*. II. *Under the Achaemenians* (3 vols.; Handbuch der Orientalistik; Leiden: E.J. Brill, 1982).

—'Persian Religion in the Achaemenid Age', in W.D. Davies and Louis Finkelstein (eds.), *Cambridge History of Judaism* (3 vols.; Cambridge: Cambridge University Press, 1984), I, pp. 279-307.

Broshi, Magen, 'Estimating the Population of Ancient Jerusalem', *BARev* 4 (1978), pp. 10-15 (repr. in idem, *Bread, Wine, Walls and Scrolls* [JSPSup, 36; Sheffield: Sheffield Academic Press, 2001]).

Brueggemann, Walter, 'Psalms and the Life of Faith: A Suggested Typology of Function', *JSOT* 17 (1980), pp. 3-32.

—'Unity and Dynamic in the Isaiah Tradition', *JSOT* 29 (1984), pp. 89-107.

Carter, Charles E., 'The Province of Yehud in the Post-exilic Period: Soundings in Site Distribution and Demography', in Tamara C. Eskenazi and Kent H. Richards (eds.), *Second Temple Studies 2: Temple and Community in the Persian Period* (JSOTSup, 175; Sheffield: JSOT Press, 1994), pp. 106-45.

Catlett, Michael Lee, 'Reversals in Hosea: A Literary Analysis' (PhD dissertation, Emory University, 1988).

Champion, T.C. (ed.), *Centre and Periphery: Comparative Studies in Archaeology* (One World Archaeology; London: Routledge, 1989).

Childs, Brevard S., *Introduction to the Old Testament as Scripture* (Philadelphia: Fortress Press, 1979).

Clements, R.E., 'Beyond Tradition-History: Deutero-Isaianic Development of First Isaiah's Themes', *JSOT* 31 (1985), pp. 95-113.

—'The Unity of the Book of Isaiah', in J.L. Mays and P.J. Achtemeier (eds.), *Interpreting the Prophets* (Philadelphia: Fortress Press, 1987), pp. 50-61.

Conrad, Edgar W., *Reading Isaiah* (OBT; Minneapolis: Fortress Press, 1991).

Coogan, Michael David, 'Canaanite Origins and Lineage: Reflections on the Religion of Ancient Israel', in P.D. Miller, Jr, P.D. Hanson and S.D. McBride (eds.), *Ancient Israelite Religion: Essays in Honor of Frank Moore Cross* (Philadelphia: Fortress Press, 1987), pp. 115-24.

Cook, J.M., *The Persian Empire* (New York: Schocken Books, 1983).

Cowley, A.E., *Aramaic Papyri of the Fifth Century B.C.* (Oxford: Clarendon Press, 1923).

Cross, Frank Moore, *Canaanite Myth and Hebrew Epic: Essays in the History of the Religion of Israel* (Cambridge, MA: Harvard University Press, 1973).

Culler, Jonathan, 'Reading and Misreading', *The Yale Review* 65 (1975), pp. 88-95.

Dandamaev, M.A., *A Political History of the Achaemenid Empire* (Leiden: E.J. Brill, 1989).

Dandamaev, M.A., and V.G. Lukonin, *The Culture and Social Institutions of Ancient Iran* (Cambridge: Cambridge University Press, 1989).

Davies, Graham I., *Hosea* (NCB; London: Marshall Pickering, 1992).

Davies, Philip R., *In Search of 'Ancient Israel': A Study in Biblical Origins* (JSOTSup, 148; Sheffield: JSOT Press, 1992).

Davis, Ellen F., *Swallowing the Scroll: Textuality and the Dynamics of Discourse in Ezekiel's Prophecy* (JSOTSup, 78; Sheffield: Almond Press, 1989).

Day, John, 'Asherah in the Hebrew Bible and Northwest Semitic Literature', *JBL* 105 (1986), pp. 385-408.

—'A Case of Inner Scriptural Interpretation: The Dependence of Isaiah Xxvi.13–xxvii.11 on Hosea Xiii.4–xiv.10 (Eng. 9) and its Relevance to Some Theories of the Redaction of the "Isaiah Apocalypse"', *JTS* NS 31 (1980), pp. 309-19.

Dever, William G., 'The Contribution of Archaeology to the Study of Canaanite and Early Israelite Religion', in P.D. Miller, Jr, P.D. Hanson and S.D. McBride (eds.), *Ancient Israelite Religion: Essays in Honor of Frank Moore Cross* (Philadelphia: Fortress Press, 1987), pp. 209-47.

—*Recent Archaeological Discoveries and Biblical Research* (Samuel and Althea Stroum Lectures in Jewish Studies; Seattle: University of Washington Press, 1990).

—'"Will the Real Israel Please Stand Up?" Part I: Archaeology and Israelite Historiography', *BASOR* 297 (1995), pp. 61-80.

—'"Will the Real Israel Please Stand Up?" Part II: Archaeology and the Religions of Ancient Israel', *BASOR* 298 (1995), pp. 37-58.

Edelman, D.V. (ed.), *The Triumph of Elohim: From Yahwisms to Judaisms* (Grand Rapids: Eerdmans, 1996).

Eisenstadt, S.N., *The Political Systems of Empires* (Glencoe: Free Press, 1963).

Elliger, Karl, *Die Einheit des Tritojesaia (Jesaia 56–66)* (BWANT, 9; 3rd series; Stuttgart: W. Kohlhammer, 1928).

Engel, D.W., *Alexander the Great and the Logistics of the Macedonian Army* (Berkeley: University of California Press, 1978).

Eph'al, Israel, 'The Western Minorities in Babylonia in the 6th–5th Centuries B.C.: Maintenance and Cohesion', *Or* NS 47 (1978), pp. 84-87.

Eskenazi, Tamara Cohn, *In an Age of Prose: A Literary Approach to Ezra–Nehemiah* (SBLMS, 36; Atlanta: Scholars Press, 1988).

Evans, Carl D., 'Cult Images, Royal Policies and the Origins of Aniconism', in Steven W. Holloway and Lowell K. Handy (eds.), *The Pitcher is Broken: Memorial Essays for Gösta W. Ahlström* (JSOTSup, 190; Sheffield: Sheffield Academic Press, 1995), pp. 192-212.

Fewell, Danna Nolan, *Circle of Sovereignty: A Story of Stories in Daniel 1–6* (JSOTSup, 72; Bible and Literature Series, 20; Sheffield: Almond Press, 1988).

Fish, Stanley, *Is There a Text in This Class? The Authority of Interpretive Communities* (Cambridge, MA: Harvard University Press, 1980).

—'Literature in the Reader: Affective Stylistics', in Jane Tompkins (ed.), *Reader-Response Criticism: From Formalism to Post-Structuralism* (Baltimore: The Johns Hopkins University Press, 1980), pp. 70-100.

—*Doing What Comes Naturally: Change, Rhetoric, and the Practice of Theory in Literary and Legal Studies* (Durham, NC: Duke University Press, 1989).

Fishbane, Michael, *Text and Texture: Close Readings of Selected Biblical Texts* (New York: Schocken Books, 1979).

Frye, Richard N., *The History of Ancient Iran* (Handbuch der Altertumswissenschaft; Munich: C.H. Beck, 1984).

Gadd, C.J., 'Inscribed Prisms of Sargon II from Nimrud', *Iraq* 16 (1954), pp. 173-201.

Galling, Kurt, *Studien zur Geschichte Israels im persischen Zeitalter* (Tübingen: J.C.B. Mohr, 1964).

Glazier-McDonald, Beth, 'Intermarriage, Divorce, and the *bat-'el nekar*: Insights into Mal 2:10-16', *JBL* 106 (1987), pp. 603-11.

Gledhill, John, *Power and its Disguises: Anthropological Perspectives on Politics* (London: Pluto Press, 1994).

Gledhill, J., B. Bender and M.T. Larson (eds.), *State and Society: The Emergence and Development of Social Hierarchy and Political Centralization* (One World Archaeology, 4; London: Routledge, 1988).

Gottwald, Norman K., *The Tribes of Yahweh: A Sociology of the Religion of Liberated Israel, 1250–1050 B.C.E.* (Maryknoll, NY: Orbis Books, 1979).

Grabbe, Lester L., *Judaism from Cyrus to Hadrian*, I (2 vols.; Minneapolis: Fortress Press, 1992).

—*Priests, Prophets, Diviners, Sages: A Socio-Historical Study of Religious Specialists in Ancient Israel* (Valley Forge, PA: Trinity Press International, 1995).

Hadley, Judith M., 'The Khirbet el-Qom Inscription', *VT* 37 (1987), pp. 50-62.

—'Some Drawings and Inscriptions on Two Pithoi from Kuntillet 'Ajrud', *VT* 37 (1987), pp. 180-213.

Halpern, Baruch, ' "Brisker Pipes Than Poetry": The Development of Israelite Monotheism', in Jacob Neusner, Baruch A. Levine and Ernest S. Frerichs (eds.), *Judaic Perspectives on Ancient Israel* (Philadelphia: Fortress Press, 1987), pp. 77-115.

Handy, Lowell, *Among the Host of Heaven: The Syro-Palestinian Pantheon as Bureaucracy* (Winona Lake, IN: Eisenbrauns, 1994).

—'The Appearance of Pantheon in Judah', in D.V. Edelman (ed.), *The Triumph of Elohim: From Yahwisms to Judaisms* (Grand Rapids: Eerdmans, 1996), pp. 27-43.

Hanson, Paul, *The Dawn of Apocalyptic: The Historical and Sociological Roots of Jewish Apocalyptic Eschatology* (Philadelphia: Fortress Press, rev. edn, 1979).

—'Israelite Religion in the Early Post-exilic Period', in Patrick D. Miller, Jr, Paul D. Hanson, and S.D. McBride (eds.), *Ancient Israelite Religion: Essays in Honor of Frank Moore Cross* (Philadelphia: Fortress Press, 1987), pp. 485-508.

Harris, William V., *Ancient Literacy* (Cambridge, MA: Harvard University Press, 1989).

Hayes, John H., and J. Maxwell Miller (eds.), *Israelite and Judean History* (Philadelphia: Westminster Press, 1977).

Hodge, Robert, *Literature as Discourse: Textual Strategies in English and History* (Cambridge, MA: Polity Press, 1990).

Hoglund, Kenneth G., 'The Achaemenid Context', in Philip R. Davies (ed.), *Second Temple Studies 1: Persian Period* (JSOTSup, 117; Sheffield: JSOT Press, 1991), pp. 54-72.

—*Achaemenid Imperial Administration in Syria-Palestine and the Missions of Ezra and Nehemiah* (SBLDS, 125; Atlanta: Scholars Press, 1992).

Holladay, William L., *Jeremiah*, II (2 vols.; Hermeneia; Minneapolis: Fortress Press, 1989).

Iser, Wolfgang, *The Act of Reading: A Theory of Aesthetic Response* (Baltimore: The Johns Hopkins University Press, 1978).

Japhet, Sara, *I & II Chronicles* (OTL; Louisville, KY: Westminster/John Knox Press, 1993).

Jeremias, Jorg, *Der Prophet Hosea* (Göttingen: Vandenhoeck & Ruprecht, 1983).

Kaufmann, Yehezkel, *The Religion of Israel: From its Beginnings to the Babylonian Exile* (New York: Schocken Books, 1960).

Keck, L.E., and G.M. Tucker, 'Exegesis', in *IDBSup*, pp. 296-303.

Kenyon, Kathleen, *Archaeology in the Holy Land* (London: Ernest Benn, 1960).

Knapp, Steven, and Walter Benn Michaels, 'Against Theory', in W.J.T. Mitchell (ed.), *Against Theory: Literary Studies and the New Pragmatism* (Chicago: University of Chicago Press, 1985), pp. 11-30.

Kooij, G. van der, 'Tell Deir 'Alla (East Jordan Valley) during the Achaemenid Period', in Heleen Sancisi-Weerdenburg (ed.), *Achaemenid History*. I. *Sources, Structures and Synthesis* (Proceedings of the Groningen 1983 Achaemenid History Workshop; Leiden: Nederlands Instituut voor het Nabije Oosten, 1987), pp. 97-102.

Kraus, Hans-Joachim, *Psalms 60–150* (Continental Commentaries; Minneapolis: Augsburg, 1989).

Kreissig, Heinz, *Die Sozialökonomische Situation in Juda zur Achämenidenzeit* (Berlin: Akadamie Verlag, 1973).

Kuhrt, Amélie, 'The Cyrus Cylinder and Achaemenid Imperial Policy', *JSOT* 25 (1983), pp. 83-97.

—'Nabonidus and the Babylonian Priesthood', in Mary Beard and John North (eds.), *Pagan Priests: Religion and Power in the Ancient World* (London: Gerald Duckworth, 1990), pp. 141-46.

—*The Ancient Near East c. 3000–330 BC* (2 vols.; London: Routledge, 1995).

Kuhrt, Amélie, and Susan Sherwin-White, 'Xerxes' Destruction of Babylonian Temples', in Heleen Sancisi-Weerdenburg and Amélie Kuhrt (eds.), *Achaemenid History*. II. *The Greek Sources* (Proceedings of the Groningen 1984 Achaemenid History Workshop; Leiden: Nederlands Instituut voor het Nabije Oosten, 1987), pp. 69-78.

Landy, Francis, *Hosea* (Readings; Sheffield: Sheffield Academic Press, 1995).

Lang, Bernhard, *Monotheism and the Prophetic Minority: An Essay in Biblical History and Sociology* (The Social World of Biblical Antiquity, 1; Sheffield: Almond Press, 1983).

Lemche, Niels Peter, *Ancient Israel: A New History of Israelite Society* (Biblical Seminar, 5; Sheffield: Sheffield Academic Press, 1988).

Machor, James L., 'Historical Hermeneutics and Antebellum Fiction: Gender, Response Theory, and Interpretive Contexts', in *idem* (ed.), *Readers in History: Nineteenth-Century American Literature and the Contexts of Response* (Baltimore: The Johns Hopkins University Press, 1993), pp. 54-84.

Macintosh, A.A., 'Hosea and the Wisdom Tradition: Dependence and Independence', in John Day, Robert P. Gordon and H.G.M. Williamson (eds.), *Wisdom in Ancient Israel: Essays in Honour of J.A. Emerton* (Cambridge: Cambridge University Press, 1995), pp. 124-32.

Mailloux, Steven, *Interpretive Conventions: The Reader in the Study of American Fiction* (Ithaca, NY: Cornell University Press, 1982).

—*Rhetorical Power* (Ithaca, NY: Cornell University Press, 1989).

—'Misreading as a Historical Act: Cultural Rhetoric, Bible Politics, and Fuller's 1845 Review of Douglass's *Narrative*', in James L. Machor (ed.), *Readers in History: Nineteenth-Century American Literature and the Contexts of Response* (Baltimore: The Johns Hopkins University Press, 1993), pp. 3-31.

Mann, Michael, *The Sources of Social Power* (4 vols.; Cambridge: Cambridge University Press, 1986–).

Mason, Rex, 'The Prophets of the Restoration', in R. Coggins, A. Phillips and M. Knibb (eds.), *Israel's Prophetic Tradition: Essays in Honor of Peter Ackroyd* (Cambridge: Cambridge University Press, 1982), pp. 137-54.

Mays, James Luther, *Hosea* (OTL; Philadelphia: Westminster Press, 1969).

McCarter, P. Kyle, Jr, *1 Samuel* (AB, 8; New York: Doubleday, 1980).

McComiskey, Thomas Edward, 'Prophetic Irony in Hosea 14: A Study of the Collocation פחד על and its Implications for the Fall of John's Dynasty', *JSOT* 58 (1993), pp. 93-101.

Meyers, Carol L., and Eric M. Meyers, *Haggai and Zechariah 1–8* (AB, 25B; New York: Doubleday, 1987).

Meyers, Eric M., 'The Use of *toru* in Haggai 2:11 and the Role of the Prophet in the Restoration Community', in Carol L. Meyers and M. O'Connor (eds.), *The Word of the Lord Shall Go Forth: Essays in Honor of David Noel Freedman in Celebration of his Sixtieth Birthday* (Winona Lake, IN: Eisenbrauns, 1983), pp. 69-76.

—'The Persian Period and the Judean Restoration: From Zerubbabel to Nehemiah', in Patrick D. Miller, Jr, Paul D. Hanson and S.D. McBride (eds.), *Ancient Israelite Religion: Essays in Honor of Frank Moore Cross* (Philadelphia: Fortress Press, 1987), pp. 509-21.

—'Second Temple Studies in the Light of Recent Archaeology: Part I: The Persian and Hellenistic Periods', *CRBS* 2 (1994), pp. 24-42.

Miller, D., M. Rowlands and C. Tilley (eds.), *Domination and Resistance* (One World Archaeology, 3; London: Unwin Hyman, 1989).

Miller, J. Maxwell, 'Is it Possible to Write a History of Israel without Relying on the Hebrew Bible?', in D.V. Edelman (ed.), *The Fabric of History: Text, Artifact and Israel's Past* (JSOTSup, 127; Sheffield: JSOT Press, 1991), pp. 93-102.

Miller, J. Maxwell, and John H. Hayes, *A History of Ancient Israel and Judah* (OTL; Philadelphia: Westminster Press, 1986).

Miller, Jr, Patrick D., 'Israelite Religion', in Douglas A. Knight and Gene M. Tucker (eds.), *The Hebrew Bible and its Modern Interpreters* (Philadelphia: Fortress Press, 1985), pp. 201-37.

Moore, S.D., 'Negative Hermeneutics, Insubstantial Texts: Stanley Fish and the Biblical Interpreter', *JAAR* 54 (1986), pp. 707-19.

Morgenstern, Julius, 'Further Light from the Book of Isaiah upon the Catastrophe of 485 B.C.', *HUCA* 27 (1956), pp. 1-28.

—'Jerusalem—485 B.C.', *HUCA* 27 (1956), pp. 101-79.

—'Jerusalem—485 B.C. (continued)', *HUCA* 28 (1957), pp. 15-47.

—'Jerusalem—485 B.C. (concluded)', *HUCA* 31 (1960), pp. 11-29.

Niehr, Herbert, 'The Rise of YHWH in Judahite and Israelite Religion: Methodological and Religio-historical Aspects', in D.V. Edelman (ed.), *The Triumph of Elohim: From Yahwisms to Judaisms* (Grand Rapids: Eerdmans, 1996), pp. 45-72.

Noth, Martin, *The Deuteronomistic History* (JSOTSup, 15; Sheffield: JSOT Press, 2nd edn, 1991).

Oded, Bustenay, 'Judah and the Exile', in John H. Hayes and J. Maxwell Miller (eds.), *Israelite and Judean History* (Philadelphia: Trinity Press International; London: SCM Press, 1977), pp. 435-88.

Olmstead, A.T., *History of the Persian Empire* (Chicago: University of Chicago Press, 1948).

Olyan, Saul M., *Asherah and the Cult of Yahweh in Israel* (SBLMS, 34; Atlanta: Scholars Press, 1988).

Petersen, David L., *Haggai and Zechariah 1–8* (OTL; London: SCM Press, 1985).

—'Israel and Monotheism: The Unfinished Agenda', in Gene M. Tucker, David L. Petersen and Robert R. Wilson (eds.), *Canon, Theology, and Old Testament Interpretation: Essays in Honor of Brevard S. Childs* (Philadelphia: Fortress Press, 1988), pp. 92-107.

Porten, Bezalel, 'The Jews in Egypt', in W.D. Davies and Louis Finkelstein (eds.), *Cambridge History of Judaism*, I (4 vols.; Cambridge: Cambridge University Press, 1984), pp. 372-400.

Porten, Bezalel, and Ada Yardeni, *Textbook of Aramaic Documents from Egypt*, III (4 vols.; Jerusalem: Hebrew University, 1986–99).

Pratt, Mary Louise, 'Interpretive Strategies/Strategic Interpretations: On Anglo-American Reader Response Criticism', *Boundary* 2 11 (1982–83), pp. 201-31.

Rad, Gerhard von, *Deuteronomy* (OTL; London: SCM Press, 1966).

Ray, J., 'Literacy in Egypt in the Late and Persian Periods', in A.K. Bowman and Greg Woolf (eds.), *Literacy and Power in the Ancient World* (Cambridge: Cambridge University Press, 1994), pp. 51-66.

Rendtorff, Rolf, *The Old Testament: An Introduction* (Philadelphia: Fortress Press, 1986).

Richard Coggins (ed.), *Israel's Prophetic Tradition: Essays in Honour of Peter R. Ackroyd* (Cambridge: Cambridge University Press, 1982).

Roberts, J.J.M., *Nahum, Habakkuk, and Zephaniah: A Commentary* (OTL; Louisville, KY: Westminster/John Knox Press, 1991).

Rowlands, Michael, Mogens Larsen and Kristian Kristiansen (eds.), *Centre and Periphery in the Ancient World* (Cambridge: Cambridge University Press, 1987).

Rudolph, Wilhelm, 'Präparierte Jungfrauen? (Zu Hosea 1)', *ZAW* 75 (1963), pp. 65-73.

Schmidt, Brian B., 'The Aniconic Tradition: On Reading Images and Viewing Texts', in D.V. Edelman (ed.), *The Triumph of Elohim: From Yahwisms to Judaisms* (Grand Rapids: Eerdmans, 1996), pp. 75-105.

Schmitt, Rüdiger, *The Bisitun Inscriptions of Darius the Great: Old Persian Text* (Corpus Inscriptionum Iranicarum; London: School of Oriental and African Studies, 1991).

—'BISOTUN Part iii', in *Encyclopaedia Iranica*, IV (London: Routledge, 1990).

Schniedewind, William M., *The Word of God in Transition: From Prophet to Exegete in the Second Temple Period* (JSOTSup, 197; Sheffield: Sheffield Academic Press, 1995).

Seitz, Christopher R., 'Isaiah 1–66: Making Sense of the Whole', in *idem* (ed.), *Reading and Preaching the Book of Isaiah* (Philadelphia: Fortress Press, 1988), pp. 105-26.

Seow, C.L., 'Hosea 14:10 and the Foolish People Motif', *CBQ* 44 (1982), pp. 212-24.

Skehan, P.W., 'Qumran and the Present State of Old Testament Text Studies: The Masoretic Text', *JBL* 78 (1959), pp. 21-25.

Smith, Mark S., *The Early History of God: Yahweh and the Other Deities in Ancient Israel* (San Francisco: HarperSanFrancisco, 1987).

Smith, Morton, *Palestinian Parties and Politics that Shaped the Old Testament* (London: SCM Press, 2nd edn, 1987).

—'Jewish Religious Life in the Persian Period', in W.D. Davies and Louis Finkelstein (eds.), *Cambridge History of Judaism*, I (4 vols.; Cambridge: Cambridge University Press, 1984), pp. 219-78.

Smith, Sidney, *Babylonian Historical Texts Relating to the Capture and Downfall of Babylon* (London: Methuen, 1924).

Spek, R.J. van der, 'Did Cyrus the Great Introduce a New Policy towards Subdued Nations? Cyrus in Assyrian Perspective', *Persica* 10 (1982), pp. 278-83.

Stager, Lawrence E., 'Climatic Conditions and Grain Storage in the Persian Period', *HTR* 64 (1971), pp. 448-540.

Steig, Michael, *Stories of Reading: Subjectivity and Literary Understanding* (Baltimore: The Johns Hopkins University Press, 1989).

Stern, Ephraim, 'Seal Impressions in the Achaemenid Style in the Province of Judah', *BASOR* 202 (1971), pp. 6-16.

—*Material Culture of the Land of the Bible in the Persian Period, 538–332 BC* (Israel Exploration Society; Warminster, England: Aris & Phillips, 1982).

—'The Persian Empire and the Political and Social History of Palestine in the Persian Period', in W.D. Davies and Louis Finkelstein (eds.), *The Cambridge History of Judaism* (4 vols.; Cambridge: Cambridge University Press, 1984), I, pp. 70-87.

—'The Archaeology of Persian Palestine', in *Cambridge History of Judaism*, I, pp. 88-114.

Stuart, Douglas, *Hosea–Jonah* (WBC; Waco, TX: Word Books, 1987).

Taylor, J.G., *Yahweh and the Sun: Biblical and Archaeological Evidence for Sun Worship in Ancient Israel* (JSOTSup, 111; Sheffield: JSOT Press, 1993).

Therborn, Göran, *What Does the Ruling Class Do When It Rules? State Apparatuses and State Power under Feudalism, Capitalism and Socialism* (London: NLB, 1978).

Thompson, Thomas, *Early History of the Israelite People: From the Written and Archaeo-logical Sources* (Studies in the History of the Ancient Near East, 4; Leiden: E.J. Brill, 1992).

Tiffin, Chris, and Alan Lawson (eds.), *De-Scribing Empire: Post-Colonialism and Text-uality* (London: Routledge, 1994).

Tigay, Jeffrey H., *Deuteronomy* (Jewish Publication Society Torah Commentary; Philadelphia: Jewish Publication Society of America, 1996).

Tompkins, Jane (ed.), *Reader-Response Criticism: From Formalism to Post-Structuralism* (Baltimore: The Johns Hopkins University Press, 1980).

Torczyner, Harry, Lankester Harding, Alkin Lewis and J.L. Strakey, *Lachish I: The Lachish Letters* (London: Oxford University Press, 1938).

Tucker, Gene M., 'Prophetic Superscriptions and the Growth of a Canon', in George W. Coats and Burke O. Long (eds.), *Canon and Authority: Essays in Old Testament Religion and Theology* (Philadelphia: Fortress Press, 1977), pp. 56-70.

—'Hosea', in James L. Mays (eds.), *Harper's Bible Commentary* (San Francisco: Harper & Row, 1988), pp. 707-15.

—'Sin and "Judgment" in the Prophets', in Henry T.C. Sun and Keith L. Eades (eds.), with James M. Robinson and Garth I. Moller, *Problems in Biblical Theology: Essays in Honor of Rolf Knierim* (Grand Rapids: Eerdmans, 1997), pp. 373-88.

Tufnell, O., *Lachish III (Tel ed-Duweir): The Iron Age* (London: Oxford University Press, 1953).

Wallerstein, Immanuel, *The Modern World System. I. Capitalist Agriculture and the Origins of the European World-Economy in the Sixteenth Century* (New York: Academic Press, 1974).

Waltke, Bruce K., 'Superscripts, Postscripts, or Both', *JBL* 110 (1991), pp. 583-96.

Ward, James M., *Hosea: A Theological Commentary* (New York: Harper & Row, 1966).

Weinberg, Joel, *The Citizen–Temple Community* (JSOTSup, 151; Sheffield: JSOT Press, 1992).

Weinfeld, Moshe, *Deuteronomy and the Deuteronomic School* (Oxford: Clarendon Press, 1972).

Wellhausen, Julius, *Die Kleinen Propheten* (Berlin: Georg Reimer, 3rd edn, 1898).

Westermann, Claus, *Genesis 1–11: A Commentary* (Continental Commentaries; Minneapolis: Augsburg–Fortress, 1984).

—*Isaiah 40–66* (OTL; London: SCM Press, 1969).

Widengren, Geo, 'The Persian Period', in John H. Hayes and J. Maxwell Miller (eds.), *Israelite and Judean History* (Philadelphia: Westminster Press, 1977), pp. 489-538.

Wildberger, Hans, *Isaiah 1–12* (Continental Commentaries; Minneapolis: Fortress Press, 1991).

Willi-Plein, Ina, *Vorformen der Schriftexegese Innerhalb des Alten Testaments: Untersuchungen zum Literarischen Werden der auf Amos, Hosea und Micha zurückgehenden Bücher im hebräischen Zwölfprophetenbuch* (BZAW, 123; Berlin: W. de Gruyter, 1971).

Wimsatt, W.K., and M.C. Beardsley, 'The Intentional Fallacy', *Sewanee Review* 54 (1946), pp. 468-88.

—'The Affective Fallacy', *Sewanee Review* 57 (1949), pp. 31-55.

Wolff, Hans Walter, *Hosea* (Hermeneia; Philadelphia: Fortress Press, 1974).

—*Haggai* (Continental Commentaries; Minneapolis: Augsburg, 1988).

Yee, Gale, *Composition and Tradition in the Book of Hosea* (SBLDS, 102; Atlanta: Scholars Press, 1987).

INDEXES

INDEX OF REFERENCES

OLD TESTAMENT

INDEX OF AUTHORS

JOURNAL FOR THE STUDY OF THE OLD TESTAMENT
SUPPLEMENT SERIES